The Cows Came Home

A catalogue record of this book is available from the British Library

First Edition: December 2003

ISBN: 1-84375-070-8

To order additional copies of this book please visit: http://www.upso.co.uk/paulchambers

Published by: UPSO Ltd
5 Stirling Road, Castleham Business Park,
St Leonards-on-Sea, East Sussex TN38 9NW UK
Tel: 01424 853349 Fax: 0870 191 3991
Email: info@upso.co.uk Web: http://www.upso.co.uk

Best wishes

Paul [illegible]

The Cows Came Home

by

Paul Chambers

Chapter 1

COUNTDOWN

Thirty minutes, we'd agreed earlier, give them time to get to sleep. It should be safe then. "Thee can sleep int' spare room toneet," her mam had said. "T'spare room," her dad had repeated. We all went upstairs together, her mam and dad leading the way. Their favourite daughter opened my bedroom door.

"There you are, Paul. Have you got everything you need? I'm going to have a quick bath." She looked at her watch, "It's ten twenty-five."

'That's almost the way you put it when you synchronise watches,' I thought. 'She's clever, my lass.' I checked my timepiece and did a quick conversion - 22.25. Then I patted the packet in my pocket.

"Yes, I think I've got everything I need, love," giving her a conspiratorial look.

"Goodneet, Paul," shouted her parents, shutting their door.

I closed my bedroom door and undressed to my army underpants. Thirty minutes we'd agreed. Give them time to settle she'd said. 22.55 was zero hour then. Don't let me get confused with this 24-hour clock thing; I don't want to mess it up. Think proper time, think 10.55, think five to eleven.

I looked at my watch again - 10.32.

I took the pack of three out of my trouser pocket. Then I took a little packet out of the bigger pack and placed it on the bed. Mm, perhaps I'd better not take any sort of a packet into her bedroom. If it was left lying about in all the excitement, her mam might chance upon it. I took the smooth object out of the packet and put it on the bed. The empty packet I then put back in my pocket.

"Packet in the pocket," I sang to myself, "'thingie' on the bed." It was one way to pass the time.

I checked my watch again - 10.37. Eighteen minutes to go. It was more nerve-wracking than waiting for United to kick off.

I went to the window and peeped through the curtains. It was moonlight. I could see her dad's garden. There wasn't much growing, not in November.

I closed the curtains, returned to the bed and checked that the 'thingie' was still there. It was.

I peered at my watch again - 10.46. Nine minutes to go.

I put my ear to the door and listened for a moment. No sound. Then suddenly I heard snoring. I hoped that wasn't my girl. It couldn't be! I'd never forgive her. I breathed a sigh of relief. It was her dad. That was hopeful, he was out of the equation. My uneasy vision of a meeting on the landing - me in my underpants carrying a 'thingie' - was dispelled. I went back to the window and peeped out again at the garden. Still not much growing. It was still November.

I tried not to look at my watch for a bit. I failed, it was 10.52. Three minutes. I started counting down from 180 but my thoughts wandered to the girl in the next room, minus her nightie. I lost count.

Now it was 10.54 and I watched the second hand slowly moving. I picked up the count. Five, four, three, two, one,

zero.

Gently, I switched the light off, turned the door handle and stepped onto the landing. There was a hint of moonlight. There was also something missing - the 'thingie' was still on the bed. Carefully I retraced my steps not daring to switch the light back on. I found the bed - I stubbed my toe on it. I groped for the dratted thing and at last my hand located it. Success! But I was running late now.

Hold on; hold on there, Paul Potts. You can't start your story in the middle. No matter how much you'd like to. Who are you? Who is this girl? God! You can't start your story in the middle! Discipline, Paul, discipline! Let's try again, let's start at the beginning. Let's not get carried away.

There goes my alter ego again! Why can't it mind its own business? You mean I can't start by writing about that night? O.K. O.K., keep your shirt on, if you say so, I won't. Where do I start then? Where do I start? The day I was born in 1925 in that small flat on the other side of the tracks?

Other side of the tracks? That's overdoing it a wee bit. Anyway, you can't start there; you can't remember that day. What were your first memories?

Oh! I get it now. First memories? Let's think. I vaguely remember an old aunt and uncle.

There you go then, let's start again. Once upon a time. . .

Chapter 2

FISHY GOINGS ON

I vaguely recall Aunt and Uncle.

They lived with us in a two-bedroom downstairs terraced flat in grimy Gateshead. I was about four years old at the time. My older brother Donald would be about seven and younger brother Malcolm Cecil, who was nicknamed Babe, *was* just a baby then. He must have been in his teens almost, before the family started to call him Cecil. That was a name he wasn't happy with either. I believe 'Babe' derived from Babe Ruth who marked Cecil's year of birth by hitting a record sixty home runs for baseball team New York Yankees.

To get back to Aunt and Uncle. They invariably wore black; I think it was a legacy of the Victorian days. It couldn't have been because of the Wall Street crash, they wore black long before that.

When I think of those days, I try to puzzle out how Mam, Dad, Don, me (Paul Dennis), Babe, Aunt and Uncle, and a guy called Vincent could all live in a two-bedroom flat. Did Vincent sleep in the coalhouse? I wasn't curious at the time, and later, when I would have liked to know, the people who could have told me weren't around anymore. Head-in-the-clouds Don was always blissfully unaware of what was happening outside his own world, so he was never able to explain the sleeping arrangements.

The other peculiar thing about Uncle and Aunt, they didn't have names! They were always just plain Uncle and Aunt, or Aunt and Uncle for that matter. That may not have been true, they might have had names - I suppose they must have had names when you come to think about it and I have to admit that's another gap in my knowledge. I know something for nothing, Don was no help on this one either. Well, in no time at all, just when I was getting used to having an Uncle and Aunt, an Uncle I thought was about ninety and an Aunt probably a hundred at least, something happened. Aunt took to her bed, and an Uncle who used to give me piggybacks if I first got up on the table because he couldn't bend and who was always saying, "When I was in Darjeeling, Don," suddenly stopped giving me piggybacks. He still prattled on about being in Darjeeling, though. It must have been pretty exciting in this Darjeeling place, wherever it was, for him to keep on about it. I wonder if it was about this time that Don got the idea of going on and on about nothing at all. No mistake, things were happening. In no time at all Aunt died and was closely followed by Uncle. At least I think they died. Well, they went missing from their favourite armchairs anyhow and when Aunt disappeared everyone wore black for a week or so. I had just got accustomed to the grown-ups wearing everyday clothes again when, blow me down, Uncle also went absent and black was again the order of the day.

So that's what happened to them - exit Aunt and Uncle. I was positive they had died, although I wasn't too sure what dying really meant. Come to think about it, I still don't know.

Well, they didn't leave a fortune that's for sure, perhaps because of the Wall Street crash, so we continued to live in our little flat. The overcrowding was reduced by twenty-five percent, however, and nobody went around in tears for very long, which was good for us kids.

Now what about this mysterious Vincent? What did I know about him? Who was Vincent? What was he doing in our house? A very good question, but I have to admit here and now - I haven't a clue.

Why didn't I ask someone who knew the answer when I was four or five? I suppose I never gave it a thought and perhaps I sensed that if I asked my mam - "Mam, who's Vincent?" I might have got a sharp retort - "Mind your own business, Den."

Vincent, a dapper young fellow, must have been well known in the neighbourhood though, because, one day, a policeman knocked at our front door.

Mam nearly collapsed when she opened it and saw the tall

copper. "Excuse me, missus, is your Vincent in?" She was too flummoxed to tell him that he wasn't her Vincent.

"What on earth has he done?" she gasped. "Vincent!"

Vincent was just on his way out to meet his friends, I knew he was going out, it was a Sunday and he had his bowler hat on. He always wore his best headgear on the Sabbath. When he saw the arm of the law at the front door he went a peculiar shade of grey.

"What's up?" he asked nervously.

"Nothing to worry about, sir". Vincent's face returned more or less to normal colour, 'not to worry' and 'sir' seemed hopeful signs.

The policeman then proceeded to explain that they had found a stolen car in the next street and as the only officer who drove a car was on a day off, would Vincent kindly drive the vehicle to the local police station? They knew he was a chauffeur, you see, and he would be doing them a big favour. Panic over.

That little story doesn't help to explain Vincent's identity though. I'll tell you what I believe now. I think that he was my Dad's son from a previous relationship. Vincent was about twenty years old at the time I am speaking of and he told us kids that he was a chauffeur to a millionaire in Gateshead. I didn't believe him then and I don't believe his story now, millionaires and Gateshead would never juxtapose in those days. He was a chauffeur, though; the policeman had confirmed that.

But to get back to my theory - he was Dad's son and his mother had deserted him, so Dad had left his home in Maidstone in Kent, bringing with him Vincent, and an Aunt and Uncle with no names, to keep him company.

O.K., it's a flimsy story, pure speculation I'm afraid, so we will have to leave Vincent's antecedents as an unsolved mystery. Sorry about that.

I do know something about Dad, surprisingly. Grey-haired Dad. Then in his mid-forties, he had the look of a benevolent Albert Einstein. He was born in 1887 and his father had moved the family from Yarmouth to Kent when Dad was a toddler to set up a wet fish and game shop in Maidstone. Previously, Grandfather had run a similar business in Norfolk.

I remember my Dad showing me a sepia photograph of his many relatives outside the shop in Maidstone - 'Potts' Fresh Fish and Game Shop by Royal Appointment to Her Majesty the Queen'

- so his father must have had the best wet fish shop in Kent. I imagined the shadowy figure of old Queen Victoria sitting down to a plateful of pickled herrings especially delivered by my grandfather, or even delivered by Dad! I felt quite proud every time I looked at that photo. Dad was an expert on fish and shellfish and how to prepare them for the table, he knew a thing or too about game birds too, the feathered variety that is.

He loved telling stories of his early days. Of trips to London on the train to see Buffalo Bill and his Wild West Show starring Annie Oakley, of Little Tich and Florrie Ford in the music halls, Barnum and Bailey's Circus.

But in those stories he gave never a hint of how he came to bring the lad Vincent, together with Aunt and Uncle, to the North-east of England around 1920. Or never an explanation of why he had left a settled slot in the 'Garden of England' to come to industrial Gateshead and drive tramcars. That was his new occupation - a tramcar driver!

How he met my mother I don't know, possibly on the tramcar, but they married in 1921. Why would Mam marry Dad in the first place? She was in her twenties; Dad was in his mid-thirties. She came, just herself, Dad had accoutrements, namely, Aunt, Uncle, Vincent. Quite a challenge for a young bride. It seemed to work out - I don't remember any blazing rows during their years together. In fact, rather the opposite.

Chapter 3.

THE DAY MAM FELL OFF HER PEDESTAL

That was a day for a seven-year-old! The date? I can't remember. It was the summer holidays though - August 1933? Dad had a day off, a weekday. How do I know? 'Cos Sunday we went to Mass, Saturday we had bacon and fried bread.

"Would you like to go to Saltwell Park this morning and have a game of cricket?" he asked the three of us as we ate our toast and marmalade.

The response was unanimous and raucous. "Yes, Dad, yes please, Dad!"

Mam wasn't coming, she had her housework to do and besides, she had her 'rags' in. Women married to tramcar drivers knew their husbands wouldn't go off the rails which was a blessing, but couldn't afford proper hair curlers which was not. So, in between their rare perms, they used ribbon-like rags cut into short lengths to curl their hair. The rags seemed to work because Mam became very smart when she took them out and styled her auburn locks.

Anyhow, we knew she wouldn't come to the park with her rags in. Saltwell Park! She wouldn't even go to the front door! So off we went. We took with us our cheap cricket bat, old tennis ball, four stumps, a bottle of water and a paper bag full of sticky black bullets. (Dad carried those; we could trust him.) It was a hot sunny day so we would need the water *and* the black bullets. Our school holidays were full of hot sunny days as I remember them. Our summer holidays that is, not Christmas - when it always snowed.

We walked along our cobbled street, up Derwentwater Road and along Spencer Terrace. The London to Edinburgh railway line, the old L.N.E.R., ran parallel to the terrace on the other side of the wooden fencing. Every time Don heard a train, he dashed across the road and peered through gaps in the fence. He was a fanatical train number catcher and name collector, in particular those of Gresley Pacific locomotives. In his mind they were the cream of the bunch.

We hurried on leaving Don to catch up in his own good time. Babe also had difficulty keeping up with me and Dad, so Dad gave him a piggyback. We got as far as the tram stop in Saltwell Road just as Don came dashing up.

Dad said, "I'll wait at the stop here and Babe and I will get the next tram to the park, we don't have to pay you see. You two big lads can walk, you've got strong legs, we'll meet you at the park gates."

Strong legs! I looked down at my skinny knees. Strong legs! Was he kidding?

Don looked at my legs, I looked at Don's; we weren't completely fooled. In fact it didn't seem quite fair but I thought if Dad was going to save two pennies we might get ice-creams in the park.

So off we went, sturdy Don was carrying the bat. It *was* his! With great difficulty, I was carrying the stumps. Well, I had small hands, like any seven-year-old.

It was about half a mile to the park but it seemed a lot further that day. I kept dropping a stump, which held us up somewhat, but we ran as fast as we could, looking over our shoulders now and then to see if Dad's tram was coming. The day was getting hotter and the sweat was running off me, which made me think of that lovely bottle of water and the black bullets that Dad had with him. I bet Dad and Babe were having a drink of water while they were waiting for the tram. I hope they were leaving some for us. I wouldn't put it past Babe to have scrounged a black bullet or two as well.

Don was getting impatient to move on, but I stopped again to take off my jersey, which I then tied around my waist. That was a bit cooler for me. Then off we ran again, getting to the tram terminus at the park before Dad's tramcar was in sight. We were dead chuffed.

We were just getting our breath back when a tramcar arrived with a clang and a clatter. Dad appeared at the exit, helping Babe down the tram steps, Babe looked quite taken aback when he saw us waiting. "We beat you," I cried gleefully.

"We've been here hours," added Don.

"Well, for that you can all have an ice-cream from Gazilli's," he laughed, "before we play cricket."

Gazilli had a stall near the park lake, I'd heard he came from Italy, I thought that must have been a long journey to the park every day. His ice-cream was famous the whole length and breadth of Gateshead according to my Dad. Knowing that made the taste even nicer as I licked the cone delicately to make it last longer than Don's and Babe's.

I don't remember a great deal about the cricket game, I know Dad was out first ball every time, caught and bowled by me. I suspected it might have been deliberate; on the other hand, perhaps I was too good for him. Don said he had broken Don Bradman's Test Match record. He claimed he got 350 runs but with a short boundary and only two fielders (Babe deserted us and went to play on a swing), in my mind it didn't count as a record. I got about a 100, roughly.

When we got tired we drank from the bottle of water and sucked a few black bullets. We didn't go on a rowing boat. That treat was usually reserved for when Dad was on his proper week's holiday, but we did go to see the ducks. There were lots in the big lake. Babe wanted to feed the ducks with black bullets, but Dad said no, they would probably choke if he did. Babe said in that case if one died we could take it home and have it for dinner. He was only about four years old then remember, so you had to excuse him for thinking things like that.

We set off for home. Dad said he would walk with us all the way this time.

As we walked along Don said, "I broke the record."

"Just like the other Don - Bradman," Dad laughed.

"Who was I like?" I asked.

"Well, Den, you're left-handed, you couldn't be Bradman, you were Frank Woolley, the Kent and England all-rounder."

There must have been a serious blank in my cricket knowledge, I hadn't heard of Frank Woolley, so I wasn't too pleased to be him. As we walked along Saltwell Road a cloud came across the sun and soon I was feeling quite chilly. It was then I realised my jersey was missing from around my waist.

"Dad," I gasped, "I've lost my jersey!"

Apart from the hand-me-down one from Don, the horrible blue one with holes in the elbows, it was the only jersey I possessed, I wasn't going to be very popular with Mam and Dad. The future looked dismal, I could see dark clouds on the horizon.

Dad frowned, perhaps this mishap could spoil his day too, after all he was in charge of us, jerseys and all. "Now I come to think about it, you didn't have it on when we got off the tram. You didn't take it off and throw it away?" he added ironically.

It wasn't like Dad to be sarcastic. My tears welled up, threatening to run down my cheeks.

"It was hot so I took it off and tied it around my waist," I said mournfully.

"You must have been careless," his face was unusually stern, "jerseys don't grow on trees, you mustn't have tied it on properly and it's fallen on the pavement. What on earth will your mother say? This could spoil my day, as well as yours."

I knew perfectly well that jerseys didn't grow on trees, did he think I was daft or something? But I could see he was just a little bit worried about Mam.

I walked along disconsolately when suddenly Babe, who was riding on Dad's back, shouted, "Look, Daddy, what's that on the railing there? It's a jersey! It's a jersey!"

His little face was beaming; the little fellow didn't like upsets. "I know where jerseys grow now, they grow on railings not on trees!" he chuckled. He was in tucks of laughter.

Even Dad was smiling now, "Well, knock me down with a feather! There are some honest people in the world, even in Gateshead!"

I ran and grabbed it, quickly putting it on; even though the sun had come out again, I wasn't taking any more chances. 'Fancy happiness being a jersey,' I thought. I started to sing and Don and Babe joined in as we walked along. Dad was laughing and singing too, when there was no one else around.

The songs we had heard on our gramophone - 'We're Only Painting the Clouds with Sunshine' and 'Ta Ra Ra Boom Dee Ay, Ta Ra Ra Boom Dee Ay'. We didn't sing 'Ta Ra Ra BUM Dee Ay', not with Dad there anyway. He might have told us not to sing about bums in a public place.

Of course when we got to Spencer Terrace, guess what? Don was train spotting again. This time an express train went rattling by and Don came running after us yelling, "I've got Pretty Polly, I've got Pretty Polly!"

Dad thought he was talking about a parrot but having been inculcated into Don's hobby at one time, I knew it was the name of a Gresley Pacific, and from the commotion he was causing it was the first time he'd sighted this rare bird.

That wasn't the end of the excitement however, for as we turned into our street, behold! A couple of gigantic steamrollers were puffing up and down laying tarmac on the cobbles. The smell of the tar was pungent and pervading. Dad explained that they were making the street smooth for cars and bicycles.

"And smooth for bogies as well!" I shouted.

A bogie in our town was generally a homemade, ramshackle orange box knocked together amateurishly by some of the older kids with wobbly wheels. The orange boxes had the wobbly wheels, not the kids.

Of course there was no motive power to speak of other than a push from a pal, or a steep hill. Gradients were required to generate high speeds but if the bogies hit a bump the chassis would invariably collapse and the wheels would fly in all directions, followed by the driver. Fortunately he just went in one direction and usually on his bottom.

Those contraptions however were the tin lizzies of the bogie world. Earlier that summer Dad had made us a Rolls Royce of a bogie, with top grade orange box timber and Silver Cross pram wheels picked up from a rubbish tip in the vicinity. Unhappily, we weren't allowed to go on the 'bank', as Derwentwater Road was usually called in our street. It was out of bounds to Don and I because of the heavy volume of traffic, about ten motorcars an hour with the odd charabanc at weekends.

As the cobbles in our street made it impossible for bogies, the pavement was the only racetrack available. That was alright most of the time, but on nice days we kept dunching into gossiping women out enjoying the sunshine, or crashing into their babies in prams. The prams not the babies. These accidents caused a many a song and dance from neighbours and a resultant bogie ban from Mam.

Hence our delight at the tarmacking - the bogie might be able to come out of quarantine.

Wide-eyed, we watched the steamrollers for some minutes, until Mam called us in for our meal. It was dinnertime, midday dinner and we had one of my favourites - salmon fishcakes made from finest tinned pink salmon.

Mam had taken her rags out, she did look smart, her hair all wavy.

"Did you have a good game?" she asked, as we all sat down to eat.

"I broke the record, three hundred and fifty," boasted Don.

"I was Frank Woolley," I piped up, not to be outdone.

I was pretty certain Mam didn't know Frank Woolley from Hughie Gallagher, the Newcastle United centre-forward.

"Frank Woolley?" she said. "You must have been good!"

"And who were you?" she asked Babe.

He chuckled, "I was 'The Man on the Flying Trapeze'." (We had the gramophone record of the song.)

"You were only on a little swing," said Don, pushing his plate away and smiling.

It was about then that Dad yawned and looked at Mam.

"Now, you three, Dad and I are going to have a nap, we're tired, so don't make a noise in the house. Go and play in the yard it's a nice day."

I wondered why it was, that whenever Mam and Dad went for an afternoon nap, Mam always took her 'rags' out and looked smart, but later when she came out of the bedroom she was always slightly dishevelled. I thought that she mustn't sleep very well on an afternoon. All the same she always seemed to look forward to their naps.

After they disappeared to bed, Don asked, "What shall we do now? You're usually full of bright ideas, Den."

"Well," I said, "we can either watch the steamrollers in the street or flood the yard. Mam said we should play in the yard."

"What on earth do you mean 'flood the yard'?" Don looked puzzled. "How can we do that?"

"I know how," I said mysteriously, "just let's do it."

The day had been quite exciting so far; I didn't want it to flag already.

"Let's watch the steamrollers instead," said Don cautiously.

Babe was listening to this conversation with interest. At the suggestion of splashy water in the yard I could swear his ears pricked up.

"Let's flood the yard, let's flood the whole yard!" he cried.

I considered the casting vote had been made, so I dashed into the scullery and came out with two thick floor cloths. I pushed them into the drain, putting a couple of old bricks on top.

"Turn the tap on, Don."

I wanted him to be an accomplice in case of trouble later and Don fell for it. Still mumbling about steamrollers he turned the tap full on. He came outside again shaking his head pessimistically, but looking at the drain as the water started to overflow into the yard.

Miraculously the pool rose and rose, growing wider, it was almost like watching the tide come in.

"And what do we do when the yard's full, clever clogs?" Don asked.

"It's a hot day," I said. "We can take our socks and shoes off and paddle, then we can sail our boats."

At the word 'paddle' Babe acted. In two shakes he had taken his sandshoes and socks off and put them on the parlour windowsill overlooking the yard, and was splashing in the water.

"Don't fall down, Babe," I said anxiously, suddenly realising that there could be snags in this enterprise. "Don't fall down!"

Perhaps if I could have kept my mouth shut the whole thing might never have happened. Within the blink of an eye I was helping a drenched Babe to his feet. Me and my bright ideas, I was thinking.

The afternoon was suddenly turning into some sort of catastrophe and worse was to follow. Nobody had noticed that the water had risen above the scullery step and was seeping into the house. Perhaps seeping was not the word, pouring was a better description.

"Crikey Moses!" I shouted at Don, "Look!"

Don looked and panicked. He dashed to turn the tap off in the scullery and plodged through the water in his sandshoes and socks. I was cooler under pressure, or perhaps I didn't want to get my footwear wet. Dry footwear might be an important factor in my defence in the inevitable inquest that was going to take place in an hour or two. My guess was that Mam would be both judge and jury.

So I took my shoes and socks off and pulled the floorcloths out of the drain allowing the water to subside, except for the pool around Babe. 'What next?' I thought. Babe was soaking, Don was slopping about like a penguin and the scullery floor was under water.

I hadn't realised how time had flown. 'What next' arrived in the shape of Mam in the parlour doorway, fastening her cardigan and looking a little flustered after her nap.

"What on earth is going on?" she shouted.

I remember thinking at the time that she was more than a little upset.

Until this flood in the backyard incident I had always thought that Mam was nigh perfect, her judgement impeccable. She never raised her voice to us without good cause; you had to admit she was in the right when she lost her temper. Metaphorically I would hold up my hands and say O.K., I deserved that telling off.

But she lost her halo that day as far as I was concerned. She picked on me as the culprit without any concrete evidence - only the word of sneaks Don and Babe, that the whole thing was my idea.

It was true I may have suggested that we flood the yard, that I couldn't deny, but I wasn't the one who carelessly fell down and got soaked. Also I wasn't the other one who turned the tap on in the first place, setting the whole disaster into motion and then capped it all by stupidly plodging through the water. Furthermore, I was just one of three that hadn't noticed that the water was getting into the scullery. In fact when I thought of it, it was I, the accused, who did eventually see what was happening. It was I, who acted in time to stop the water pouring into the parlour, then into the bedrooms and out the front door into the street.

Unfortunately, I got no chance to present a coherent defence, not in the face of the tongue-lashing I was receiving. It was that day I suppose that I came to realise that life could be so cruel.

Time is a great healer they say. All the same, it took a good hour before things had settled down. We had helped Mam to clean up the mess, I working assiduously head down in a contrite manner. Babe couldn't help; he was wrapped in a towel, wearing his sandshoes and socks for decency, waiting for his clothes to dry out. Don of course spent the rest of the day in bare feet.

It was when quiet had descended, that Dad emerged from the bedroom having had his nap. (He always seemed to take a while to pull himself together.) Mam told him the whole story.

You wouldn't believe it but Mam was laughing now and so was Dad. I just didn't understand it - either the flood was a major disaster which was the strong impression that I was given an hour or so ago, or it was a storm in a teacup - it must have been a mighty big cup.

The three of us were tired when we went to bed that night. As I dozed off I still hadn't puzzled out the attitude of grown-ups. What I did know for certain, it had been a roller-coaster sort of a day.

Us kids all slept in a double bed in Mam and Dad's room; Vincent had the other bedroom to himself. Don and I slept at the head of the bed and Babe in between us at the foot. It wasn't a bad arrangement provided nobody continued to grow. That couldn't be guaranteed as none of us surpassed a height of five feet at the time. Unless we were going to be dwarves.

My little mind didn't think that was a possibility. But in any case that problem, the problem of sleeping three in a bed indefinitely, never arose.

Chapter 4

TIN HUTS AND BROLLIES

Shortly after that day, the sleeping arrangements took a turn for the better. Vincent got married and left home, Don moved into the second bedroom and Babe could now sleep the right way up. It was a pleasure now to be able to kick my feet about without the danger of giving Babe a poke in the eye. He was a canny lad really.

It was disappointing to miss my drink of Tizer at Sunday dinner though. On the Sabbath, we always had a roast, with veg, potatoes and gravy, then rice pudding or stewed prunes and custard. This was good, but our drink was always tap water. Until one Sunday. That day, Vincent came in, took off his bowler hat and carefully placed it on the sideboard. Then, rather grandly, he produced a large bottle of fizzy Tizer, the new super drink, and put it on the dinner table. "That's for you, kids," he smiled. I think he'd had a pint or two. I also think he'd had a rise, because a bottle of Tizer was on the table every Sunday after that.

Then he got married and left home and the Sunday table looked kind of bare without the Tizer. What his marriage did mean was that we became a normal family - just a mam and dad and children. No old people without names, no mysterious chauffeur of dubious antecedents. I felt very happy with the new set-up, despite the lack of Tizer.

I was also content that we were a Catholic family - Mam's father and mother were both born in Southern Ireland, immigrating to England before Mam was born. As you would expect they were 'of the faith'. For me, there was only one disturbing thing about being a Catholic - our awesome parish priest. He used to visit us when least expected. So fearsome was he, that when I heard him talking to Mam at the front door, I would scramble to hide under the big parlour table draped with the big, red cloth. Without fail, Babe would tumble in beside me.

The priest's long black cloak, the strange Irish brogue of his god-fearing voice and his bushy, black eyebrows were all so scary. Even Mam was a bit wary of him. I could tell - she spoke to him all namby-pamby.

When I was about eight, I ceased hiding under the table. I was a big, brave boy now and besides I sensed that the tablecloth was really too small to hide us properly. I changed my tactics - when I heard Mam and the priest at the front, I was out the back door and into the back lane for a bit of fresh air, always with Babe at my heels. That was O.K. on a fine day, but one time when we heard him shaking his umbrella at the front door, we flew out the back and into the lane before we realised we were getting soaked. We returned into the yard 'toot sweet' as Dad would say (he had been in France during the war), and rushed into the outdoor netty.

The air wasn't as fresh in there, mind. We stood in the dim light after fastening the door latch, shivering and wet, praying that the man of God would not want a wee. He had never had a wee before at our house, but it would be just our luck for him to want one now. Unless of course priests didn't need to wee, they were a bit different!

To calm my nerves, I picked up a copy of the Daily Herald (the paper was in the netty for our bums), tearing it into squares and pushing them on the hook. Babe helped, but he was hopeless. I wouldn't have liked to have used his little squares. We had just finished our self-imposed task, when Mam rescued us as soon as the 'Father' had gone.

When I say we were a Catholic family that is not strictly true - Dad wasn't a Catholic, but he allowed us to be brought up in the faith. His philosophy perhaps - let Mam have her say on this issue and he would have more influence in the important things, afternoon naps for example.

The priest never visited when Dad was at home, no matter what shift he was on. I suspected it was the hand of God. Either that, or Dad popped his shift rota through the priest's letterbox.

Dad was one of those marvellous dads. When we started to play with lead toy soldiers, he made a super fort with a proper drawbridge, battlements, everything. The snag for Babe and me was that Don always commandeered the fort and the cream of the soldiers - the Grenadier Guards regiment. Half of the Grenadiers, though, were bandsmen playing bassoons, trumpets and drums. With their hands full of musical instruments, I couldn't see what good they would be in a proper fight. Not only that, three of them were headless. It was no use arguing with Don, though. He insisted they were fighting men, and as long as they could stand up, they counted just as much as a Red Indian chief with full headdress, a tomahawk and bow and arrows. That didn't seem right.

Babe and I always lost these contests. The Grenadiers were sheltered by the stout walls of the fort whilst our motley army of cowboys, Redskins and a few Zulu warriors, were exposed to enemy marble-attack unprotected, whereas our marbles just bounced off the walls of the fort.

Dad also made a marvellous model of an ocean liner - the Lusitania - complete with masts, funnels, and captain's bridge with a wheelhouse, the lot. Sadly, we couldn't sail it. It was too heavy to take to the park lake and flooding the yard was now strictly taboo. I don't know what happened to that liner, it probably finished up on the fire when we were short of coal. If so, I wish I had been there - the towering inferno of the Lusitania!

Then there was the model theatre. Dad had made a work of art if ever I saw one. Imposing proscenium, orchestra pit with cutout musicians, plush velvet curtains and valance (the material purloined, no doubt from Mam's sewing box), and a safety fire curtain displaying advertisements for Rinso, Ovaltine, Bisto and the ilk.

The actors and players were assembled from cutout cards bought at Johnson's Toy Shop. They entered and exited the stage slotted into thin wooden strips. Dancing, therefore, was very much left to the imagination. Of all the cardboard characters in the ensemble, the one I particularly liked was the ventriloquist. He was unique, he could say 'bottle of beer' without his lips moving, not even if you looked at his mouth through Dad's magic magnifying glass. It was no secret that the ventriloquist's voice, and indeed every voice, was that of one of us kids. Somehow, though, the theatre wasn't a howling success as a plaything. Speaking the dialogue from backstage, not one of Don, Babe or me seemed to be cut out for the thespian profession. The audience of Mam, Dad and the cat, sitting in the stalls, had difficulty in hiding their yawns. In fact the cat didn't bother to stifle his and unashamedly went to sleep on Mam's knee.

I'm sure a less cultured audience would have booed and hissed as we fouled up the voices - a deep baritone for the Good Fairy and a squeaky soprano for the Demon King, was the sort of mishap that was prone to happen.

No, the family were not impressed with the theatre in action, so after one or two flops, the curtain was rung down and the whole project was aborted.

I was about ten years old when Don said, "Why don't we go to the Tin Hut this morning?" Babe and me looked blank.

"The Tin Hut? What rubbishy talk is that?" I asked.

"You've never heard of the Tin Hut? My pal Humpy is always talking about it, he says it is a corking place. You can get old Wizards and Hotspurs in good condition for a penny each and tatty ones for a ha'penny. What's more, when you've read them, you can take two back and swap them for another one."

"Your pal Humpy is humpy," I said, "that sounds too good to be true."

His pal's real name was Geordie Williams - hence Humpy - I didn't get it either, unless Humpy meant stupid.

"How much money have you got?" Don asked. "I've got fourpence."

I turfed out my pockets. "I've got two candy cigarettes, two buttons, an elastic band, a piece of chewing gum, but only a penny."

"I haven't got a penny," chirped up Babe, "but I've got two ha'pennies, that's about the same, isn't it?"

Don chose to ignore that remark. "So that's sixpence altogether," he said. He was quick at maths for a thirteen-year-old. "Let me see, that's six Wizards or Hotspurs."

"Or three Wizards and three Hotspurs," said Babe. He was only six; I excused him for counting on his fingers.

I nearly said you could get four good Wizards and four tatty Hotspurs with that fortune, but I didn't, we'd had enough arithmetic for one day. Besides, for a change, I wasn't in a showing off mood. The outcome was that we decided to go. This Tin Hut was in Redheugh Road, about a fifteen-minute walk from our house. We soon saw it - if this was a Tin Hut I was a Chinaman. It was more like a big engine shed on the railway. A huge Nissen hut made of corrugated iron. There was a ramshackle canopy at the front, under which were dozens of accumulators (batteries) and myriads of car tyres and bicycle wheels, there were even brooms and broomsticks. Not the sort of place that I thought would stock Wizards, except those of the occult variety.

I discovered later, that the accumulators were hired by people to power their wireless sets. In our area at that time few streets had electricity cables installed. The accumulators must have been charged up elsewhere, for there was no electricity on these premises either. We soon discovered that not even gas mains had reached the Tin Hut. It looked a mysterious sort of building to me.

"Go on, you wise one, you friend of Humpy," I said to Don. "Go in and find the comics, we'll be behind you." (Not too close though.) He looked a little dubious, but I think he knew he had burnt his boats; his reputation was at stake. Bravely, he stumbled inside and we followed. It was dark after the bright sunlight; there were only flickering oil lamps for illumination. We brushed past hammers and chisels, saws and files, spanners and screwdrivers, garden spades and forks (these seemed incongruous - there were no house gardens in a mile radius of the Tin Hut). Babe knocked over a row of spades, which fell to the floor with a clatter. I was about to run for it, when I glimpsed a counter to the right, stacked with comics. Hovering at the main counter was a stern man with a grey moustache and beard. Don backed into me, standing on my toes in the process, eyes glued on the fellow. Suddenly the apparition smiled through cracked teeth.

"It's all right, sonnies, I'll put the spades back." Babe, who had retreated hurriedly to the door at the noise and clamour of the falling spades, came in again when he saw the smile.

"The Wizards are over there," I said to Don, trying to sound cool.

"Aah," he said gratefully, as we made our way to the comics

section. Humpy was right. There were piles of Wizards and Hotspurs - piles in good condition, and piles somewhat the worse for wear. Even better, there was another heap of what turned out to be American comics, comics I had heard of but never seen before, they even smelled American to me, a Wrigley's Spearmint kind of smell. I scanned them greedily, Dick Tracy, Orphan Annie with funny eyes, Li'l Abner, Dagwood, all of these in colour at a penny each. I would have one, that was me spent up.

Don was more conservative by nature and spent tuppence, keeping half of his available funds in reserve until he got his thruppence pocket money at the weekend. Being younger, Babe and me only got tuppence a week, so we hadn't the same scope to juggle our finances.

Don got two Wizards. One of the stories in the Wizard at that time was called the Wolf of Kabul. The Wolf was a tough Englishman of the bulldog breed who was the scourge of wicked Afghan tribesman in the Khyber Pass. Why was he the scourge? Simply because he carried a heavy cricket bat studded with nails - the 'clickyba' was its fearful name. It was a weapon that the 'Wolf' wielded fiercely, scattering infidels in all directions. Infidels were easy meat in those days, particularly Afghan infidels.

Don was fascinated by the 'clickyba'. He was a sucker for cricket bats since his Bradman feats in the park.

With his penny, Babe got an American Comic. That was no surprise. No doubt I would have to explain some of the American words, like Gee Whiz meant Crikey Moses and Li'l Abner meant Little Abner (who unfortunately for Babe's comprehension was very big). That kind of thing.

Anyhow, that was most of the afternoon sorted. We sat on the netty steps in the backyard, and read our comics. It was a beautiful day (school summer holidays again), but after an hour or two I started getting restless. I had been reading in one of Don's Wizards, a story about these soldiers who had parachuted behind enemy lines - sometimes these kids' comics held the most amazing prophecies.

"I've got an idea," I said.

Don groaned, I must have interrupted him reading about a critical moment in a Wolf of Kabul adventure. "Oh no, not another idea!"

Not to be distracted, I said, "Listen, it's a good wheeze. You know Mam's brolly? I bet if I jumped off the coalhouse roof with the umbrella open I would float down to the ground like someone, a spy perhaps, jumping out of a plane with a parachute."

"I've got a better idea," said Don, "shurrup and read your comics." (He sometimes lapsed into a bit of Geordie, under stress.) "Besides, Mam wouldn't let you have the umbrella for such a crazy scheme."

"She's not in. You know she's gone to the library. I'm sure she wouldn't mind me borrowing it for a scientific experiment."

"Go on," said Babe, who was always aiding and abetting me. "Mam won't mind if it's a sitific expemiment, I want to see you float down."

Well, I couldn't disappoint the little fellow, could I? He looked up to me so much. I dashed into the house, rummaged in the wardrobe, found the umbrella and put it up to see how big it was. There were two things wrong with that. One, I shouldn't have put the umbrella up in the house, I'd forgotten Mam had said it was very unlucky, and two, it wasn't very big and didn't look much like a parachute, which could also be unlucky for me.

A thought crossed my mind, Babe was lighter than I was, perhaps he should do the jump. But then I decided, no, if anything happened to Babe, Mam and Dad would have my guts for garters, whereas if I was hurt, although it might be painful, at least I would get some sympathy. Don was still shaking his head when I appeared with the umbrella. That was no surprise. He was always shaking his head, after the flooding the yard fiasco. Anyway, I climbed onto the banisters at the top of the steps and clambered towards the coalhouse roof, which was about ten feet above the ground. I had been on to the roof many a time, but not with a brolly and I had one or two scary moments with the ferrule poking into vulnerable parts of my anatomy.

Eventually I made it to the sloping tiled roof, stood up precariously and opened the umbrella. Looking down it seemed more than any ten feet.

"Go on, clever clogs," said Don, "Go on, jump, we're waiting!"

If I had jumped up high straightaway, any braking effect the umbrella might have had, could have come into play, but I sort of slithered off. Crash! My ankle went over, my head hit the concrete yard - and the brolly! When I looked up, the umbrella had smashed into the dustbin with a clatter and a clang, and now looked like a skeleton. The material was all torn off the frame. I felt something very much like warm blood trickling down my forehead, but thought, 'The umbrella! That's the worst part of this disaster - even if I have a broken ankle and a fractured skull!'

There was a ray of hope, the ambulance might come and take me to the infirmary before Mam came back from the library. In which case I would be safe, Mam couldn't scold me in hospital with all the nurses and doctors around, or fuss on about a mouldy umbrella, could she? Then after six months, when I came out of hospital fully restored, with my skull repaired, my broken ankle fixed, and the broken umbrella collected by the dustbin men long ago, the whole affair would surely be forgotten.

The ambulance didn't come, however, Mam came instead just as Don was picking me up. And do you know what?

"My bairn!" she cried, taking me in her arms. "Are you all right? What's happened?"

Don explained that I had fallen off the coalhouse roof and got entangled with her umbrella, which just happened to be in the yard at the time. Bless the lad. Do you know, Mam accepted this explanation without question? Don went up in my estimation for a day or two.

As it happened, after staunching the head wound and applying Germolene and a bandage, and putting a coldwater press to my ankle, Mam decided that I would soon be O.K.

Nevertheless, I walked around with a bad limp for a few days, thinking that if she continued pitying me, she wouldn't have time to think about brollies.

Unfortunately, she would soon have more to worry about than umbrellas.

Chapter 5

SHADOWS

Christmas 1936 - the last of the carefree laughter and happy innocence of childhood. Our life was to change. Yuletide had always been a joyous time for we lads. Santa had come up trumps, bringing presents every year. Stocking fillers were goodies such as chocolate selection boxes, painting books, sweets. Then there were the presents we had specially asked Santa to bring.

The previous year was the Christmas of the Escalado, the horse race game - a combined present for the three of us. From the moment I saw it in Johnson's shop, I hankered after it. I knew it was too expensive for me alone, but convincing Don and Babe that they wanted it too was easy. I say the three of us, but Mam and Dad almost commandeered the game. The horses rattled across the table, we betted with tiddlywink counters, we shouted our fancies home. Dad acted as bookie, always finishing up with the biggest stack. Useless to him - he never played tiddlywinks.

Number one gambler was Mam. She liked a bit of a flutter in real life too. Many's the time I'd taken bets across the back lane to the bookies runner who lived at number thirteen. Thruppence up and down, that was her favourite bet. Judging by the few times I went for winnings, number thirteen wasn't unlucky for Jefferson the bookie. Except on one glorious sunny day. The local bobby caught Jefferson taking bets sitting at an old desk in his backyard. A rainy day, and he would have been inside, he and his desk would have been in his scullery.

Another Christmas, Don and I got Hornby train sets. By

combining the two sets of track, the railway had one terminus in the front bedroom and the other in the parlour. The only snag was, that because there were so few straight rails, the trains snaked erratically, first curving one way and then the other. Don thought there was another drawback - if we both set off our clockwork trains at the same time, there would be a whopping crash in the passage. I didn't think that was a fly in the ointment, the disasters were the best part of the game.

Then there was the one when Don got a bus conductor set. When we were all seated, a captive audience around the fire, Babe and me on the fender seats, Dad and Mam in the armchairs, he would walk up and down shouting, "Fares please, fares please." At the same time, he would be pinging away merrily, punching tickets in his toy machine. "Room for six more upstairs," would be his cry.

What the devil he was talking about was beyond me. Our flat was a single-decker, you couldn't go upstairs unless you went next door and there were only four of us anyway, so why six? He would prattle on about fares and room upstairs for hours. I was glad when he had used up all his tickets.

For this Christmas, the Christmas of 1936, Don and I both got Meccano sets, Babe's main present was a butcher's shop with candy legs of pork, joints of beef and lamb, and sausages, all very realistic. We opened our parcels and then had a quick breakfast of crispy fried bread, bacon and egg. It *was* a special day. The table cleared for action, Don and I were soon sat messing about with our Meccano. Babe was on the floor, setting out his butcher's shop. With the help of the instruction booklet, I soon had the rudiments of a crane arising from the bits and pieces. Don was having a few problems with the tiny bolts and nuts. He kept dropping them on the floor and started to get ratty.

I looked up, Babe seemed to have his shop sorted; it looked quite realistic.

"Is your shop open, Mr Butcher?" I asked.

"Yes, I'm open now."

"I'll tell you what," I said, laying aside my spanner and getting down on the floor. "This construction work makes you hungry, I'm ready for dinner. Have you a nice piece of beef and some sausages?"

"This is beef, isn't it?" his blue eyes questioned.

"Smashing," I said. (I wasn't too sure, mind, I was no expert.)

Don was scratching his head, trying to puzzle out how to fix the wheels on his tramcar contraption. He pushed his handiwork to one side; I thought he looked pleased to have an excuse to stop. "I think I'll knock off for a bit and come to your shop, Babe, I'm starving. I'll have a couple of legs of pork," he said.

'That's going over the top a bit,' I thought, but Babe was delighted to make the sale.

"It's a good job your butcher's shop is handy, Babe," I said, "we couldn't have done without it." His smile said it all.

We had a bit of a rest then and watched Dad lighting the Christmas tree candles and then the candles in the paper Chinese Lanterns he had hung up in the passage. Our house must have been a veritable firetrap. It was taking him longer to carry out tasks these days, always breathless and often coughing. I know Mam was very concerned and always trying to persuade him to go to the doctor's.

"Soon," he would say, or, "After Christmas," or, "After your birthday." It was a visit he was dreading to make.

Christmas dinner that year, as every year, was roast pork, stuffing, potatoes and veg, followed of course by Xmas Pud. We washed it down with a bottle of Tizer this time.

Mam and Dad drank homemade wheat wine, a potent brew it seemed, for they both became very merry. Dad had been making wheat wine for ages; he seemed to prefer it to a bottle of Newcastle Brown Ale from the off licence at the bottom of our street.

At night, Mam's mother came with Uncle Matty and Aunt Winnie (Mam's half-brother and half-sister), both in their twenties. Mam's dad had died at an early age and Grandmother had married again. Her second husband fathered four more children for her and then followed her first husband to the grave. She didn't marry a third time; she'd had enough of children I think (and of husbands). Grandmother we called her - she would never be a Grandma or Grannie, she was much too stern and serious. We didn't see much of her, she spent a lot of her time involved in local Labour Party politics and only recently had been elected a Gateshead councillor. She had lived in a small terraced house not far from us. It was just after that Christmas she moved into a brand new council estate - a lovely house with a garden was hers to rent.

"Could that be just luck?" Dad had asked.

That Christmas night the atmosphere was somewhat quiet at first. Grandmother, in a dour mood as usual, asked me when I was going to sit my exams for the Gateshead Grammar School. "You're sure to get in," she said, "you're always top of the class, so be sure to stick in my lad and you could go far."

The last thing I wanted to hear about on Christmas Day was exams. Thankfully, Dad produced a bottle of port and what with that and the wheat wine the party warmed up considerably. Dad even got Grandmother laughing at least twice that night. What a shock that was.

In the spring, Don got his first job. It was only temporary, delivering leaflets for Northern Rediffusion Cables. They were wiring up houses to their network and renting radio-type boxes at two shillings a week. Cable radio perhaps? Great swathes of Tyneside were still without electricity in the late thirties and by renting from Rediffusion, people could receive B.B.C. programmes without messing around with accumulators. Electricity cables didn't come to our street until just weeks before World War II.

In that same spring, Mam finally persuaded Dad to go to the doctor's; his health was getting worse with each day that passed. It was a struggle for him to continue working. I think Mam and Dad expected the diagnosis, but it didn't lessen the blow - Dad had T.B., then more commonly known as consumption, the dreaded killer disease of the thirties. Another setback, if Dad's news wasn't enough, Mam told us that she was expecting a baby. 'What a time to order a baby!' I thought. In those far off days, ten was an innocent age for most children; certainly it was for me. I hadn't a clue where babies came from. That stork mullarkey was unbelievable but I certainly didn't connect afternoon naps with baby production. The whole concept was a mystery. I began to understand part of the riddle when Mam's belly started to swell. It triggered a memory, a vague recollection of the big belly she had before Babe was born. The baby was in Mam's belly! What a funny thing! How it got there was a puzzle. I didn't like to ask, if only grown-ups were supposed to know. How would it get out?

Through her belly button? Not having a baby sister was a drawback here.

Dad struggled most of the year to get to work and bring his wages home. During the summer the doctor arranged for him to go to Barrasford Sanatorium for four weeks, a convalescent home in rural Northumberland. The theory was that fresh country air could help T.B. sufferers. Those from the working class were sent to the English countryside; the more well off ones would travel to Switzerland or some other Alpine region. In the majority of cases, relief, if any, was temporary and the symptoms unchanged.

Soon after coming home from Barrasford, Dad accepted that he would have to give up work. Winter was approaching and the disease was spreading in his lungs.

The new baby arrived in late summer, a boy, and lo and behold! Mam did become thinner again pretty quickly. The bad news - the baby was discovered to have one leg shorter than the other. Stephen, as he was christened, would always have a pronounced limp. With Dad out of work, our family income was now much reduced, Mam mainly reliant on the parsimonious Board of Guardians. Her sister, Sally, also helped. About once a month, on a Sunday afternoon, we would go to see Aunt Sally. She and her husband, Leslie, had a grocers shop with house attached, in Newcastle. Every visit, Mam was given a parcel of groceries - dented tins, damaged packets, that sort of thing. We would catch the electric train to West Jesmond station and walk to Aunt Sally's house. I noticed that there were trees in some of the streets. Until these visits, I believed that trees only grew in parks, or out in the country.

"Why are there trees here, Mam?" I would ask.

"It's a posh area of Newcastle, Den, a bit like Low Fell in Gateshead, only more swanky."

"Posh, oh! Is everybody rich in Jesmond, then?"

"Well, most of them have a bit of money."

"Has Aunt Sally got a bit of money, Mam?"

"You're always asking questions. Why don't you be quiet, like Babe?"

'Aunty must have a canny bit of money, all the same,' I thought. They had a wireless for one thing, in fact it was one of those fancy radiogramophones, I bet that cost a bob or two.

Their house was at the back of the shop, which was closed on Sundays, so Aunt Sally was a lady of leisure when we visited. We would get there in time for tea and unsold stale cakes, and listen to the radio. The programmes were dull on a Sunday afternoon, that was until 'Les Miserables' came on. The play was being serialised. It was difficult to keep up with the story though, just hearing an episode every four weeks. It was also a bit hard to hear the radio above the noise of Aunt Sally's voice gabbling on.

"The bank manager came in yesterday," she would say. Or, "The editor of the Chronicle told us a good story the other day, but said he couldn't publish it for fear of libel." Or, "The stationmaster at Jesmond told me he was being promoted to a good position at Newcastle Central. He'll be stationmaster there before long. You see Agnes, with us being 'High Class Grocers' we have an interesting clientele."

High Class Grocers! Clientele! Our top shop just had customers and half of them got their groceries on tick. Jesmond was different it seemed. Peopled by luminaries apparently. Good for Aunt Sally. Three cheers for Aunt Sally!

Don had graduated from leaflet distribution to butcher's boy and before the year-end, he climbed another dizzy rung of the ladder when Dad got him a job in the tram sheds. He was making a small but useful contribution to the family income now. Don, who was quite a good-looking lad in a sort of way, had his idiosyncrasies. One was at the dinner table. If he could, he avoided using his knife to eat, instead, keeping it bright and shiny. That way, he could use it as a mirror. He would hold the knife up and take sly looks at his reflection, then smile in a self-satisfied way.

About that time, I joined the public library; it was a revelation after knowing only the one at school. The Gateshead library was a veritable Aladdin's Cave to me. After a visit there, I could hardly wait to get home to read my treasures. As Dad couldn't walk uphill to the library now, I would always select a couple of books for him too.

He had more time to read now and I was happy to know that I was helping him to take his mind off his illness. He liked wildlife books, cricket books and books about the oldtime music halls and circuses. "You're a good lad to bring me these," he would say.

I hoped being a good lad would help a lot in my next experience, that was, to be confirmed in the Catholic faith. It meant that I was judged now to be capable of sins, sins of both the mortal and venial variety. Now I would have the worry of going into the Confession box, confronting the awesome Father O'Malley at the other side of the grill. He had already told us the difference between mortal and venial sins but fascinated as I was with his bushy, twitchy eyebrows, I hadn't paid much heed at the time. So I thought I would look up the terms in our tattered dictionary.

'Mortal sin' - a complete loss of grace. So then I had to look grace up, I was sure it didn't mean some girl. 'Grace' - to be favoured or sanctified by God; I wouldn't like to lose grace then. Mortal sin appeared to be pretty serious. On the other hand venial sin seemed to be quite a harmless sort of sin - 'a sin easily forgiven', I could cope with those kinds of sins any day. My much-thumbed 'Catechism' indicated the mortal sins, most from the Ten Commandments - 'Thou shalt not kill' - I could steer clear of that unless killing flies with a rolled up Daily Herald came into it. But, 'Thou shalt not commit adultery'. What was that? The 'Catechism' was no help there, neither was our tatty dictionary with it's cover missing. I was pretty sure some of the pages were missing too. Talk about bad luck - the first word in the book was 'adventure'! All the same, I decided I was fairly safe with adultery unless I accidentally stumbled into committing it without knowing.

Weekly confessions became a bit of a problem for me; I racked my brains to think of venial sins that I had been guilty of. After two or three weeks of repeating myself, confessing minor misdemeanours, I began to think that the priest was wasting his time with me.

The fourth time I was in the confessional box things changed. Until then Father O'Malley had given me a penance of three Hail Marys, which was a doddle, but my fourth confession went something like this:

"Father, forgive me for I have sinned."

The grave voice came through the grill, "Hend whott are your sins?"

"Er, I slept in and was late for school."

"Hend whot helse hev ye to say?"

"I told my pal John Brown that he was stupid and he isn't, that was a lie."

"Henything helse, boy? His that haal? God will know if you've missed henything." To me, he sounded almost disappointed.

I hadn't anything else on my list; it was a spur of the moment outburst. "I've had lewd thoughts, Father." Lewd thoughts, what were lewd thoughts? I didn't know, unless wishing I could pee higher up the wall than Lofty Wilson was one. He was the champion in our class. The priest, however, had ranted and raved at the congregation from the pulpit the previous Sunday. He had said that men and women shouldn't have lewd thoughts, so I presumed that boys shouldn't have them either. But as I knelt in the confessional, I started to panic; lewd thoughts might be a mortal sin!

One word he uttered, "Begorrah!" Then there was silence from the other side of the grill. I was glad I couldn't see his eyebrows twitching. At last he spoke in sepulchral tones.

"How hold are you, my son?"

"Eleven, Father, going on for twelve."

"Bejabers! You know what lewd thoughts har, to be sure?"

"Yes, Father, they're things you shouldn't have, they're pretty serious." I was getting really worried now. "I had just two or three of them, Father."

"Ha won't ask ye whot they were son." Phew! That was a relief; apart from the peeing theory I had run out of ideas. "But they har serious, they're halmost akin to adultery."

I'm not sure, but I think I might have blacked out for a few seconds. The next thing I heard were those grave tones again in the middle of a sentence - "almost mortal sins."

Phew! I was relieved, 'almost'!

Was I hallucinating? Or did I detect a hint of laughter in his voice now. Surely not!

"For your penance son, say three Our Fathers hend twelve Hail Marys."

'My big mouth again,' I thought. Now I would have to make time in my busy life for this huge penance, so big it must be a record. I vowed there and then to stick to confessing run-of-the-mill venial sins in future.

I was becoming more aware of events happening in the outside world now that I was reading Mam's 'bible' - the Daily Herald, the voice of the Labour Party.

Adolf Hitler had reoccupied the Rhineland and the threat of war was again casting a shadow over Europe, another shadow! Gas masks were now being mass-produced for the civilian population.

The abdication of Edward VIII was followed by the coronation of George VI on the 12th of May, 1937. I remember that there was a street party, flags and bunting flying and best of all a holiday from school. All of us children had been presented with a Coronation mug so I had a container to receive dollops of the pop that was flowing like water.

That same year Joe Louis, the 'The Brown Bomber' beat the German, Max Schmeling, for the heavyweight boxing championship of the world. That was one in the eye for Hitler!

Babe and I were now going to the matinees at the Bensham Picture House. It was known as the 'fleapit'. Sometimes, when I was scratching my belly, I thought I knew why. 'The Pictures' became a weekly treat and used up most of our pocket money. First we would watch a cowboy picture, and then there would be a serial.

Our favourite was 'Flash Gordon'; he would finish up at the end of each episode in a perilous predicament. As far as we could see there was no escape. It was a bit of a worry to have to wait seven days to see how cleverly he turned the table on his enemies. Our relief only lasted twenty minutes, though before the daredevil was threatened with death or worse again. Another harrowing week was in store for us!

In time, we did get a little blasé about the whole thing; it only took a couple of years or so.

The cowboys! They seemed so brave and dashing with their cowboy hats, neckerchiefs - Tom Mix, Buck Jones, Ken Maynard. They had such clever horses, such handsome white stallions. It was all action, they didn't mess about with soppy girls much, as they seemed to do in the one or two grown-up cowboy pictures I had seen with Mam.

After the picture show we would ride our imaginary horses down Derwentwater Road or was it the Deadwood Trail? We fired our six-shooters at the bandits who always appeared on Saturday afternoons in Gateshead. It did not matter one jot to us, that in reality they were innocent citizens going about their legitimate business. Luckily we only had percussion caps in our pistols, not bullets, otherwise a special edition of the 'Evening Chronicle' would have rolled hot off the press - 'Massacre in Gateshead' the headline, thus relegating the 'Football Final' to a Sunday morning print. That would not have pleased football fans eager to read about the exploits of Tynesiders, Newcastle United, or even Gateshead F.C., whilst also hoping to find that Wearsiders, Sunderland, had suffered another defeat.

Saturdays were exciting. After tea, we would accompany Mam to Coatsworth Road - apart from the High Street, the busiest and best shopping thoroughfare in Gateshead. Most of the shops stayed open until nine or even ten o'clock on a Saturday night. The brightly lit pavements were crowded with people jostling and laughing as they hunted for bargains. For many, it was the highlight of the week. Babe and I soaked up the excitement; our favourite shop was Johnson's Toys. We pressed our noses to the plate-glass window, longing to be able to buy some of the thrilling things.

Mam would let us drool for a few minutes, then, "Come on, boys," she would say, "life's not all beer and skittles." Beer and skittles! It wasn't even all pop and tiddlywinks! We would then concentrate on the main purpose of the expedition, the search for bargains in the food shops. Money was tight, so whether it was the butcher selling off sausages, broken biscuits from the grocers, or bruised fruit and wilting vegetables from the fruiterers, we were to the forefront. I got great satisfaction in pointing out to Mam some bargain that she'd missed.

We helped Mam carry our goodies home and would then show them to Dad who was usually sitting in Uncle's armchair (the armchair was still called Uncle's), sipping a glass of wheat wine to help him forget his illness. Dad would always say "By, you've got some good bargains this week!" That was in between painful bouts of coughing and his gasping for breath.

Don didn't come with us on our Saturday night forays, he was almost sixteen, and at the weekend he and his pals were off to Low Fell to parade up and down the main street. They would warily eye similar groups of lads and admire with awe bevies of teenage girls. From what I could gather, nothing much happened on these nights. If he clicked with a girl, he certainly never told me, he probably never tried to click anyway. It would have altered his comfortable routine. Before he went on 'Low Fell Parade' I would catch Don at Saturday tea looking at himself in his knife and appraising his coiffure of short back and sides. After tea, his pals would call for him all dressed in best suits, with Brylcreemed hair - Humpy, Jonesy, Stewart, and Stewart's cousin. Stewart's cousin was a recent addition to the squad; I didn't know his real name.

"Who is that lad?" I would ask.

"That's Stewart's cousin," he would say. My guess was that Don didn't know his name either. He was a bit like that.

By the spring of 1938 Dad was spending more and more time in bed, listening to his favourite gramophone records, Caruso, Gigli, Gilbert and Sullivan, or dozing restlessly. Even reading was becoming an effort, although he always seemed pleased to hear about our exploits.

He had received one disappointment; I had failed to earn a grammar school place to the surprise of family and teachers. I suppose I was doing so well at school that expectations were high. I wasn't too worried, I was more concerned about Dad. At least I would be able to go to work in a year or so and earn some much-needed money.

In the meantime Mam got a part-time job as a barmaid at the Honeysuckle on Coatsworth Road and our Saturday night shopping expeditions ended. Saturday now, was one of the many nights that I stayed at home to look after baby Stephen who was now two years old. Dad couldn't do more than give advice and Don was excused to continue his Low Fell jaunts and visits to the Coatsworth Cinema. This was a slightly upmarket movie house when compared to the flea ridden Bensham. Don could afford the extra threepence admission you see, he was a breadwinner.

Little Stephen wasn't any bother, I would put him to sleep in his rackety cot early in the evening and have a few games with Babe, before he too went to bed. Then I would read a book whilst waiting for Mam. It was very quiet for an hour or two apart from Dad's coughing spasms.

"Please make Dad better," I prayed.

Chapter 6

DAD'S BEST SUIT

My prayer seemed in vain on the day that Mam and I were in the front bedroom talking to Dad.

Painfully, he raised himself up on his pillow. "Agnes." It was strange to hear him call Mam by her Christian name, it was usually 'pet' or 'dear'. "I've been thinking, I know how you can get a bit of money." He paused for breath, "I want you to pawn my suit, you should get a pound for it at least, I've hardly worn it."

Mam was taken aback for a moment. "No, Albert." This use of Christian names sent a shiver down my spine. "You'll need it again when you begin to feel better."

Dad smiled wanly, "I don't think so, and you don't either, dear."

Mam burst into tears, "Oh, Albert, I don't want to pawn your suit, it'll feel awful."

I'd heard enough; I couldn't listen any more to their sombre talk. Sobbing quietly, I rushed out of the room to hide my grief. Dad must have persuaded Mam to do as he wanted. Next day, I found her wrapping up the suit in brown paper, the tears running down her cheeks.

"You're going to the pawn shop then, Mam?" I asked. "Do you want me to come with you?" I wasn't keen on going, but I thought that she would like someone with her on this sad mission, even if it were only me.

The pawnbroker's wasn't too far away - along Askew Road and then down a little side street. I knew we'd found it when I saw the three brass balls over the doorway. Mam looked around to make sure that no one she knew was in the vicinity, no one to witness her ignominy, before she opened the door. The inside of the shop was funereal, both in appearance and atmosphere. I gave a start, as a man with a black beard and moustache appeared from a curtain behind the counter. He was wearing spectacles with thick lenses.

His voice was gravelly. "Yes, m'dear? What can I do for you?" he said, eyeing the parcel, knowing full well what he could and would do.

Mam spoke hesitantly, "How much will you lend on this?"

He raised his glasses to his forehead and meticulously unwrapped the parcel, putting the paper and string under the counter. He squinted as he examined the suit, shaking his head, as though finding faults.

"Ten shillings. Then you'll have six months to redeem it."

"Is that all you can give me? I was expecting at least a pound, it's a good suit."

"Times are hard, m'dear."

"I can't take as little as that," Mam said. "Fifteen perhaps? Or I'll have to take it back."

"Look dear, twelve and six is as much as I can give," he said with a spurious smile on his face.

"And I'll have six months to redeem it?" I was sure that she knew she would be doing no such thing.

"You'll have six months, I'll give you a chitty."

After giving her the pawn ticket, he counted out five half-crowns. "And there's sixpence for the lad."

Wonders never cease; I wouldn't have believed the old skinflint would have done such a thing. I suppose he was inviting us to bring further business his way. As we walked down Askew Road, Mam said, "Don't tell your dad that we only got twelve and six for his nice suit."

"No, Mam," I said, fingering the tanner in my pocket. I'd never had a sixpence of my own before. It was only then that I discovered one reason why Mam had agreed to let me go with her to the pawnshop in the first place.

"We'll go round by Coatsworth Road, I'll buy you a pair of shoes. I was going to buy Babe a pair as well, but now he'll have to wait. He'll have to have hand-me-downs, that pair you grew out of a couple of years ago."

Mam bought me a pair of stout shoes. I had tried them on,

they seemed alright, all shiny and new. I wanted to wear them there and then, but Mam said no, they might have to be changed yet, if I found them too tight. I think she wanted to make sure there was room for growth. So I walked down Derwentwater Road carrying my shoes, instead of proudly wearing them.

"Talking about Babe, Mam," I said as we walked over the railway bridge. "He's called Cecil at school and he doesn't like to be called Babe at all, so why don't we call him Cecil from now on?"

Mam laughed. "What a good idea, we'll tell him and your dad straightaway when we get home. It'll take his mind off not having a new pair of shoes!"

As we turned into our street Mam gave me her last half-crown.

"Nip into Dick's and get a couple of barley wines for your Dad. Don't forget to get the change."

Dick's was our local off licence; Richard Law was the licensee. He was a tall, smart ex-policeman with an Errol Flynn moustache. No one called him Dick, or by his nickname - 'Law and Order' - to his face.

"How's your dad? It's a bit since I saw him on the trams."

"Not too good, Mr Law, he's had to give up work."

"Well, tell him I'm asking after him, will you?"

"I will, Mr Law," I said. He didn't offer to treat him to the two bottles of barley wine, though. When we got home, we showed Dad my shoes and gave him his barley wine.

"You shouldn't have got the barley wine for me, the money was for you," he said, pausing for breath. Then he added, "Thank you, Agnes, all the same, I'll have one tonight and one tomorrow night. Was the pawnbroker alright?"

"A bit funny, but not so bad," she said, giving me a knowing look and changing the subject quickly. "Den and I have made a decision between us this afternoon, I know you'll agree. You'd better," she threatened, jokingly. "We want to start calling Babe, Cecil, he's getting too big for that silly name."

"That's good," he said, "it is about time we dropped that name. Mind, he'll always be Babe to me."

Mam laughed. "Babe," she shouted. He was in the parlour. "Come in here, pet."

"What do you want, Mam?" he asked, coming into the bedroom.

"Well, the three of us here have been talking about you and we have decided we are not going to call you Babe any more, but Cecil, the name you're called at school. Babe's a daft name for a big lad."

"Oh good," he said, although mingled with delight at losing the stupid Babe name, I sensed he was disappointed at not being called by his first name - Malcolm. How he got to be called Cecil at school I don't know. It was the same with me, why Dennis and not Paul?

Chapter 7

LOSS

That was a minor worry in the greater scheme of things. The Daily Herald was telling us of the Nazis marching into Austria, and of their claim to the Sudetenland region of Czechoslovakia. Hitler seemed hellbent on building a greater Germany. We were all fearing that war was not far away.

Mam was now finding that her money no longer lasted from one meagre Friday payday to the next. She knew that Danny the grocer at the top of our street allowed credit to reliable customers, and the time came when Mam added her name to his list.

It was usually the Wednesday of each week that Mam would say something like, "Den, get the basket and take this note to the 'Top Shop'. Ask Danny to give you the things on it. I've only asked for flour and yeast and some marge and jam. I've written I'll pay him on Friday as usual. When you come back from the shop I'll be able to bake some bread."

Wednesday was the norm for this arrangement, but sometimes when things were more desperate it was a Tuesday. 'Tick at the Top Shop' was a regular thing now. I don't know why it was called the 'Top Shop' in the first place. We didn't have a bottom shop in our street. Unless you called the off licence a shop.

I was always going 'messages' - on a Saturday with a bit of money still in the kitty, it was off to the butcher's for a cheap joint. Wednesday it was just 'twopennorth of lap'. Lap? Some part of a sheep? I daren't imagine, but Mam said it was a tasty part. With potatoes and a few veg, though, it made a dinner for the family. Ham shank was another cheap buy Mam made use of – "The basis of a many a good broth," she said. It was, especially if there was a little extra meat left on the bone. Mam's note for the butcher sometimes asked for a 'quarter of brawn', if I'd had a pencil I would have crossed it out. Brawn was a strange jelly-like substance; I didn't like it. I didn't like mysteries; the lap puzzle was enough for me. Besides, 'brawn' sounded too much like brain, ugh!

Other times, I'd be asked to go to the fish and chip shop on a Saturday night, for twopennorth of chips with plenty of scranchions, plus a couple of dollops of mushy peas. That would be a real supper treat. I was a busy shopper in those days. "Mr Reliable," Mam called me. She was good at the blarney.

In September of 1938, two things happened. The first, the family, like almost everyone in the country, were issued with gas masks. War looked more and more likely as Hitler launched another tirade against the Czechs. Now he was accusing them of discriminating against their German-speaking minority. A Nazi invasion of Czechoslovakia seemed imminent and that could involve Britain and France - they had guaranteed the Czech border. The other thing - I discovered that our class, at least those that wanted to, could go to school camp. If I went, I would dodge a week's tour of the shops.

We were to go to Blackhall Rocks, a village on the Durham coast. I tried to look it up in my school atlas, but couldn't find it marked. I'd been told it was near Hartlepool; that place was on the map, so now I knew it wasn't all that far from Gateshead.

Even so, I wasn't desperately keen on going away with twenty boys and twenty squealing lasses, particularly as my best friend John Brown had cried off. Mam and Dad, however, had set their minds on me going. "It'll do you good," they said - I was fighting a losing battle there.

I had never been away from home before, my knees knocked when I boarded the coach. A multitude of gossiping mothers came to see us off. Mam and Cecil were looking anxious. I thought, 'Shall I jump off and shout, "Mam, I've changed my mind. I don't have to go. They can't make me go, Mam, can they?" No, I'd be scoffed at by my schoolmates for years.' Instead, I stayed in my seat and just waved miserably to Mam. I called myself all the names under the sun for being so soft; it was only a week away from home, after all.

After what seemed a long journey on the swaying coach, with kids making a racket and one lad being sick, we turned off the main road and lurched down a sort of dirt track to our destination. I was puzzled, it was just a collection of wooden huts, I thought a camp would be a lot of tents. I saw the signs on some of the buildings, 'Dining Room', that sounded promising, 'Boys Dormitory' and 'Girls Dormitory'; I was pleased about those signs too. At least we would be segregated! No strange giggling girls messing things up. I must have been a late developer.

The rest of the day passed in a flurry. We had put our few goods and chattels in the lockers in our dormitories and then had a big tea. After the meal, our form master, 'Chronic' Waters, gave us a talk on do's and don'ts. There seemed a lot more don'ts than do's. One don't, he made a point of stressing - we must not go down to the beach without a teacher, there was danger in the tides.

I could think of one don't that Chronic should have observed himself - don't sneak up behind pupils in the classroom and clip them across the lughole, just because they weren't concentrating on their work. We were all a bundle of nerves at school when he hovered at the back of the class. We always wondered who he was going to pounce on next. He caused many an epidemic of red ears.

It was rumoured that a piece of shrapnel was embedded in his skull, a relic of his time on the Western Front in the war. It seemed as good an excuse as any for his unreasonable behaviour, mind. I remember walking to school with John Brown one day. "Brownie, why does such a fiend as Chronic go to Mass every Sunday?" I asked, expertly kicking a tin can under a passing tramcar.

John had a theory. At least his mam did. "Me mam says it's so he can pray to God to give him strength to wallop us on a Monday. I'm glad me mam doesn't pray for that. She's bigger than Chronic."

"The things people will pray to God for!" I gasped. Anyway, after Chronic's talk we watched a Laurel and Hardy film in the Main Hall. The girls all screamed at their antics, but that was to be expected. There was no need for sensible lads to do the same though, was there? Main Hall! What a grand name for a wooden hut. After the Stan and Ollie bit of excitement, it was off to bed in our dormitories.

I had a pair of Don's hand-me-down pyjamas; they were a bit big for me. Some of the lads didn't have any at all and slept in their underpants. It was strange to be in a bed on my own, but I was so tired I was asleep in no time.

The next thing I knew, Willie Duff, another pal of mine, was shaking me.

"Gerrup, Pottsy, wa deein' P.T. befower brekkie, wiv gorra git dressed, gerra move on, Chronic's cummin' roond."

I jumped out of bed at the mention of Chronic; I didn't want a blow from him, my left ear had been singing since before the school holidays as it was. I got dressed and staggered sleepily with the others into the Main Hall.

Fortunately P.T. was only a light work out, although Duffy wasn't amused. "P.T.!" he said. "I thowt this was ganna be a holidaa!"

After breakfast of scrambled eggs, things brightened up for a while. All the lads were going down to the beach, a couple of hundred yards from the camp. It was a nice day for late September and we chattered in the sunshine on the way.

Chronic would never have made a Redcoat at Butlins, the happy campers wouldn't have put up with him for an hour, never mind a day. "Hurry up, you lazy lot, stop straggling," he said waving a cricket stump at us. Suddenly there were no stragglers, the threat of the stump and the crazy person brandishing it did the trick.

We were going to play cricket and some of the lads were carrying the gear (minus Chronic's stump). "Are we playing here, sir?" someone asked.

"No, not here," he shouted, "the girls are using this part of the beach for netball. Come on, move along."

"What about here, sir?" stupid Stevie Lawrence said, inviting a crack on the shins.

"Will you rabble shut up? We'll play where I say so!" We skirted around a couple of rocky outcrops below the cliffs and finally he seemed happy, if he ever could be. There was a lovely stretch of smooth sand, which, although it was blackened by coal dust from nearby collieries, was ideal for beach cricket.

"Right, lads," he said. "You, Duff, and you, Jameson, will be captains, I'm going up to the back for a rest, so get yourself organised. I had a busy day yesterday, sorting out you lot, and then to thank me for it, you kept me awake with your snoring all night."

It took ages to pick two teams. Duffy picked me as vice-captain; well he had to, didn't he? It took about twenty minutes messing about, before we finally got to playing cricket. When we started the game, there was a wide stretch of sand down to the sea, but the tide had turned and began to encroach on our playing surface. Scoring boundaries became much easier, mind. Some of the lads lost interest in the cricket and started paddling. Eventually we all joined in, splashing and kicking water over each other.

Nobody had noticed the effect of the tide, until Jameson shouted. "Look, lads, wa ganna be curoff. Grab ya shoes and the cricket stuff and mayk a dash forrit!"

He was right; the sea was already a foot high around the small headland. The cliffs at the rear of the beach looked almost impossible to scale, we had to get through the water.

We all dashed for our shoes. Some of us, and that included me, couldn't swim. At school, the procedure was that the more academic pupils were assigned to a shorthand class, whilst the rest got to enjoy the municipal swimming baths. So that left me and a few others with what could turn out to be a slight disadvantage. Pitman's shorthand wasn't going to help - long legs would have been more useful.

It was when I picked up my shoes that I suddenly thought of our beloved teacher sleeping at the back of the beach. If we left him, he might drown. Oh dear! My first instinct was to run for it, but after a short tussle, my better self won out. "Duffy," I shouted, "Chronic must be asleep, we should wake him."

Like me, Duffy hesitated for a second, "Do ye think so?" Then, "Aal gan, ye canna swim," he said.

"I'll wait here, then," I shouted stupidly.

Duffy dashed to the back, I could see him shaking Chronic and hear him yelling. In the circumstances I thought that our teacher appraised the situation with commendable quickness, showing remarkable agility for someone with a piece of metal in his head. He was on his feet, hopping and taking off his socks and shoes, at one and the same time.

With one brief look behind to see that Chronic was following, Duffy and I waded through the rising water. With some difficulty we managed to get to the next little bay. The other lads were already paddling around the second promontory way ahead. It appeared to be even deeper there.

It was! Minutes later I was almost up to my waist in the flowing tide, my shorts were soaked. Twice I fell and twice Duffy helped me up. Then, I fell again and this time couldn't get to my feet, as I swallowed salty water.

Was I grateful when I felt firm hands grab me and lift me? The hands of Chronic, who staggered with me to dry land and safety. Was I glad then that we had woken him up?

The experience took the wind out of our sails for the rest of the day. A chastened group of schoolboys we were, as we dried out in the dormitory. As well as fresh clothes, our teacher had to dig out his spare pair of shoes. He had lost those he was carrying when rescuing me from the tide. After smartening himself up, Chronic then had to report to the powers that be in the Camp Office.

It was a very chagrined teacher who returned to supervise us. He would have been even more distressed, I thought, if the local lifeboat had been called out. I'm sure he would have hated the publicity. All the same, for the first time, I was pleased that our teacher had strong hands.

That was the highlight of our camping holiday. The next morning we were all called into the main hall to hear a special announcement.

We were to return to our homes, school camp was cancelled. The crisis in middle Europe was becoming even more serious. Prime Minister Neville Chamberlain was travelling to Munich, in an attempt to get some sort of an agreement from Adolf Hitler. Failure could mean war.

It was later that day therefore, that I arrived back home and next day was doing my shopping chores again. 'Mr Reliable' was back.

A few days later the Daily Herald displayed the infamous

photograph of Chamberlain waving his piece of paper. 'Peace in our time', was the quote.

Not many people believed that.

Dad survived only a few more months, he was very ill at Christmas. Into the New Year, he never made it to his armchair. When he could be bothered, I spent time in the front room talking to him. "Dad," I said one night, "we've got a new kitten, look."

He opened his eyes, "That's good. Your mam was telling me she saw a mouse in the scullery the other day."

"I think this kitten would be frightened of a mouse, Dad," I laughed. Dad smiled weakly.

It was the last evening of January 1939 when Dad spoke his last words to me.

When I was heading for bed that night, Dad, thinking about us as always, said, "Don't forget to keep that kitten, Den, it will get rid of any mice." Then he closed his eyes.

"O.K., Dad, don't worry I'll see that we keep it." He was in a troubled sleep when I left for school next morning. The first lesson had just ended when I was sent for by the Headmaster. I was wanted at home, Cecil would stay at school until lunchtime.

I knew why I was called home. A tearful Mam hugged me and told me the news. The news I dreaded to hear. I went into the bedroom. Dad looked peaceful at last, no more racking coughs, no more struggling for breath. I sobbed on his pillow.

I had lost a wonderful father.

Chapter 8

LONGUNS AT LAST

Life without Dad.

Stephen found it strange at first whenever he limped into the bedroom and Dad wasn't there. Until Mam explained to him that he had gone to heaven. He seemed to be happy with that. "Daddy come back soon," he would assert.

Don was now the senior man (seventeen in April), but he didn't get a man's wage. So Mam got a job on night duty at an old people's home, which helped to ease our poverty. This retirement home had, in Victorian days, been the 'Workhouse,' once home to paupers. She worked four nightshifts each week getting home about eight in the morning. That would give her time to get Cecil and me off to school. Stephen would be our responsibility during those nights and, fortunately, he slept like a log. That was just as well, because we were no slouches when it came to heavy sleep.

A red-letter day early that year was when Mam got her first pay packet. Her first act was to pay off the 'tick' owed to Danny at the Top Shop. Her second was arranging to hire a Northern Rediffusion radio at two shillings a week.

The first day's listening was glum. We heard on the B.B.C. that German troops had marched into Czechoslovakia, effectively occupying the whole country, with no resistance at all. There was no response from Britain or France, other than verbal condemnation, which Mam said was water off a duck's back to Adolf Hitler.

"So much for Neville Chamberlain's 'piece of paper'," I said. Mam was finding that now I was just as interested in the news as she was.

Although I always listened to the 'News', thankfully there were happier programmes - Arthur Askey in 'Bandwagon', 'Monday Night at Seven'. Famous dance bands. The radio highlight for me that summer was listening to the Test Match cricket commentary between England and the West Indies. They were to be the last Test Matches for seven years. Memory tells me that 1939 was not the first time we had heard a broadcast in our house, mind. Funnily enough, five years earlier, when I was eight, Mam and I had listened to a wireless. In that year there was a big Royal Wedding, the Duke of Kent was marrying Princess Marina, the 'stylish Princess Marina', according to the Daily Herald, and of course the King and Queen attended the ceremony together with dignitaries from all parts of the globe. I knew that Mam had followed the build-up to the ceremony in the paper. On the big day, Mam happened to open the door to the large cupboard in our parlour and heard voices. Curious, she put her ear to the wall, and lo and behold! John Snagg was describing the ceremony as though he was next door, which I suppose in a way he was. Our neighbour Mrs Maggs (Mad Maggie Maggs, we called her), a crotchety, rather deaf, old woman must have turned up the sound on her wireless.

"Den, listen," Mam said. "It's the wedding!"

She was right, a voice was saying - "We are gathered here together." (I guessed it was the Archbishop of Canterbury.)

I didn't hear any more because Mam said, "Let me in again," nudging me impatiently out of the way.

For the next half hour she had her head against the wall and relayed the service to me. "They look lovely," she said. She must have been psychic, our Mam. I pretended an interest, but would have much preferred to listen to a commentary on the Australian Test Matches any day.

I made frequent sorties to the cupboard when cricket commentaries were being broadcast, but there was never a sound from next door. I think our neighbour preferred royal weddings to cricket. Funny woman, I never did like her.

What I do remember about that episode, Mam was complaining of a stiff neck next day.

Now, five years on, the hire of our set did mean that there would be no longer any need to go eavesdropping in cupboards. As it happened, later in the summer of 1939, our street was wired for electricity and a real radio would now work in our house. It was just a small question of the money, though. But wasn't this electricity like magic? Light in our flat at the flick of a switch! Goodbye to matches and gas mantles.

Hello to war. On that fateful third of September 1939, like almost everyone else in Britain, we listened to Chamberlain's declaration of war with Germany.

The air raid warning sirens blared within minutes of his announcement. Thankfully, the weird wailing was closely followed by the all-clear signal. That warning sound sent shivers up my spine, wondering what horrors might lie ahead.

We checked that our gas masks were handy, and spent hours applying sticky tape to the windows, to lessen the danger of flying glass when bombs were dropping. We had organised our blackout blinds a couple of days earlier.

Stephen spent most of the day wearing his gas mask. He found that if he blew into it in a certain way he could make rude noises. He giggled uproariously, a sound which seemed uncanny under that mask. We couldn't help laughing at his antics, the poor beggar didn't realise what a solemn day it was; he was still only three.

There wasn't anything exciting on the radio that day. Sandy MacPherson, the organist, had been called upon to play solemn music. We were in a serious enough mood as it was, so we switched him off.

Later in the day I asked Mam if I could stay up until it got dark, to see what the blackout was like.

When darkness arrived, I opened the front door and looked out into the street. It was a cloudy night and almost pitch-black, except for the light shining along the passage from the parlour. It cast an exciting beam as it probed the darkness. There was a shout. "Put that light out!"

My mistake! I should have closed the parlour door. I slammed the front door shut quickly and put my back against it - to keep out the noise, I suppose. It didn't work, I could still hear the voice of Charlie Cook, our officious Air Raid Warden shouting, "Who showed that light?! Who showed that light?!"

Already his A.R.P. armband seemed to be giving him delusions of grandeur. What would he be like when he got his tin hat? I turned on the radio so Mam wouldn't hear his strident voice. Sandy MacPherson was still at it. Was he going to play that dratted organ all through the war? In desperation I tried Radio Luxembourg (usually broadcasting light cheerful programmes). All I heard was slow classical music.

Was this going to be our radio fare? If so, roll on the peace!

In disgust, I went to bed to read my Beano.

Radio-wise, after a few weeks, things did improve. 'Hi Gang', with Ben Lyon and Bebe Daniels and the comedian violinist, Vic Oliver. 'The Hippodrome', with Harry Korris and the gormless 'Enoch'. There was also 'ITMA' which was very popular, but not with me somehow.

A lot of the kids in our street were evacuated to the countryside in the early days of the war, although most had straggled home by the next spring. Mam, however, couldn't face the prospect of the family splitting up; she was still recovering from the loss of Dad. Staying at home brought some advantages, our school was closed for weeks and by the time it reopened I was nearly fourteen and old enough for work. So I didn't go back. Goodbye to classes, goodbye to Chronic. With a 'Provident' voucher, repayable over twenty weeks, Mam bought me a gent's suit - longuns at last! My short trews were put in the hand-me-down cupboard for Cecil. No bare knees and, with my new identity card, I was almost a man! Wasting no time, two days after my birthday, I set out to find a job. That's not strictly true - to my mortification Mam came with me. Our first port of call was the local employment exchange. There, I was told of a vacancy for an office boy at Caledonian Connectors Co., in the east side of Gateshead.

Mam said to the clerk. "That's just what he wants." She turned to me. "What do you think, Dennis?"

"Well," I said, trying to sound grown up, stroking my beardless chin, "If it's in an office, it's what I want alright."

The clerk gave me an introduction card to take to the factory.

"I'll come with you to this place, Den," she said.

I braced my shoulders, "No, Mam, I had better go myself, the clerk's described how to get there."

"Alright, son," she said, "but don't be scared, speak up for yourself."

In some ways I would have been a lot happier if Mam had

come with me, certainly less nervous, but I guessed that to go for a job with Mam at my shoulder wouldn't be a good move.

I found the place with some difficulty; the name board over the door could have done with a coat of paint. I paused in the dingy porch and straightened my new tie. Nervously, I knocked on the window marked 'Reception'. I waited for what seemed an age, but there was no response. My hands were moist now; I could feel beads of sweat on my forehead.

I banged again, harder this time, the sound echoed around the porch. I stepped back, trying to distance myself from its source. There was another noise now - my heart beating against my ribs.

A white-haired, hawk-like, bespectacled man in a grey overall opened the window. He looked me up and down, I felt quite small. I wasn't very big to start with. "What do you want, sonny?" he asked. "There's a bell there to ring if you want attention, you know."

I saw it now. "Sorry, sir. I've come from the Labour Exchange about the job for an office boy."

"Well, come in," he muttered in a testy voice, as though I was holding him back from more important duties. I discovered later that he was the timekeeper, 'Old Miller', and his job was of a lowly nature in the office hierarchy. Above that of an office boy, mind.

He let me in and showed me to a door on the left, just inside the small general office. 'Manager' said the sign. Mr Miller knocked and a voice bade me enter.

The most kindly looking man I'd ever met was seated at the desk. He looked like a jolly Santa Claus without the beard, chubby-cheeked with a friendly smile. His hands and his head were shaking uncontrollably. I didn't know it then, but Parkinson's disease was well advanced.

At this my first job interview, however, he put me at ease from the start. He took my introduction card and glanced at it briefly. "M-my name is S-Stewart. S-so, you did w-well at s-school?" his speech, too, was affected by his ailment. "You w-want to work in an office?"

"Yes, Mr Stewart."

"W-well we w-want an office b-boy for our b-bottom office, the w-works office," it was painful to listen to him. "Five days a w-week and S-Saturday mornings. T-ten shillings a w-week. Any q-questions, s-sonny?"

"That seems fine to me, sir. What do you manufacture, Mr Stewart?"

"B-bolts, n-nuts and r-rivets, sonny. I j-judge p-people on f-first impressions, P-Paul," he stuttered. "You c-can s-start on M-Monday, n-nine o'clock, O.K.?"

"That would be fine, Mr Stewart." He got unsteadily to his feet and held out a trembling hand. In a grave manner, trying to live up to my long trousers, I shook it firmly.

"S-see you on-on M-Monday, then, s-sonny." I walked home in a bit of a daze; ten bob a week and to be called Paul seemed alright to me.

The following Monday, I got the tram to the High Street and walked the half mile to the factory.

Jack Wood, the senior clerk in the factory office, a cheery man in his thirties, escorted me to my place of work. We walked through a large department filled with clattering machines, manned by overall-clad women, most of them young.

"This is the Screwing Shop," Jack said.

I don't think the word had the same connotation, then, that it has today, if it had I wouldn't have known anyway. The operatives were employed to cut the thread on blank bolts and nuts, that's when they weren't staring and whistling at new office boys. I sensed my face was a bright shade of red when we reached the steps up to the bottom office.

"Is there another way from the top office to the bottom office?" I asked Jack.

"You can go around outside by way of the gangway."

There and then I made a resolution - the gangway for me. Come rain or snow!

The bottom office wasn't very large, just a row of Dickensian desks, where the few staff sat on high stools. There was Anne, blondish, vaguely pretty, but with a trace of moustache, probably in her late twenties. Then Lily, a little, prim woman in her late fifties. Jack of course, and Harry, sixteen-year-old, the office junior - but junior no longer, now that I had arrived.

There was also the most important personage in the office, Duncan Cameron, the Rivet Shop manager, in his sixties. He had a cantankerous look about him, what hair he had was white, as were his eyebrows and moustache. The head office of the company was in Glasgow, so too was their main factory. Cameron had been transferred from Scotland many years before; I think he still hankered after returning to his homeland.

Over the next few weeks I learned the routine - rubber stamping tallies with descriptions and sizes of rivets or bolts, filling in the details of railway-wagon tickets, seeing to the post, answering the archaic telephone. A booth in the office housed this instrument - a fixed mouthpiece and an earpiece attached by a cord. This was my introduction to the field of high technology.

It was by no means an onerous job; Harry and I had lulls in our work, which we tried to fill in in a constructive way. For example, the sloping desks were ideally suited to our version of ha'penny football. We each in turn would flick our penny (the player), and with it, try to hit the ha'penny (the ball), so that it went through the opponent's goal (chalk marks on each side of the desk.) Oh no! It wasn't as easy as people would think. You had to allow for the slope of the desk as the coins curved in a subtle trajectory.

When we tired of our football, we would play the tally flicking game. This was more active. We would stand at either end of the office with a handful of cardboard tallies, and flick them at each other between a finger and thumb. If you were in form, they would spin gracefully through the air. The object of the game was not to let a tally hit you, and more importantly not to let a tally hit Anne, Lily, or Jack. Generally, they were understanding of our need for harmless relaxation, providing they didn't get flicked in the eye. It was a happy office.

There was quite a lot of skill involved in our games, not the least facet keeping a wary eye open for Cameron, coming back from frequent tours of inspection of his beloved Rivet Shop. Although, give them credit, Anne, Lily, and Jack, were quite good lookouts too.

"Hey up," they would shout, "here comes the gaffer."

Cameron always carried a pair of tongs with him on his trips into the works. He would pick up a red hot rivet straight from the die and examine it for quality with what purported to be expert eyes.

I hated to go into the Rivet Shop to call him to the phone. There were a dozen furnaces throwing out white-hot heat and beside each was a rivet machine. Each machine was manned by three persons - a feeder, who inserted steel bars into the furnace and, when white-hot, processed them through the cutter. The rivet maker then, with his tongs, fed the short lengths into a revolving die table where they were forged into rivets. Finally, the young picker-out, again using tongs, placed them in a container for bagging up when they had cooled.

The heat was overpowering, the noise tremendous, the sweat poured out of the workers. I marvelled at each picker-out, all young lads of sixteen or under and thought that job was not for me!

The Rivet Shop was more or less as I imagined Hell would be; only down below they would work twenty-four hour shifts instead of knocking off at five o'clock.

If that was a foretaste of Hell, I certainly didn't want to go!

The only snag was that, about this time, I was having strange sensations and thoughts. These feelings were magnified when Anne showed glimpses of stockinged thigh and more, as she slid sensuously down off her high stool. I think she was a bit of an exhibitionist, was Anne. One day, it struck me like a bolt from the blue - this was what Father O'Malley had been ranting on about that Sunday morning in church. These thoughts of mine were the real McCoy - one hundred per cent cast-iron lewd ones. I hoped it didn't mean I was going to end up in this Hades place. It was a confusing time.

It was also a bit of a worrying time for me. Usually when I finished work I would walk home at night over the Windmill Hills. The windmills had long since disappeared but the hills were still there. I wasn't the most robust of lads, about medium height when I started work, but growing rapidly. So rapidly, that I was soon taller than Don, a fact that didn't please my elder brother. I remember that for a period I became breathless climbing the bank, and had the morbid idea that I'd contracted T.B., like my Dad. It proved to be a needless worry and walking to and from work soon made me much fitter. Young brother, Stephen, was now nearly three, a very quiet lad and a daydreamer. I remember an evening when returning home from work I expected Mam to be up to her eyes in wallpaper and paste. She had told me that morning that she was going to decorate the parlour, so expect a mess. What I didn't expect was Stephen sitting in the passage with a saucepan over his head.

"Hello," I said, "what are you doing with that on your head?"

"A sodjer!" he said, "I'm a sodjer!"

"Can you get it off?" I asked.

He put his hands to the pan, then looked a bit anxious. I got a hold of it but it wouldn't budge. 'Here's where Mam comes into the picture,' I thought, 'it's rightly her problem.'

"Hello, Mam," I said, "Why is Stephen wearing a saucepan? On his head," I added superfluously. I couldn't see where else he would wear it.

"What do you mean, a saucepan?"

"You know, a pan you cook with."

"Oh, did you take it off?" she asked, busily pasting another strip of wallpaper.

"Well, I did try, but it won't come off. I thought you must have put it on for some reason."

She dropped her pasting brush. "Don't be stupid. My God! I asked Cecil to keep an eye on him. Instead, he must have gone out to play in the street!"

"Stephen!" she shouted, "Come in here at once!"

"He may not hear you," I said, "the pan's over his ears."

This remark seemed to compound what I suspected was a streak of panic.

Just then Stephen came limping into the room, the handle of the pan was at a rather jaunty, raffish angle. He didn't seem to be too worried yet. I thought he might be when he went to bed; he could have difficulty sleeping.

She rushed to him and frantically tried to take the saucepan off his head. It still wouldn't budge.

Stephen looked up at her and laughed, "Sodjer's tin hat!"

"I'll give you tin hat!" she shouted, then looked at me. "What are we going to do?"

"We could take him to the Queen Elizabeth." I didn't say hospital, I thought that word might upset the little lad. I had never been to the Q.E. in those days, but I knew it existed, didn't I just! Our grandmother, now a Justice of the Peace as well as being a Town Councillor, had laid one of the foundation stones. That was just before she moved into a grander council house.

"The Q.E.!" Mam moaned, "And who's going to take him on the

tram with a saucepan on his head? A battered old saucepan at that! Why couldn't he have put the best one on if he was going to do such a stupid thing?" I didn't think fellow tram passengers were going to notice the quality of the saucepan. They might however, wonder what mother would make a young kid wear a pan for a hat and then take him on a tramcar. I think Stephen was beginning to comprehend the seriousness of the situation at this point and started to cry. He ran back into the passage.

"We could get the Fire Brigade," I said clutching at straws.

"The Fire Brigade," she yelled, rather hysterically, "people climbing up ladders won't get the pan off his head." I think she missed the point; I made allowances for her, she must have had a tiring day.

Just then I heard the front door open. That'll be Don, I guessed from the sound of the footsteps - those of a working man returning from a heavy day in the engine sheds. He seemed to take a while to appear in the parlour, I heard him talking to Stephen.

Mam was sitting down shaking her head, trying to puzzle out what to do next, at the same time moaning, "I wish your dad was here! He would know what to do."

Don finally entered the room. It didn't register with Mam that he was carrying something.

She looked up. "Oh, Don, what are we going to do about that saucepan? What are we going to do? What are we going to do?"

"Just put it back on the shelf, I don't think you should have let him wear it Mam. He could have got it stuck on permanently." He held up the pan and handed it to her.

She accepted it disbelievingly. "How did you get it off?"

"Just twisted it a little," he said. I think it was then he realised that we'd had serious problems with the pan.

"You just needed a little strength," he smugly added.

"You're a miracle worker, Don," she said, as Stephen appeared in the doorway, wiping away his tears and coming to Mam for a loving hug.

'The red mark on his forehead will disappear in time,' I thought, watching Mam move all the saucepans to the top shelf in the cupboard.

The saying 'locking the stable door' crossed my mind.

Chapter 9

REAL WAR

Glad we were when the spring of 1940 dawned, bringing with it the promise of longer daylight hours. We'd had our fill of the dreariness of blacked-out nights. Mam was sick of the dark journey to the workhouse every evening, stumbling over kerbs and cobbles, her screened torch of little help. Soon, twilight would bring relief, and then the blessed long daylight evenings would be upon us. The expected bombing raids hadn't materialised during the first six months of the war, and the sticky tape was beginning to peel off our windows. The 'Phoney War', so named because of the standoff situation between the Allies and Germany, had lasted all winter through.

The Nazi attack, and occupation of Norway and Denmark in March, warned us that the 'Phoney War' was now over. The month of May saw the overrunning of Holland and Belgium by Panzer Divisions. Everything was happening so swiftly, always for the worse.

The country was bucked up no end when Winston Churchill became Prime Minister, replacing the inept Chamberlain. We heard Churchill's rousing, backs-to-the-wall speech offering only blood, tears, toil, and sweat. Victory and the war's end however, seemed a distant prospect. Mam still had suspicions of Churchill because of his part in defeating the workers in the General Strike of 1926. She accepted him, only because Clement Attlee (the Labour Party leader) had called for his appointment. If it was alright for Clem it had to be alright for Mam.

"He's the best man for the job, Mam," I said, "Chamberlain wasn't up to it."

"Hark at the expert!" she laughed.

Every day we listened to the radio and read the Daily Herald, searching for good news.

Dunkirk brought some relief, with many British soldiers escaping from encirclement by the German Army.

"It means they can fight another day, Mam," I pointed out.

"That's very true, Den."

I didn't tell her that I'd read that in the Daily Herald.

Things generally, were still going badly. Paris fell, and then came the armistice between France and Germany. It was a virtual French surrender, ending the fighting on the mainland of Europe and leaving us almost alone. But we were still defiant.

We followed these events with anxiety, wondering when Hitler would launch the invasion of Britain.

First, he wanted to defeat the R.A.F. and gain mastery of the air. The Battle of Britain began - daylight bombing raids to knock out our aerodromes and destroy our planes. It seemed to become a struggle for survival. We listened every day to the Air Ministry communiqués giving figures of planes lost by both sides. The Luftwaffe was losing more bombers in their daylight strikes than we were fighters, but what reserves had we got? How many pilots, how many planes?

Enough, it seemed, because we heard on the news one day in September, that the Luftwaffe had called off daylight raids, the Battle of Britain was over.

There was no respite for the people of London and the South. The German Air Force switched to a night-bombing blitz, an easier option for their Heinkels and Dorniers. The North of England suffered fewer raids; Hitler was targeting the capital.

The family did spend spells at night in the brick-built, concrete-roofed, backyard air raid shelter erected by the council during the summer. Cold nights, though, found us squashed under the dining table when bombs were dropping and our guns were firing. It was warmer inside and it seemed a sturdy piece of furniture! We dreaded any raid occurring when Mam was at work, though. Mam worried about us, and Don, Cecil and me were concerned about her. Work-wise, production at Caledonian Connectors was increased twofold - longer working hours, both in office and factory. The North East shipyards were now working flat out to build ships, for both the Royal Navy and the

Merchant Fleet. Our output was crucial. To coin a phrase, you could say that we were the nuts and bolts (and rivets) of the whole operation. Forgotten were the games of ha'penny football, tally flicking and other such frivolous amusements. Now it was all tally stamping, wagon despatching, dealing with urgent phone calls, sorting the post.

I still had time to observe the frequent flashes of Anne's thighs. She always seemed to make sure that there was an admirer around when she slid off the stool. 'Tease', would be the word to describe her. One afternoon, I was collecting her work for the post. "I've got a pain in my chest, right here," she said, pointing. "See if you can feel anything."

'A strange request,' I thought, as tentatively my hand explored. I could feel something sure enough. "It's soft," I said.

She laughed, "It's alright then." Gosh, It felt alright to me! That was the night of the mail mix up. She *was* a tease. Harry and I also began to notice that Jack and Anne seemed to spend a lot of time in the small cloakroom when they came back from lunch. Serious canoodling was suspected there.

Their behaviour, unsettling to us young lads, took place despite (or was it because?) Anne was engaged to an older man by the name of Sammy, a commitment which had already lasted for six years. Sammy seemed reluctant to name the day. Notwithstanding this, Anne was not only proud to display her thighs, she was even prouder to show off her engagement ring to all and sundry. Frankly, I thought it looked a bit tarnished. Like Anne?

Sadly, Sammy and Anne never got to the altar and Anne, finding herself jilted, had to look around for fresh fields. Despite the long hours, I got to the Regal, and the local Coatsworth picture house, once or twice a week. Sometimes with John Brown, but often on my own after John got himself a girlfriend. 'Lucky so-and-so,' I thought. When would I get a girl? I hoped I didn't have to wait until the cows came home. My social life never seemed to get off the ground.

Perhaps I was saving myself for the right girl. Ha Ha.

Meantime I enjoyed the 'flicks'. The likes of Robert Donat in 'Goodbye, Mr. Chips', John Steinbeck's 'The Grapes of Wrath', 'Kipps', 'How Green Was My Valley'.

Then there were the comedies of George Formby, Will Hay and

the like. In a bad week, I might have to scrape the barrel - 'Old Mother Riley' might be the only choice. On the radio, the inimitable Rob Wilton was a 'must listen' act. His classic - 'The day war broke out' catchphrase, and his sketches - 'The Home Guard', 'The Fireman', 'The Justice of the Peace', had the family in stitches. Fortunately, Robb Wilton's Home Guard platoon weren't asked to fight - the invasion never took place.

There was an invasion in the summer of 1941; Germany invaded Russia, to the surprise of a lot of pundits, including me. My verdict?

"Adolf's made a mistake now, Mam. He must be crazy!"

In the event, it was a close run thing. He did make a mistake, but it was more than three years, before he was finally proved wrong.

Later in the year, Mam introduced us to her new 'boyfriend', Rob Hall. (Well, he was only fifty-two.) He was a widower, with a broken nose and a Geordie accent. A cheerful fellow, he was a van driver employed by the L.N.E.R. It looked to be a serious committed relationship from the start. Pleasant as he was, to me, he would never replace Dad.

Rob had a daughter, and also a son, both married. The news had recently come through, that his son, Robby, had been captured by the Germans at the fall of Crete and was now a prisoner of war.

Food rationing was very severe now and towards the end of the year, it was extended even further - 'Points Rationing' was introduced. Each person was allocated 'points' to be used to obtain all canned foods. Like most things, these were in short supply. The sage spoke, "At least it's fair, Mam."

That same month, December, came the Japanese attack on Pearl Harbour and once again the oracle (or the know-it-all) was consulted.

"Well, Mam, make no bones about it, the Japs have destroyed a lot of the U. S. Fleet. It'll take a while for them to recover, but now that Germany's declared war on America, the 'Yanks' will be helping us in Europe. It's good news in the long run."

Cecil, who was listening, nodded his head in agreement. I thought he was becoming a sensible lad.

1942 arrived, a watershed year in our family. Mam got married to Rob Hall. It was a fait accompli. One day, she just went out, all smart. Two hours later she returned accompanied by Rob.

"We've got news for you all," Mam said. "Rob and I have just got married. We'll all be moving into his house in the Avenue as soon as we can."

Well, it was always on the cards, but to do it like that behind our backs. It took the biscuit! We three lads all went very quiet. I made a vow that day - I would never call him Dad. There was nothing we could do about it. The deed was done; it was too late to have our say. I could see one advantage, though - I wouldn't have to sleep in Mam's room any more. Now I was sixteen, that news had to be good.

The Avenue, where Rob lived, was slightly higher class than our humble street down Askew Road. Proof of that, if proof was needed - the Avenue is still standing, our old street was demolished many years ago. Our new home wasn't very far from Saltwell Park, but again it was one of a pair of flats, this time an upstairs one. There were three bedrooms, but still no bathroom, no hot water. Don and I would have to continue going to the public bathhouse. It was years now since we had used the tin bath in front of the fire.

What made the Avenue appear so upmarket to us, may have been the tiny garden plots in front of each downstairs flat. They introduced a touch of greenery to the street – an exotic sight for someone with a vivid imagination. Before the war, the green plots had been protected by iron railings, but these had been sacrificed as scrap iron for the war effort.

Within a few weeks of our move to the Avenue in 1942, Don was called up. He joined the Royal Air Force Regiment, which he always maintained was the R.A.F. equivalent of the Commandos. It seemed to please him to believe that, so as a good brother I didn't argue. Most of his duties, until he went to Normandy, involved the defence of airfields in England and Scotland, manning anti-aircraft defences. The Bofors gun was mentioned by him once or twice, although to give him credit, he only claimed one Luftwaffe plane shot down by his gun team. He collected many a story during his wartime service, some tall, but none short! I was afraid he was storing them up in his memory bank. Repetitious reminiscing was threatening the family. Could there be a hint of envy in me at this time?

Don, an active combatant, and me a seventeen-year-old civilian? What could I say? That I was a self-appointed pundit and that I fancied myself as a crooner in the Bing Crosby mould? No comparison to a near commando!

Crooner? Well, Mam said I had a canny voice, nobody walked out of the room when I joined in with Bing or Al Bowlly on the radio. On the other hand, crowds didn't rush into the room either. Whatever people thought of the singer, most liked the songs - 'The Inkspots' singing 'Do I Worry?', Bing crooning 'Trade Winds', the haunting 'Lilli Marlene'.

1943 arrived and still the war dragged on. The first glimmer of hope had been the British victory at El Alamein the previous year.

In February, the Americans achieved their first victory in the Pacific at Guadalcanal, whilst the Russians appeared to have brought the Nazi armies to a halt.

Later in the year Italy's Mussolini was deposed. With the invasion by the Allies beginning to bite, Italy surrendered in September. But the Germans showed few signs of wilting after four years of war.

We were busier than ever at work. Harry was called up to the R.A.F. He had been asked if he wanted the firm to apply for his job to be classed as a reserved occupation. If successful, he would have been in the same category as Jack Wood, exempt from military service. The cracker said no, so when I was posed the same question, for some inexplicable reason, I followed his example. Was I eager to fight? Well, the war would be over soon. Perhaps I was bored with the daily routine, long hours and no annual holiday that year. Perhaps I was getting into a rut. One plus point at work - I now had two juniors assisting, I was moving up the hierarchy!

A further piece of good news - Mr Jackson, the cashier in the front office was approaching retirement. He promised to hang on in the job until I returned from the forces. Our new manager, Mr

Patterson agreed that the position of cashier would then become mine.

Despite the Italian surrender, the Germans fought on in Italy. It was another nine months before the Allies entered Rome on the fourth of June 1945.

Two days later, the Normandy landings. 'D' Day had arrived.

That same day, a big brown envelope addressed to Mr P. Potts dropped through our letterbox.

Chapter 10

THIS IS THE ARMY?

'What's all this?' I wondered, as I opened the O.H.M.S. envelope. I hoped it wasn't what I thought. It was – call-up papers! A railway-warrant, details of the time of the train I was to catch from Newcastle to Durham on the 20th July 1944. Two weeks hence. Why Durham? All was revealed - at Durham station, an army bus would be waiting to transfer recruits to Brancepeth Training Camp. On arrival there I would report to reception.

That July day could have been a fateful day worldwide. That was the date of the failed assassination attempt on Adolf Hitler, which came very close to success. If the plot had worked, the duration of the war could have been shortened, and hundreds of thousands of lives would have been saved. Instead, it was just a fateful day in my life.

Our intake milled around at reception, there were about sixty of us - a mixed bag of callow youths. After the initial confusion, we were registered and assigned our army number. I can still recall mine - 14802039. For some peculiar reason we were then led to the Medical Section for an examination. Why, I didn't know, we had already been given a full medical check prior to call-up.

So far no one had shouted at us and the sergeant who escorted us to the stores for our army issue seemed such a nice chap. There, an R.A.C. private measured us and gave us chitties to show to the orderlies behind the long counter.

We collected about half of our kit there and then - one battle-blouse, one pair of boots, two pairs of drawers (summer), one pair of anklets, one pair of trousers, one khaki shirt, one forage cap, socks, and a 'housewife'. The latter was a small cloth bag. Inside were needles, thread, spare buttons, darning wool - no instruction book, though. At the end of the counter we collected a mess tin and an enamelled mug. Then, finally, a kitbag to hold our swag. Then it was off to our billet, just one of a row of Nissen huts. The camp was in the grounds of Brancepeth Castle, with plenty of greenery to be seen.

"This was part of the golf course," said the corporal escorting us. "They say it was the long par four." In the hut, we chose our beds and dumped our kitbags on them. I appropriated a bed in a corner, farthest away from the door. My brain was awakening from the daze caused by the first flurry of activity - I was beginning to think again. My choice would give me two advantages. One, I would have only one bed next to mine, thus halving the chance of having a snorer or a lad with smelly feet near me. Two, I would receive more warning than most, when an N.C.O. arrived like a bombshell at the other end of the hut. Surely, this laid-back approach wasn't going to last.

Having selected my bed, it was all change. We had been instructed to get out of our civvy clothes and into army uniform, 'at the double'. Although this was a small indication, the fact that 'at the double, *please*' was not the phrase used, seemed to me a warning sign.

My intuition was spot on. I was trying on my forage cap and wondering where the mirrors were (I couldn't see any at all), when a small whirlwind, or to be more precise, a sturdy sergeant, burst through the door at the other end of our billet.

"STAND BY YOUR BEDS, YOU LOT, AND LISTEN TO ME," he shouted in a parade ground voice, which reverberated off the walls. I remember thinking that the acoustics in the hut were excellent. But really, I couldn't see the need for the bawling, we weren't deaf, or we wouldn't be in the army in the first place. I could hear him more than adequately, even at the other end of the hut. I thought to tell him so, but bit my tongue; I had this gut feeling that it wouldn't be a wise move.

"STAND STILL AT THE BACK," he bawled. I looked around. Who did he mean? Not me surely? He continued a little more quietly. "I'm Sar'nt Bell, got that? For my sins you're members of my platoon for the next six weeks. Number three platoon. SO WHO ARE YOU?"

"Number three platoon." (No more than a mumble).

"NUMBER THREE PLATOON, WHO?" he bellowed.

"Sergeant!" the response was a little more distinct; I think we were getting the hang of what was required.

'By the end of six weeks we might be word perfect,' I mused.

He went on to explain, in a voice now a little less than a shout, that he was going to take us to the canteen for grub, so to bring our mess tins. There might be plates for us to eat off on the morrow. Or words to that effect. Wasn't that nice? We were going to have plates eventually!

Anyway, to the mess, in slovenly fashion, we meandered. That was a mistake.

"LOOK LIVELY, YOU UGLY LOT. MY GOD, I'LL HAVE YOU SMARTENED UP!" He was shouting again, it couldn't be very good for his throat.

We queued up in the canteen, the word came down the row - stew and a mug of tea, or no stew and tea; I selected the former. It was surprisingly tasty, but I knew now why our containers were called 'mess' tins, the stew didn't look very appetising.

We'd hardly had time to finish, when our sergeant, by the door, bellowed, "NUMBER THREE PLATOON, FALL IN OUTSIDE, AT THE DOUBLE!"

'There they go again,' I thought, 'no please!'

He trooped us back to the billet.

"Stand by your beds," he said, saluting, as a young officer came into the hut.

"This is Lieutenant Reynolds, your platoon commander. He wants to have a little chat with you lot, so pay attention," said the sergeant.

Our officer looked fresh out of university but he must have been in the army a while, to have two pips.

"Gather round, you chaps," he said, in a quiet cultured voice. A change from all the shouting.

We shuffled up the hut to listen to him.

"I just want to put you in the picture and tell you what's going to happen in the next six weeks. Well, fellows, during the time you're here you'll be doing basic infantry training. There are twenty of you in the platoon, and towards the end of the period, you'll be allocated to army units.

"From this platoon, fifteen are to be allocated to the Durham Light Infantry, three to the Royal Army Pay Corps, and two to the Commandos. That's unless there is a late change of plan. It's jolly unusual for trainees to go straight into the Commandos but the powers that be are looking for new blood. So this is by way of a one-off experiment.

"You can all volunteer for the Commandos, but as I say only two of you will be accepted. So, if you want to join that elite unit, you will have to impress your platoon sergeant here, and myself. Is that clear? In fact what will actually happen, is, that the two of you that impress us the most, will be instructed to volunteer, does that make it clearer?"

The mumble came again, "Yes, sir."

I made a mental note there and then - not to impress these gentlemen too much - the Commandos were reputed to be the death or glory boys. My ambitions led in neither direction - somewhere in between, in fact. He continued. "Now, you won't see me every day over the next six weeks, but Sar'nt here will keep me up to date. What you have got to do is knuckle down, no slacking. I want Platoon Number Three to be the smartest platoon of this current intake. Any questions?"

'He wants to be a captain,' I thought. I looked around this motley crowd. Already I was giving them nicknames. 'The Fat Boy', 'The Twitch' (every so often his head would jerk), 'Cyrano' (yes, he had a big nose), 'The Mad One' (with wild eyes), 'King Kong' (six foot four and beetle-browed), 'Little Titch', and of course myself, 'Skinny Legs'.

If he wanted this lot to be the smartest platoon, he would have his work cut out.

He repeated, "Any questions? Come on, chaps, there must be something you want to ask."

We looked at each other, waiting for someone to speak up. I passed my first big test, no questions from me. I wasn't going to be the one to stand out as a keen, eager recruit, with Commando potential.

Perhaps others were thinking the same way, because at first, no one opened their mouths. Then the 'The Mad One' spoke up.

"Will we be going to the rifle range, sir?"

The young officer smiled again, "That's a good question, what's your name, private?"

"Thoms, sir, Jack Thoms," he said, with an odd, one-sided grin on his face.

"Thoms, make a note of that name, Sar'nt."

'Oh, ho!' I thought, 'That's one for the Commandos.'

"The answer to your question, Thoms, is, that yes, we shall be going to the rifle range. Any further queries?" Nobody else raised his voice. I was beginning to think that we had, all in all, a fairly intelligent platoon. It was a pity, though, we could have done with one other keen lad.

"Right, Sar'nt, carry on." With that remark, he turned on his heels and exited the hut. We were now left to the tender mercies of the stentorian Sergeant Bell.

"Right, you lot. The washrooms and the latrines are just over the path there. Apart from the necessary, you'll stay in your billet until reveille, at six-thirty. Is that understood?"

"Yes, Sergeant," the chorus was getting louder and even more in tune, I thought, from my observation post at the far end of the hut.

"You'd better jump to it in the morning, or Corporal Jones will have you on jankers. He's a sadist, is the Corporal." He gave a macabre sort of laugh as he departed the billet.

For a full minute, there was an eerie quiet in the hut, as everyone stood immobile, except for a sniff from 'Cyrano' and a jerk of the head from 'The Twitch'.

The silence was broken by 'King Kong'. "That bleedin' Sergeant, he'd berrer not shoot at me. Aa'll knock his bleedin' block off."

Was this bravado? Or did he really mean it? I hoped the latter, it would make the next few days interesting.

There were a few more ribald comments in that vein, before we organised ourselves for an early night.

'Little Titch' had the bed next to me; he was not much over five feet in height, with the look of a Mickey Rooney.

"What's your name?" I asked. "Mine's Paul, Paul Potts. I'm from Gateshead. I worked in an office."

"Jarge Wilkins," he said, "Aam fra' Selby, Yorksheer. This lot's goan t'be a seet different ta clarkin, tha knows. Any road, there's nowt us can do abowt it."

I gathered that he thought we would have to resign ourselves to our predicament. Listening to Wilfred Pickles on the radio had given me a slight knowledge of the dialect.

"Let's 'ope wi' end oop int' Pay Corps."

Quickly interpreting his remark, I decided it was a sentiment with which I fully agreed.

"Some hope," I said. "You're a clerk and I'm a clerk, so there's not much chance of being a pen-pusher in this army. I don't believe they think like that. More likely we'll finish up in the Commandos."

"Eee by gum, not if Aa shoot me-sen int' foot," he laughed. I wasn't sure whether he was serious or not, I didn't envisage myself doing anything quite as drastic as that.

As I got into bed, I pondered, I could write a book about this day - 'One Day in the Life of Paul Potts'. Then thought, that wouldn't do for a book title, it didn't seem to have the right ring about it.

I didn't notice 'lights out'; I was asleep as soon as my head touched the hard pillow. Apparently, no one was a heavy snorer, because it was the sound of the bugle that woke me in the morning. That was just before our corporal, a bumptious little squirt of a fellow, charged into the hut. WAKEY, WAKEY! YOU LOT," came the shout. "WAKEY, WAKEY, YOU HORRID LITTLE MEN. GET TO YOUR ABLUTIONS AND BACK HERE BY SEVEN-THIRTY." Little men! That was rich coming from him! If I hadn't a headache now, I would soon have one if this shouting continued. In a bit of a daze, and not wholly sure of my bearings, I staggered to the washroom. Shaving daily was a superfluous task for me, but I thought I had better go through the motions.

Breakfast was sausage and beans, then back to the billet.

I got back on my bed, hoping for five minutes to recover from my early call. There was no peace, however, the door was smashed open as Sergeant Bell, followed by Corporal Jones, stormed into the room. Why couldn't they walk in like civilised people? I just had time to jump to my feet and hastily straighten the blanket.

"STAND BY YOUR BEDS!" It was Corporal Jones; his voice was out of all proportion to his stature. It was a toss up as to which N.C.O. shouted loudest, I gave it to the corporal by a short head.

As it happened the day passed reasonably calmly, the decibels diminishing, nevertheless, it was a busy day.

Injections, for God knows what hideous diseases. The needle was wielded by an R.A.M.C. apprentice; that was my impression anyway. Two of the lads fainted.

Hair cuts. When I saw my short back and sides in the mirror, I nearly fainted. Would the family recognise me?

Pay books were issued and the rest of our kit was collected. Then came the difficult part - after midday meal back to the billet. Objective? How to make our beds and how to store our clothes in the lockers.

Bed making seemed easy, the only snag apparently - there were two ways of making a bed. There was our way and then there was the army way, as interpreted by N.C.O.s Bell and Jones. It was soon revealed that our way wouldn't do.

Corporal Jones demonstrated the one and only method, who were we to argue? Then it was our turn and the N.C.O.s inspected our handiwork.

Surprise, surprise, only two beds passed the initial inspection. One of these was Jack Thoms. Commandos here he comes, methinks.

My bed making was approved on the third inspection, some had five attempts, so my efforts were about average. 'Good! One of the crowd,' I thought.

Time was getting on then, so putting kit away didn't get the same attention as the bed making routine and at last we were stood down to enjoy the facilities of the camp. These were bordering on the non-existent, so I had a quiet night, reading and writing home.

The next weeks were purgatory. P.T. every morning early, long before my body was attuned to sudden movements. Somehow I coped, although gymnastics were not my forte. I discovered that I had more muscles than I thought. I didn't like that, because they all ached at the same time.

Even so, I was certainly more proficient than 'The Fat Boy'. In fact, I felt sorry for the pommel horse. It was just as well that the R.S.P.C.A. Inspector wasn't in the vicinity.

Again, Jack Thoms was a star performer. "Three cheers for

Jack," I said silently, "there will be only one Commando place to avoid, that's for sure."

Parade ground drill was now every day, twice a day. That's where the shouting reached a crescendo - "ATTENSHUN! RIGHT DRESS, LEFT DRESS, ABOUT TURN, LEFT TURN, RIGHT TURN, HALT!" The whole thing left me dizzy; those N.C.O.s didn't seem to know which way they wanted us to march.

'King Kong', didn't seem to get the hang of the drill, he got shouted at regularly by our sergeant. Disappointingly, he never raised a hand to that noisy individual and went right down in my estimation.

On the fifth Sunday (no duties), I went home for the day. Getting to Gateshead meant a four-mile walk into Durham to catch the bus. I arrived at Mam's just in time for Sunday dinner. Thoughtfully, I had written to her, telling her to expect me, so dinner was soon on the table.

Rob rolled in from his Sunday lunchtime drink at the 'Azure Blue', just as the dinner was being served. A beautiful piece of timing. Everyone laughed at my new non-hairstyle, and Mam wanted to know how things were going. I tried to give the impression of unalloyed satisfaction, but I don't think I succeeded.

After dinner, I read the 'Sunday Sun', cheered by the news about the fall of Paris, hoping that victory wouldn't be far away. I had a natter to Cecil, who was now working at a sweet factory, and we gave Stephen one or two games of Ludo. Stephen had a placid disposition, always anxious to please. He couldn't seem to concentrate on anything for very long, though, which worried Mam. Mam had just received a letter from Don, and from the sound of it, he was now in Normandy, although he could only give hints in his letter, such as 'I've picked up a bit of French'. The censor must have had an off day. 'Careless talk costs lives', was the wartime warning.

I got back to camp and looked around the billet. It had been strange to be home again, it was a little different in the army. I wondered what was in store for me, before I returned home for good.

What was in store for me at Brancepeth, was a visit to the rifle range at Whitburn, which was a change from the parade ground. At the range, we fired a dozen or so rounds at targets some two hundred yards away. I scored three bulls, one of the top scores. I would have to curb my prowess. Of course, the parade ground still figured very much in our training, although now the drill was with a rifle.

It was, "SLOPE ARMS, ORDER ARMS, PRESENT ARMS, FIX BAYONETS," as these words of command were added to our vocabulary.

We'd had intelligence tests during the fifth week and in the final few days, we learned our fate.

Lieutenant Reynolds returned to our hut to be present at the announcement ceremony.

"Well, fellas, I hope you have gained some idea of army life during the last six weeks. Sarn't Bell will now tell you your postings."

We listened with bated breath.

The sergeant's voice boomed out, "I will read your names in alphabetical order, can you all hear me?"

It would be a miracle if we couldn't.

The first three were all allocated to the D.L.I. Then, "Dawson. C., Commandos." I looked pretty safe now, surely Jack Thoms, would be the other daredevil.

The sergeant continued to read the list. All, to the fourteenth man, were to be infantrymen with the D.L.I. My name was next. Thirteen now, were D.L.I. and one the Commandos. Seven to go and still no Pay Corps, good, but there was still one Commando place left, bad. Surely it couldn't be me, it had to be Jack Thoms.

"Potts, P., to the R.A.P.C." Stupidly, for a moment, nothing registered, R.A.P.C.! The Pay Corps! My heart leapt, you would think I had won the Football Pools.

I nearly missed the next announcement.

"Thoms, J., the R.A.P.C." I couldn't believe it!

The rest was a bit of an anti-climax. 'Cyrano' was the other Commando, George Wilkins got his wish, the third Pay Corps spot. I was pleased, I didn't want him walking round with a rifle bullet in his foot. He was a canny lad.

"One other thing, chaps," said the lieutenant, before leaving, "it's passing-out parade tomorrow, I want you to stand out as the best and smartest platoon in your intake, if only for the thanks you owe Sergeant Bell and Corporal Jones, for looking after you."

Looking after us? That was a new one, but I would do my best, as a thank you to God on high for looking after my posting.

I think most of us did do our best on the parade ground next day, but unfortunately, our best wasn't good enough. We finished runners-up, Jack Thoms dropped his gun. That may have cost our friendly lieutenant promotion.

So, the following Monday, Jack Thoms, George Wilkins and me were heading for York, where our Pay Corps battalion was stationed. We were to be given a lift in an army truck to Durham Station, loaded down with our kitbags and our greatcoats. The good news - no rifles for us!

I was very pleasantly surprised when Sergeant Bell and Corporal Jones stepped out to see us off.

"We'll never forget you, Sergeant," I said, "or your voice!"

He laughed, "That was the whole idea, Potts."

He turned away, bracing himself to harry the next batch of recruits. I hope his voice lasted out.

Chapter 11

THE CAT'S PYJAMAS

Destination York, a crowded train - a journey into the unknown for me, never having been farther than Blackhall Rocks. It was the last of being a proper soldier, if the information we had gleaned back at Brancepeth was true.

No more marching drill, arms drill, rifle practice, bayonet practice. Hopefully, no more shouting and bawling. All ended, now that we were in the Royal Army Pay Corps.

Sitting on my kitbag in the train corridor, I wondered why we'd had that square-bashing. Would it be of any help in my new clerical role? Surely there wouldn't be much need for arms or marching drill. I also sensed that firing rifles, or charging people with fixed bayonets, would be out of order in an office.

As fellow passengers shuffled past me on the way to the toilet, I continued my musing. Perhaps the brass hats knew something that I didn't. Possibly we would soon be transferred to Normandy, touring the front line, distributing pay packets to the troops, pay packets stuffed with French francs. That sort of operation might require us to have rifles at the ready. Somehow, though, it seemed an implausible scenario to me. I hoped it was anyway.

One thing I had learned from my Brancepeth experience, was to keep my head down and fade into the background, when sergeants, corporals, or others of that ilk, were in the vicinity. That philosophy had worked so far; I resolved to continue with it. The fact that army privates were instructed to keep their chins up and chests out was surely only a minor snag.

We had been told that there would be an army truck waiting

at York station, to take us and our equipment to our reception point. Surprisingly, there it was, manned by an R.A.P.C. private. "Grosvenor House," my pal, George Wilkins said, looking at our posting instruction, as we sat in the back of the truck. "That's t'place reet next t'Betty's, that's a posh caff, thaa knows."

George knew York pretty well, his hometown, Selby, was only a few miles away. We stopped outside Grosvenor House - a block of offices that had been commandeered by the Pay Corps. The driver helped us with our kitbags and greatcoats, and we entered through a side entrance leading to the basement. There, we left our goods and chattels as he showed us up to the second floor. "Where the admin section is," he'd explained.

We were greeted by a bespectacled Sergeant. "Phillips is my name," he told us. His affable manner conflicted with the three stripes on his arm.

"So, you're Privates Potts, Thoms and Wilkins. Well, look you, you'll be working in this building until further notice, you will."

Two things struck me immediately - he was Welsh, and more pertinently, he was speaking quietly, thus confirming to me that he was, indeed, a sheep in wolf's clothing. After telling us we would be allocated one to each section on the ground floor, he gave us a briefing on the office hours and billeting arrangements. We would be lodged in private homes in York, and would normally be free from duty each weekend starting Saturday midday, unless otherwise advised. Already this seemed like my sort of army.

Then we met Lieutenant Young, a forty-something, stout gentleman, who explained that we were now members of the second company of the R.A.P.C. York Battalion. We would, of course, be subject to Army Regulations at all times.

That was it; that was our induction.

"Dismiss, chaps," said the officer. Jack Thoms saluted, so George and myself thought that we'd better follow suit. The lieutenant looked a little surprised, as though he was not used to this behaviour in the office. He didn't return our salute, and a touch confused, we turned and walked out of his sanctum. Back in the main office, Sergeant Phillips told us saluting wasn't the done thing inside the building. He did say that we must salute any officer whom we passed on the street, whether he be army, navy or air force, Canadian, Pole or Yank. With so many airfields situated in the flat plain around York there was a cosmopolitan mixture of airmen coming into the city. The dreaded M.P.s, were, apparently, actively policing in York, especially at night - nabbing Pay Corps privates was their favourite amusement. "They have it in for us office wallahs," the Sergeant had said.

After that lecture, he took us down the stairs into the ground floor office. There were three distinct sections; three rows of double-banked desks, each clerk facing another. The sergeant assigned Jack Thoms to the first section, passing him on to an A.T.S. Corporal. I gathered she was section leader. Then George to an R.A.P.C. Lance-Corporal, and finally myself to a Corporal Dixon. He seemed a friendly sort, he could be O.K. as my immediate boss.

I glanced around at the other members of the section, there were seven, all females. Two A.T.S. girls of rather drab appearance, and five civilians. 'I should be able to have some influence here,' I thought, as a member of the Pay Corps in a Pay Corps office. (That was a joke to start with.)

Bill Dixon ("Call me Bill, unless t'officer's abaht", he had said) showed me to my place and introduced me to my fellow clerks. The A.T.S. girls still looked drab, perhaps it was their uniforms; most of the civvies were also of a commonplace appearance. Apart from one. The girl who would be opposite me. She was the cat's pyjamas!

This vision was certainly an exception. She was about my age, a bonny girl, with soft brown hair and a good natured, eager smile. She was wearing a smart blue sweater, which helped to emphasise her cuddlesome figure. To say that I fancied her, even at first glance, would be an understatement.

"This is Joan Speed," said the corporal. "Watch out! She's fast!" he joked.

She could be as fast as she liked with me.

"Hi," she smiled, in a tinkling voice.

'She can tinkle one syllable,' I thought. 'That takes some doing!'

I sat down at the desk Bill had indicated. My luck was changing, changing fast. From the good (landing an office job in an army of tough fighting regiments), to the brilliant (sitting across from this nubile bundle of girlhood.)

Then came the blow.

"You'd better let Joan pass over all her filing, now that you're the junior on the section," Bill said, grinning.

I grunted to myself, this idea of pulling rank on civilians had not lasted long. Yet, if I was to be instructed by anyone on how to file the mass of documents that had quickly dropped on my desk, who better than Joan?

I looked down at the pile in some dismay, then caught her eye. Not surprisingly, she was smiling, pleased to relinquish the lowly task. For the first time I noticed the dimples in her cheeks and the way her brown eyes twinkled.

"I'll come round there and show you the ropes." Her voice had just a trace of Yorkshire accent.

Moments later, she was leaning over, gently brushing my shoulder, as she explained the simple procedures. I tried to follow her words, but, at first, the meaning was lost in the music of her voice. I made a big effort to concentrate, but now it was the pervasive quality of her perfume that distracted me.

"Say that again," I said, landing back on earth. "When you get letters from the troops querying their pay, you just file them?" I looked up at her, "I must have misheard you!"

"No," she laughed, "that's correct. We've been so busy, that we have had to do that, just to cope. You see, some complaints are so minor, that a lot of men don't follow up their grievances. Those that do, those that complain about a lack of reply, well, then we dig out their first letter and deal with it. That system cuts down on our workload and stops us getting absolutely snowed under."

"Well, I'll be blowed!" I said.

"I don't think it's right, myself, mind. Anyway, the first and second letters are then passed to Vera to reply to. She's upstairs, she's the correspondence clerk. I presume she answers them," she chuckled.

"She might file them," I suggested.

"Don't be a soppy 'aypporth. Anyroad," she smiled, "just concentrate on the job, that's the best thing."

As if I could, when she was leaning over me, with her tinkling tones, pleasant perfume, and brushing bosom.

Me, an unworldly, callow young lad! It was about then that I had the feeling that I might be falling in love. I had no previous experience in the matter, but it felt like something of that kind. If it wasn't love, it was as near as dammit.

She went back around to her desk. I was sorry she was no longer close, but at least I could still admire her across the desk.

"Where do you come from?" she asked.

"Gateshead, do you know where it is?"

"Gateshead! Why! I've been there, would you believe! My dad once took me to see York City beat your team. We went to the ground in a funny tramcar, I remember it well. Down a very dingy road. It seemed a poor area, that part."

I felt humiliated, going down Askew Road, she must have passed the mean street where I was born and brought up. What would she say if she knew that? It was fortunate that we didn't live there any more. (I was thinking well ahead.)

At the same time, I was pleased. She liked football. Things were getting better all the time.

"Yes, I know Askew Road," I said. (Don't I just!). "It's not so bad where we live."

'Not so blooming well good either, when you come to think about it,' I mused.

"Where are you billeted?" she asked.

"Gordon Street, I've been told it's just off Haxby Road."

"Well, what do you know?! That's only a quarter of a mile from our house in Burton Lane. Let's see, you want the number two bus to Haxby, you'll get off at the Gordon Street stop. You can catch the bus at Exhibition Square. I'll walk up to the bus stop with you tonight if you like."

If I liked! I jumped at the offer. 'She's very friendly,' I thought, 'perhaps she's beginning to like me.' In my short life, I hadn't been used to friendly girls. Come to think of it, I wasn't accustomed to girls at all, not even the unfriendly variety.

I knew what! I was getting more and more convinced that I could be in love, although I hadn't a pain in the heart yet. Perhaps that would come later, when I got more into this romance thing.

It was about then that the Corporal broke in to interrupt our conversation.

"Will you two 'ushup, and gerron wit' work? Yer bashin me lug 'oyl."

"Yes, Corporal Dixon," laughed Joan. She seemed to have a

rapport with Bill, he took her mock respect in good part. The rest of the working day passed quickly, some of the letters I was filing were amusing, some were quite distressing. Joan had told me to pass any that seemed really urgent to Bill, for swifter action. I thought there were a few that were in that category.

Knocking off time arrived and Joan and I went down to the basement containing the cloakrooms, storage space for bikes, etc. Joan collected her bike, I picked up my kitbag containing most of my possessions. My greatcoat and spare boots I left until next day.

"How far is it to the bus stop?" I asked, humping the kitbag on my shoulder. I tried to give an impression of a strongman, but my wobbly knees were reluctant to join in the pretence.

"Oh, only a couple of hundred yards or so."

Getting up the stairs to the exit and trying at the same time to appear nonchalant was difficult. Out on the street I settled into a grim rhythm, not adding much to the conversation. You needed breath for that. A commodity that I found was in short supply. Joan was concentrating on pushing her bike, so hopefully didn't notice that I was beginning to stagger.

At last we arrived at the bus stop, just as a red double-decker bus pulled up.

"Here you are," she said, "just in time!"

With about my last ounce of strength, I dropped the kitbag on the platform and rolled it under the stairwell.

"Good look with your digs!" she shouted. I gave a weak wave before flopping into a seat.

I found my billet easily, and what's more, it wasn't too far from the bus stop, that was a welcome stroke of luck. The street consisted of terraced houses, most seemed to be well kept, one of these was my lodgings.

I spent a minute or two gathering my breath before I knocked. A buxom, thirty-something, dark-haired woman, rosy cheeked and wearing spectacles, answered my knock. She seemed O.K. at first sight.

"Mrs Crow?"

"Yes, that's me. You must be Paul Potts, cum in lad."

Soon she was showing me my room. Upstairs I went with my kitbag, it was a smallish room, entered through a larger bedroom. She explained that the bigger room was Len Wright's, who was also in the Pay Corps working in an office in Salem Chapel. She explained that there were R.A.P.C. offices spread around York. Len was on leave at the moment, he would be back next week.

Although mine was a small room, it would do me. I could close the door and drift off into uninterrupted dreams of Joan. Golly, a room of my own! Later, after I had unpacked that cursed kitbag, Mrs Crow called me downstairs to meet her husband, Charlie (her name was Maureen).

Charlie was henpecked, I could see that. He was half her size, wore glasses, and blinked a lot. "That's Charlie," she said, almost disdainfully, then, "this is Fido!" she crooned.

She lifted up a sort of indeterminately coloured, small, hairy bundle. There were eyes and a nose in there too, I could just spy them.

Fido was a dog.

What kind, I had no idea, except he was a miniscule example of the canine species. I wasn't well up on the nuances of breeds and suchlike. "He's a Long-haired Chihuahua, he was very expensive," Maureen seemed proud.

My knowledge of dogs was expanding already. There must also be a Short-haired Chihuahua.

When I say she lifted it up, that wasn't all, she kissed it with an overwhelming show of affection. This seemed to me to be going too far, even for a Chihuahua! It must be exceedingly special judging by the fuss she was making of it. This singular animal enfolded in her ample embrace, gave me a haughty look. It surprised me that such a tiny face could display such scorn.

"Fido comes to bed with me every night - he's my little diddums."

'A teddy bear might have been cheaper,' I thought.

"And Charlie?"

"He sleeps at the other side of Fido, don't you, Charlie?"

Charlie gave a sigh and a nod. He didn't seem to say much, but I guessed he wasn't her big diddums. Surely not?

"Any children?" I asked.

She gave me a funny look, I thought, for such a harmless question. Instead of answering, she changed the subject.

"If you want a bath before we eat, the water's hot. We usually eat about six but we'll have it a bit later tonight."

A bath! In a bathroom, in a house! There's a first time for everything. I smiled, as I ran the bath. Soon I was luxuriating in this unexpected pleasure.

Spruced up, I answered her call to go down for the meal. "High Tea", she had said, high tea, it was. Small letters was all it deserved.

Maureen, Charlie, Fido and myself sat down to what would be a filling repast, at least that's what I was hoping. Some hope!

Fido had his own chair, heightened by a couple of cushions so that he could see the table. I was sitting opposite this bizarre arrangement.

He lacked a knife and fork, he didn't need one. Maureen fed him from her piled-up plate. Charlie and I didn't have piled-up plates. We had rather skimpy portions of boiled potatoes, reconstituted dried eggs, fried; and tinned peas. Pathetic, even for a wartime meal.

Fido was luckier, Maureen and Fido shared two sausages, which I thought was manifestly unfair.

I had one consolation - the army allocated thirty-five shillings a week for personnel billeted in civvy digs. Bill Dixon, however, had said - "Give the landlady thirty bob a week. All the landladies in York believe the army allocation for digs is thirty bob. Don't rock the boat."

So that's what I had agreed with Maureen earlier, when I handed over my newly acquired billeted personnel ration book. That arrangement would leave me with an extra five shillings. That was enough to take a girl to the pictures, twice a week, and that girl surely had to be Joan Speed. Moreover, I would still have my own army pay, to fund further outings. The future was looking very rosy.

Maureen and I sat in the parlour, after the meal, Maureen nursing Fido and chatting. That was in between billing and cooing at the doggie. Charlie came in after he had washed the dishes and he switched on the wireless. We sat and listened to ITMA - Tommy Handley and his gang, Mrs Mopp – 'Can I do you now, sir?' and 'Funf speaking', had Charlie chuckling.

"It's reet funny," he said. "Dos't thee like it?"

"It's quite good," I replied, not wishing to disagree.

Maureen broke into the conversation, "Fido likes it."

Fido, to me, seemed to have the same haughty look that he had when I first saw him, so how could Maureen say that? 'It must be telepathy,' I thought.

When Maureen started kissing her doggie, I decided to go up to my room, her excessive adulation was making me feel a little queasy. Moreover, I wanted to be alone with thoughts of Joan. In bed, my mind was in a ferment.

What a day it had been!

What about tomorrow? Should I ask Joan out? Would she think I was jumping the gun, if I did?

Should I wait a few days? God! She might have a boyfriend already. No, she couldn't. Was this not the fickle hand of fate serving me an ace? She liked me - I think. I didn't sleep much, mind.

Chapter 12

DUEL IN THE CELLAR

I jumped out of bed next morning - the first time in living memory that I had done more than crawl out. Except Christmas mornings, when I was a kid.

Downstairs for breakfast. "Good morning, Mrs Crow."

"Just call me Maureen, lad."

"Good morning, Maureen," I grinned. I had a feeling it was going to be a good day.

It didn't start very well. When I sat down at the table, in front of me was a revolting looking bowl of watery porridge. Somehow, I gulped it down. The toast and homemade jam that followed, tasted almost delectable.

Maureen, who had been doing her kitchen chores, came into the parlour. "Finished?"

"Yes thanks, Mrs - Maureen. Is Charlie at work?"

"Yes, he starts early, he works just up t'road at Rowntrees."

"And the - and Fido?" Why did I ask that? I wasn't interested, except in a macabre sort of way.

"He's havin' a lig-in bed, he's had a funny sort of night."

Good God! I guessed Charlie must have had a funny one, too.

I shot off to work before Maureen could bring Fido down for his breakfast. I bet he didn't have watery porridge.

I was first in the office - yet another record. To crown it all, I started work before time. Soon I was engrossed in filing servicemen's plaintive letters into folders. Joan had told me the day before that we were a fortnight behind schedule. She'd said that she had been on holiday, and no one had kept the work up to date.

Strangely, I was getting concerned. Flippantly, perhaps, I perceived a danger that we would receive 'why no reply?' letters, before I had got the original ones out of the way.

What sort of a rumpus would that cause?

These ponderings ceased the moment that Joan took her seat opposite.

"Hello, Paul," she smiled, "you're in early!"

Thoughts of filing went out of my head as soon as I saw her cheerful face. "Hello, Joan, you look bright this morning."

"Thanks, I don't feel it. What're your digs like?"

"Not bad, if you forget the dog and the porridge," I laughed.

"You don't like dogs and porridge?" I noticed her voice still tinkled.

"Not much, when the dog runs the house and the porridge runs to water!"

She chuckled, "You daft lad!"

'Let's find out more about her,' I thought. "Do you go out much, Joan?"

"Oh, yes," she said, "I was at the Regal last night."

My heart sank - with a boyfriend? I hoped not!

"I went with Helen, the girl on the end, there." I looked at the A.T.S. girl. She was no oil painting. I pondered - why did plain girls always have pretty girls for friends? "We saw 'Top Hat' with Fred Astaire and Ginger Rogers. I've seen it three times now. There's some good dancing and good songs. 'Isn't It a Lovely Day?', 'Cheek To Cheek', others, of course."

My heart had leapt up again - she hadn't been to the pictures with a lad. It could be a lovely day yet for me, although it might be too much to hope that I would get cheek to cheek with her.

"There's a good picture on at the Odeon this week," she added. "'For Whom the Bell Tolls', with Gary Cooper and Ingrid Bergman."

I nearly asked her there and then if I could take her to see it. However, I thought better of it, Bill Dixon had just taken his seat. She might rebuff me in front him. I'd have to wait now. Instead - "I like that sort of film, adapted from a book, 'Goodbye Mr Chips' or 'Kipps'. Do you, Joan?"

"I do, 'Love on the Dole', is another."

We might have gone through the whole gamut of screen adaptations, if our friendly corporal had not piped up then.

"Reet you two, never mind Chips and Kipps, just button thy lips, th'as given usens enuff English literature lessuns for naa', let's get stuck in, reet?"

A bit of a spoilsport, was our Bill.

I spent the rest of the morning plucking up the courage to ask Joan for a date, I might get a chance at lunchtime. That plan fell through, though. "I'm popping next door to Betty's, I'm meeting a friend – Zena," she said, closing her ledger. I felt deflated, the moment gone. On the other hand it's a girl friend again. She can have as many of them as she likes. They can form fours, that wouldn't worry me. As Joan disappeared, I went across to talk to George Wilkins. Mad Jack was there too.

"How's it going?" I asked.

"Reet well," said George. "It's a seet better than beein' in Normandy."

"I wouldn't mind being in Normandy with the Commandos myself - that's who I wanted to join - not the Pay Corps," said Jack. Further confirmation that he was a bit mad.

"By the way," he continued, "by the way, she's a smasher you're sitting opposite to. I fancy her."

"Well, fancy away," I said hotly.

The rest of the day, I smouldered - that bloody Jack Thoms! He'd better not have any plans concerning Joan. Joan was out of bounds for Jack Thoms. "You hear that, Jack?" one time I muttered to myself, "Keep off."

"Did you say something, Paul?" Joan asked.

I looked across at her, "Er, no, not really."

Joan was not at her desk when work ended, she had been called upstairs. Another opportunity lost. On the way out I brushed past Mad Jack shuffling papers. Queer devil! After partaking of high tea with the Crow family (I got a sausage *and* a piece of bacon), I went up to my room to read. I wasn't terribly annoyed that Fido had eaten the best part of a pork chop, I was already resigned to being the poor relation.

I tried to read, but the words were meaningless. I paced the small room impatiently. I wanted tomorrow to arrive. It was to be the big day.

Next morning, by great good fortune we were first in the office, this was my chance - I nerved myself.

"Joan," I spluttered, "can I take you out this week? Have you a free night? Where would you like to go?"

"Hang on, Paul," she laughed, "one question at a time, I've already been asked out, as it happens."

"What?" I couldn't hide my dismay.

"Jack Thoms asked me out last night - your pal," she said mischievously.

"He's no pal of mine. What did you say? Jack Thoms! Jack Thoms! He's mad," I shouted in disbelief. "What did you say?"

"Shush," she said, "he's just coming in, he might hear you!"

"I don't care if he does," I said hotly.

"Hold on, I didn't say yes," she chuckled. "Perhaps I was waiting for a better offer. He did pester me though."

"Look, Joan, you don't want to go out with him? You can't."

"Well, no," she admitted, "but he was persistent. He does seem a bit peculiar, mind."

"A bit peculiar! That's an understatement. He's a bit barmy more like it. Then you'll go out with me? Say you'll let me take you out."

"What a bully you are, and me thinking you were a nice looking, well-behaved lad. There's Jack though, I don't think he's going to take no for an answer," she teased.

"Don't worry any more about Jack, I'll sort him out at lunchtime. He'll take no for an answer, alright!"

Where did this rash response come from? I certainly didn't make a habit of sorting people out, I wasn't built for it for one thing. Moreover, why did I have to start with an athletic type like Jack? Why couldn't it have been little George? Other staff started arriving. "Leave it to me, Joan," I said, "I'll bone him." The rest of the morning, I wasn't thinking too much about work, my mind a confusion of ideas. Was I Paul the intrepid or Paul the unwise? I set my plans, I would confront him in the cellar. But how do you sort someone out exactly? The chances were that I would come off the worse. A vision of him in the gym at Brancepeth displaying his athletic prowess kept intruding in my mind's eye. God! Apart from bulging biceps there was also that manic look. Lunchtime seemed to arrive about ten o'clock, but when I looked at my watch it was twelve. My plans were still not finalised. I saw Jack go down to the cloakroom. I looked across the desk. "I'll see you later, Joan." I felt like one of those soldiers going off to war saying goodbye to their womenfolk. 'Well, here goes,' I said to myself, 'in for a penny in for a pounding. Keep your fingers crossed, young Paul.' I was going to play it by ear, I hoped it wouldn't be a thick ear.

I followed him downstairs to the cloakroom.

"Jack", I said. He turned around, he was taller than me, more importantly he was heavier. Most people were. I nearly asked him, "How are things, mate?" But I didn't - I screwed up my courage when I thought of his rough hands mauling Joan.

"Joan Speed," I said, "she's my girl. I want you to keep off her - she's not going out with you, tonight, or any other night. Get it?" I almost snarled, this wasn't like me at all.

I was mastering my role quickly, this was a surprise.

"Oh!" He sneered, like a proper villain. "You and whose army is going to stop me?"

I grabbed the lapels of his army jacket, I had seen this happen often in the films. It usually seemed to work. I hoped he was a picture-goer. If he wasn't and didn't know the script, I was heading for a punch on the nose as well as a thick ear. Joan wouldn't like the look of me then!

My performance must have been convincing, I suppose there was good reason for that. What do they say? When love walks in the door, common sense flies out of the window? He was muscling in on my act, I was getting furious and it must have showed. Mind, it wasn't often I lost my temper - it had to be something serious, and this seemed serious enough to me.

"Just back off, Jack," I said, trying to outstare those wild eyes.

For a minute, I thought he was going to hit me; I prepared to duck, then, suddenly, he laughed. "O.K. Don't get so uppity. If that's how you feel she's all yours, mate. I don't really fancy her anyway."

Not fancy Joan! He was kidding. If he wasn't he must be mad! It was quite a relief all the same to know that he'd backed down. I released my hold on his jacket and felt my heart cease thumping.

It was scarcely credible, I had sorted him out! This sorting out of people was easier than I had feared. In a way, I felt like a knight in shining armour who had vanquished his rival and gained the hand of the fair maid. What a colourful imagination!

I danced up the stairs two at a time, Joan was going out the door with Helen.

"Joan!" I shouted, "It's sorted. I'll explain tonight, after work."

"You've got me curious," she said. "We'll talk afterwards, then."

"Are you going to tell me what it is that's sorted?" This was at our desks in the afternoon.

"All in good time, I can't explain now. It's sorted though," I smiled, enigmatically.

I teased her throughout the afternoon. 'It's sorted' I mouthed, knowing she would lip-read my words. She shook her fist at me in frustration.

She smiled, however, when five o'clock finally arrived.

As we walked together out of the front door, I said. "You haven't got your bike today, have you? Can I walk you home? It's a nice evening."

She punched me playfully in the chest. "You certainly can walk me home, and I want a full explanation. I want to know what's sorted, and I want to know fast!" she threatened.

Apparently we walked up to Exhibition Square, along Bootham and down Burton Lane. I didn't notice that at the time, I was too busy embellishing my tale of derring-do. It was sounding a little too heroic, I began to think I should play it down a bit.

"It was nothing really, Joan. He's all bluster. He won't bother you any more though. You'll come out with me now, won't you?"

"I was going to, anyroad," she laughed, "and even more now that I know you'll chase off any pests!"

We had reached her home. It was a council house, a semi, in what seemed a very pleasant area. Well-tended gardens, back and front.

"Tomorrow night's O.K. then, Joan?" I asked. The Odeon, eh? You want to see that picture, don't you?"

"You're a fast worker!" she smiled. A fast worker! I nearly looked over my shoulder to see if she was talking to somebody else. If I was such a fast worker why had I waited until I was eighteen and a half before making my first date?

Seven o'clock, she'd said, meet her at the bus stop opposite the railway station. Joan had insisted that I should get the Haxby bus to the station, rather than call round for her. I'd have to rush my 'high tea' if I made the detour. What a thoughtful lass.

I finished another one of Maureen's repasts in good time. Already, I was finding that they didn't take too long to eat. I could have made it to Joan's and caught the bus from there easily. Instead I had plenty of time after the four of us had eaten our mince and dumplings. (Dumplings predominated.) So, seven o'clock it was. Well, perhaps not seven, say twenty to seven, I'd made sure that I caught an early bus. Sitting upstairs on the double-decker, for the first time since arriving in York, I was able to observe some of the sights of the city, with the evening sunlight, playing on the mellow stonework - Bootham Bar, York Minster, the city walls. In my euphoric mood it all looked very imposing. A scenic overture for what would surely be a very pleasant night.

Providing Joan turned up! Perhaps she was having me on. "Don't be daft, Paul," I said to my reflection in the bus window. Getting off the bus, I sat on a low wall to wait for her and tried to banish such brainless thoughts. A number twelve bus arrived but no sign of Joan. She had told me that it would be the number twelve or the number four.

Two military policemen walked towards me, I stood up and tried to look smart. They gave me a disdainful look from below their peak caps and marched on.

I looked at my watch and then at the station clock. It was one of those funny ones that jump the minutes. Five past seven, whoops! Six minutes past, whoops! Seven. Waiting for the pointer to move had a hypnotic effect. I nearly missed the arrival of a number four bus. A crowd were streaming off the double-decker. Anxiously, I looked for Joan. Ah, there she was! My! She looked attractive in a casual fawn jacket and yellow roll-necked jumper. She cheerily waved and dashed up to me, apologising.

"Sorry I'm late, that's just like the buses! They're never there when you want one." She looked at her watch. "The last show starts at quarter to eight, there's sure to be a queue so we'd better dash. The Odeon's not far, it's near Micklegate Bar."

She grabbed my arm, I loved that. We hurried along.

"Were you waiting long?" she asked.

"Oh, no," I laughed, "only about forty minutes. I would have waited all night, I nearly did!"

"Get on with you," she said, squeezing my arm.

She was right, there was a queue.

"We'll go in the circle," I said, getting my money ready.

"The circle? Are you sure? I'll pay for me."

"You certainly will not. Don't you dare!!" I said in Cary Grant fashion, as we joined the long queue.

We stood waiting in line, our arms still linked. I looked around. There wasn't another girl as smart and as fetching as mine. I hadn't felt so proud since that day when, as a little lad, I discovered that my grandfather's shop was by appointment to Her Majesty the Queen. In fact I was prouder now. Was it my imagination, or did I spy one or two men glance admiringly at Joan and then look enviously at me? Soon people were pouring out of the cinema with the previous programme now ended. We shuffled forward to the ticket office.

"Two one-and-threes," I said, plonking a half-crown down and collecting the tickets.

Upstairs, in the darkness of the cinema, we were ushered to our seats. Pathe Newsreel was showing damage caused by V2 Rockets in the south of England. Unlike the V1 'doodle bugs', they landed and exploded without warning.

"They're terrible," Joan whispered.

"It's Hitler's last fling, hopefully," I said, still the sage.

The news ended and the credits started rolling for the big picture. I glanced at her in the dim light. She smiled, those cheeks dimpling.

'Ingrid Bergman, Gary Cooper in For Whom the Bell Tolls'.

Soon we were engrossed in the story with its Spanish Civil War setting. Joan was more absorbed in the film than I was. From time to time I gave her sidelong glances to make sure she was still there. It wasn't as daft as pinching myself, anyway.

I thought Ingrid Bergman was great in her part, the Technicolor impressive. I hadn't read Hemingway's novel, I would join the York library and borrow it sometime. Midway through the film Joan put her hand on mine, probably thinking that she had waited long enough for me to make the first move. I was fast? That was a joke, I wasn't attuned to the subtleties of cinema courtship, or any other kind for that matter.

When I felt her fingers searching for mine, I lost the thread of the story for a few minutes. Was I disappointed when the show ended? "It was good, wasn't it?" she said.

"Yes, it was." I laughed, "And the film was good too," I said, squeezing her hand, as we stood up for the playing of the National Anthem.

We came out into the street, the stars were bright, the moon shining in a cloudless sky. A night when the blackout enhanced the scene. "What a nice night! Shall we walk or get the bus?" she said.

I looked at her, "Let's walk, moonlight becomes you!"

She dug me in the ribs, "You've been seeing too many Bing Crosby 'road' pictures. You'll be singing to me next," she chuckled.

I started to warble, "Moonlight becomes you . . . ."

She giggled, "Well I never! That's the first time I've been serenaded!"

"I could have just said the words, they would still have been true, Joan. You see, you've got me moonstruck," I said, earnestly. I was getting the hang of this courting thing. It was easy - just tell the truth.

"Let's change the subject," she laughed. "You'll get me embarrassed."

We walked over Ouse Bridge and up Coney Street, it probably took half an hour or so to reach her home. She told me something of her family; her dad was an engine driver, she had an elder sister, Liza, and a brother.

Her brother, Philip, serving in the Irish Guards, had received a severe leg wound during the Anzio landings in Italy. Joan said that it had been feared that amputation might be necessary. However, the prognosis was now more hopeful, although he was still in military hospital.

I could have listened to her pleasant voice and admired her profile all night, as we walked along, linking arms in the moonlight.

"Have you had many boyfriends?" I asked.

"Oh! That would be telling!" she chuckled.

"Come on," I said, "out with it!"

"Well nothing serious, Paul, that's all I'm saying! Certainly not one that's serenaded me, anyroad," she smiled.

Too soon we reached her gate. "This is it, Paul, thanks for a nice night. See you tomorrow, then."

"Thank you, Joan, it was lovely."

"You can give me a goodnight kiss," she said. "You deserve one anyway for that song!"

"If you don't watch out, I'll sing a few more, then," I said, putting my arms around her and clumsily searching for her lips, our noses bumping.

She laughed. "Don't you know where noses go?"

"I haven't much experience of those technicalities, Joan," I breathed.

"Something like this," she murmured as I found her soft lips at last. Our kiss was a shy and tentative affair. A bit like my other kiss from a girl. That was in our upstairs neighbour's backyard. It was Mary Naylor's seventh birthday party - I was five going on for six at the time. She took advantage of my youth. I say a bit like Mary Naylor's kiss, but I sensed that Joan's meant more. I didn't cry and run away this time. I walked on air, back to my billet thinking of Joan. I would have to hold on to her, I could do it - I was sure a rapport was building up between us. Everyone was asleep when I got back to my digs, although I thought I heard a high-pitched woof from the doggie. Perhaps it was dreaming of the mince and dumplings it had eaten at teatime.

I didn't dream of dumplings of any kind, not that night, anyway. I dreamt instead of a girl with moonlight in her eyes.

Chapter 13

A CURIOUS LODGER

In the office next morning, the empathy between us was evident. Because of the proximity of others, not in words did we express our feelings, but in glances and smiles. Sometimes I would pass a letter of complaint across to her, ostensibly to obtain her opinion, but truthfully contriving to touch her hand.

Walking her home that night, we made plans for another outing. 'Babes in Arms' was showing the following week. "I've seen it", I said.

"That's funny, so have I! It was good," she laughed.

"It'll be twice as good if we go together, Joan!" Going back to Gordon Street, I skipped and hopped over the bridge. Two little girls came around the corner hand in hand and looked at me funny. I slowed to a sedate walk as they passed. Turning round, there they were, hands on hips, shaking their heads at the antics of a grown-up. I didn't care, I had another date!

In the digs, I got a bit of shock, a Pay Corps private was sitting on the parlour sofa beside Charlie and Fido. This must be my fellow lodger, Len Wright, returned from leave. In my ebullient mood, I'd forgotten that Maureen had told me that he would be back in time for the meal. Charlie and Len stood up. "This is Len, Paul." Len would be about thirty, his age was difficult to guess. My first impression - this guy's no run-of-the-mill soldier, not even of the Pay Corps variety - not the way he was mincing about. Had I ever encountered such a man before? I don't think so. No! Hold on, what about that dame in Jack and the Beanstalk at the Gateshead Empire? Len held out a limp hand

and spoke in an odd falsetto. "Hello, young Paul," he said, gushingly. "You look a nice young man, I've heard a lot about you already from Maureen and Charlie. How do you find this life, working in the Pay Corps?" His eyelashes fluttered winsomely.

Maureen or Charlie hadn't warned me to expect this, though I might have guessed he would be unusual. Whenever I passed through Len's bedroom, there was always a subtle, fragrant scent in the air.

"O.K., Len. The work's alright. Not only that," I added, "I've found a girlfriend."

The way he was eyeing me up and down, I thought that I had better wise him up straightaway.

He looked disappointed. "Oh dear, I hope you haven't been too impetuous, Paul. I hope we can be nice friends."

Not too nice, I trusted.

"Do you know, Paul, the last fellow lodger we had here was a beast?! Not at all refined, quite ghastly and rough, would you believe? It will be lovely to have a nice young man in the next room."

Charlie who had been fidgeting quietly, butted in then, "I'd better go and see if Maureen wants any help with the tea." I think he was glad to get out of the room.

Len, however, was in full flow now. "I've had to leave a dear friend in Middlesborough today," he said. "We had a positively lovely few days together, I'll miss him a lot. It's awful that I've had to leave him fretting. You know, Paul, I hate this army and the coarse uniforms. Ooh! The sergeant we have in Salem office, he's really, really, frightful! He's an absolute brute! The upstart seems to have taken a dislike to me already and he's only been with us a month."

Thankfully, Maureen came in with the tea - Spam, chips and beans. Len sat next to me and opposite the doggie.

"What do you think to Fido? Isn't he precious?"

I nearly choked, it couldn't have been a bone - no bones in Spam.

"Mea culpa, mea culpa," simpered Len, "I shouldn't have asked you when you're eating." He patted my thigh.

In my sheltered life, I had no experience of the Lens of this world, but an innate sixth sense told me to beware or I could find myself heading down a strange path. A world completely divorced from my vision of Joan and I, perchance on the road to love and marriage.

I started thinking - was there a bolt on my bedroom door, or a lock and key? One grain of comfort, there was a chair in my room - a chair I could wedge under the door handle. Upstairs, I discovered that I didn't need the chair, there was a bolt on the door. That night, and every night, I locked that door slowly and silently, I didn't want to upset Len, more than needs be. I suppose he was harmless, I hoped so, anyway.

Now that I had worked out my defences, Len faded into the background. Or he did, until I told Joan about him. We were in the queue waiting to see 'Babes in Arms'. She burst out laughing when I mentioned the name Len Wright and lodger in the same breath.

Her merriment increased when I told her the story of the locked door.

"You did right, mind," she said, in between giggles. "Len Wright! He-he, ho-ho-ho, he's well known in the Pay Corps! Although I only know him by sight, he-he, I've heard, he-he, all about him." The couple in front of us turned around with a 'what's so funny?' look, but her chuckles continued. "I didn't know he was in your digs, though, I could have warned you!"

Her mirth intensified, "I would put your chair against the door knob, as well as fastening the bolt!"

That laugh was so infectious. "Will you stop it?" I begged, "It's not funny!" But it was - I could see that now. I tried to remain dignified. I gave up, it was too difficult. So I joined in the merriment.

"In fact," her sides were splitting, "in fact, hee, hee! I would get a key for the door lock as well!"

By now half the queue, were looking at us, wondering what was so comical, what were they missing? The tears were streaming down her face. "You see what you've done now?" she said, trying to recover her equilibrium. "You've spoilt my makeup," wiping tears of laughter from her cheeks. Then she burst out again - "Len Wright! Ho ho! Len Wright and Paul Potts! What a lovely couple they could be! I'll be jealous next!"

"Give up, Joan," I chuckled, "or I'll strangle you!"

We were filing towards the box office by now, I was glad that the film wasn't a tearjerker. We would have had to walk out if we had started giggling again, say, at a poignant moment in a Bette Davis saga.

Thankfully, she quietened down, but then I pictured Len scratching his head after trying my door and finding it locked. That started me off again. "Shush," she said, as we took our seats, "let's have some decorum."

"What a nerve!" I chuckled, "You didn't show much decorum in the queue!"

We finally contained our giggles and settled down to enjoy the picture. 'Our love affair' sang Mickey and Judy in the film. Was ours a love affair? It was certainly turning out to be fun. Afterwards, I walked her home. No moon, this night, just dark and cloudy. Joan had brought her torch with her and we navigated our way through the city centre and down Bootham. Joan knew where we going, I was lost - in every sense. Now and again, we bumped into fellow pedestrians. I heard about her first job at Rowntrees - she had soon left that one - she didn't like the smell of chocolate! Then there was her first boyfriend, Peter Towers. Apparently, that was a friendship that started at school, their family were neighbours. Her mam and dad had hoped that it would be serious, but Joan had other ideas.

"I'm glad you had," I said, pulling her closer.

That caused a lull in the conversation as she returned the hug. We walked down a dark street parallel to the railway line. I guided her into an even darker archway.

"What are you up to?" she laughed.

"I want to tell you something, Joan."

"What can you tell me here that you can't in the street?"

I put my fingers to her lips. "Careless talk!"

I could hardly see her face, yet her eyes were bright. "I just want to say simply, that I've fallen in love with you, Joan. Even though you laughed at me in the queue, it might be because you laughed at me in the queue, you minx. I might have fallen in love with your laugh." Her cheek was cool to my lips.

She sighed gently, "That's happened a bit quick, Paul. Golly," she murmured, "I like you too, mind."

Inevitably, we kissed - this time without bumping noses - it was a kiss filled with fervour, her lips pliant and inviting. She gasped for breath, "Gosh, you have hidden depths, Paul!" but she was soon silenced by my renewed attentions.

She came up for air. "We'd better get moving, we're going to be late."

Reluctantly, we moved on, her hand finding mine. She was quiet for a while, I think she had been taken aback by my sudden avowal. Then she spoke softly.

"Shall I tell you something?" she said, squeezing my hand, as we stumbled over a kerb. I steadied her.

"Yes, please, when you squeeze my hand like that, I know you're going to say something nice!"

"Well, Paul, I think I love you. You won't get a big head, if I say I liked the look of you when you first walked into Electricity House?"

"You'd marked me down had you? Hang on, though, you only think you love me?"

Her voice was warm. "Let's say that I have never felt this way before about anybody."

Inevitably, we kissed again, tenderly, with newly awakened affection. "Paul," she said, catching her breath and taking my hand. "We'll have to go." We reached her home much too soon. We didn't linger, Joan was anxious not to be too late and I suppose, so was I.

She had one parting shot, as she opened her garden gate. "Be careful of Len Wright!" Her laughter followed me on my way. I turned and shook my fist, then realised that she wouldn't see it in the blackout.

Stumbling back to Gordon Street, I did just as she had said. I carefully negotiated the hurdle of Len's bedroom, with my boots in my hand, safely sliding in the bolt, and settled down to my reverie, in which Joan was the star turn.

The next few weeks passed with my head in the clouds - cinema visits two or three times a week, followed by my walking her home. The walks were amorous endings to perfect nights, for, even if some of the films disappointed, Joan's company never failed to delight me.

We did see some enjoyable films - 'Jane Eyre', another adaptation! Bing in 'Going My Way', 'Girl Crazy', with Judy Garland and Mickey Rooney. Judy was one of Joan's favourites.

We both thought there were some catchy songs in 'Girl Crazy' - 'Embraceable You', 'Not for Me'. I remember Joan humming, 'Embraceable You' on our way home one night. I embraced her, but wished that it had been a balmy summer's evening and she wearing a thin frock, rather than a winter coat in the cool autumn air.

"Listen, Paul, my mam and dad go to the pictures on a Monday night, that's when dad's not at work. Would you like to come around? I warn you I have to do the ironing every Monday, it's my contribution to the housework. It might be boring for you!"

"No, it wouldn't, darling, I'd love to come."

"I think there's a snag, mind. I think Mam and Dad would like to meet you first, Dad particularly, he likes to know what I'm up to, and with whom!"

"Oh! Would I pass the test?" I teased.

"Well, you've passed my test! So there's a chance!"

So the following Sunday, we arranged to go for a walk, and then to her house for tea. She took me to explore the city walls, I was surprised how much of the medieval ramparts were still intact. We didn't have anything like them in Gateshead. Just back lane walls mainly. Joan seemed nervous of the impression I would make on her parents. Her usual happy mood was more subdued. Perhaps she was also concerned about what I would think of them.

She got her front door key out. "I should warn you, Paul, Mam and Dad talk more broadly than I do. I hope you'll understand them!"

"Oh! I think I'll be alright, Joan. Don't forget I slept in the next bed to George Wilkins for six weeks!"

"This is the parlour, sit down while I find Mam." She called out, "Mam, we're here!"

A stout woman with a pleasant face and straight, no nonsense, black hair appeared. Shrewdly, I guessed that she had been in the kitchen; she wiped her flour-covered hands on her apron and brushed a stray lock off her broad forehead.

She smiled at me. "So this is Paul, then. 'Ello lad, Aa'l not shek 'ands, A'am just mekin' a few scones. 'Ave ye 'ad a big dinner?"

"Well, not a big one, Mrs Speed. Big dinners are a rarity in Gordon Street."

"That's grand then, lad, ye'll ate all't more for thy tea, then," she laughed. "You're a Geordie, Joan tells us, you doan't speak like a Geordie, mind."

"My dad was a southerner, perhaps that's why I don't."

Joan's father came through from the garden. He put me in mind of a film actor - not Clark Gable, was it Guy Gibbee? Bald-headed with an amiable countenance just like whatshisname. "So this is your lad, Joan? Grand to meet thee," he said, shaking me firmly by the hand. "I said to your mam, the lad must 'ave some gumption for Joan to like 'im."

"Don't be daft, Dad," said Joan, blushing.

"D'ust like sport, lad?"

"Yes, especially cricket and football."

"You doan't 'ave Rugby League, up there, do's thee? Wi've got 'Steam Pigs', that's York rugby, tha knows. The steam cums off t'scrums int' winter. Then, of course, there's t'City."

"We've been to Headingley, to the cricket, Dad. Don't forget Yorkshire!"

"Aye, lass, roll on the peace, so we can see the tykes winnin' the championship agen."

"I've been going to Newcastle United and Gateshead the last couple of seasons," I said. "I'm hoping Newcastle get back into the First Division after the war."

"We went to Gateshead's ground, didn't we lass? That tramcar went down a poor area."

"Paul doesn't live near there, Dad."

'Why does that outing keep coming up?' I asked myself.

Mr Speed changed the subject. "'As thee a job t'go back to after t'war? There shud be plenty up theer int' Gateshead," he added, laughing. "Where there's muck there's money, th' say."

"Dad! That wasn't very nice!"

"It were only a joke, lass, Paul knows that."

"I have a job as a cashier to go back to," I said.

"There's plenty of jobs int' York, tha' knows."

'He's thinking well ahead,' I thought.

Just then, Joan's mam came in with a large plateful of sandwiches. "Bring t'scones and t'tea in, Joan. Sit theesen down at the table, lad," she added. "Get stuck in! Tha' looks as if a square meal will do thee good."

Joan came back with the scones just then. "Mother!" she said, "You shouldn't say such things! What will Paul think?"

I laughed, forgivingly, one eye on the table. It was a square meal alright - egg sandwiches, cheese sandwiches, pork sandwiches. 'Mrs Speed must have farming contacts,' I thought. I got stuck in as instructed. This was a change from Rose Street fare!

"Mam, can Paul come tomorrow night, when I'm ironing?"

"Our Joan! Do you 'ave to ask? I think Paul seems a sensible lad, dun't he George?"

"Aye, Ida, he does that. But he'd better look after our lass." There was a hint of a warning there!

"Why doan't you tek lad int' front room after tea, Joan, you can listen t't radio, or play some records," said her mam.

'What a wonderful person!', I thought.

"You can 'ave t'electric fire on."

Marvellous, she was!

Joan turned to me, "Do you want to stay, Paul?"

"Well, I would only be on my own, so it would be nice, yes." I didn't want to sound too eager in front of her mam and dad. They might have second thoughts.

A little later, Joan showed me into the front room. My spirits soared, Joan's mam had switched the electric fire on and bang in front of it was a sofa!

"Right, before we go any further, I have a bone to pick with you, Paul Potts! What do you mean? 'I would only be on my own', 'It would be nice'," she laughed, digging me in the ribs. She was getting this digging me in the ribs thing off to a fine art.

"Well, I couldn't say it would be fantastic, could I? Your dad might have thrown me out of the house! Anyway, is this an early Christmas present, being in the front room with you?"

"Sit yourself down on the sofa, while I put some gramophone records on."

"Something romantic," I suggested.

She laughed, "You'll just have to take pot luck!" She came beside me. There were just a couple of lamps shining, casting a pleasant, romantic glow. She was wearing the yellow roll-necked jumper with the smart skirt that she had worn on our first date.

She took my hand. "What do you think to my mam and dad, then?"

"Proper champion!" I said, laughing. "They must be if they produced you!"

There came that dig in the ribs again. "Don't scoff!"

"No," I said, "they were nice. Honestly, Joan, I can understand your dad's viewpoint. Can I tell you here and now darling, I don't think I'll ever ask you to do anything - you know - that you wouldn't want me to do. On the other hand," I added, laughing, "I hope there's a lot that you do want me to do."

She gave me a warm kiss as I put my arms around her.

"Do you think I passed the first test?" I asked.

"I think so," she laughed, "or you wouldn't be here in this room now!"

"Have I got my feet under the table?"

"'Od your 'osses, lad!" she mimicked, "Let's not jump t'gun!"

The night passed swiftly, as I discovered an abundance of charms. There were some caresses, I sensed, that would be taboo, after all, we had only known each other a matter of weeks. There were opportunities, however, for embraces and cuddles, opportunities to express my feelings for her, to revel in her nearness. As a novice, I was certainly venturing into unknown territory.

Our excitement was interrupted by a knock on the door.

It was her father. He didn't come in. "Joan, are thee two cumin' through for a bite of supper, befower Paul goes?"

"Yes, Dad," she flustered.

Unfortunately, it looked as though our delightful evening had come to an end. We straightened ourselves up and tried to calm down.

A little later, I was at the front door with Joan.

"Thanks for a lovely evening, darling," I said. "Tomorrow night, about seven then?"

"Yes, Paul, but it won't be like tonight, mind. I really have a lot of ironing to do!" she said, as she gave me a fond goodnight kiss.

Chapter 14

TO THE RESCUE

The following night a smiling Joan answered my knock. "Hello, love," I said, giving her a hug, "I'm here, ready for the ironing. Lead me to it."

She responded in kind, then pushed me away with a laugh.

"That's enough!" she said, "*You're* not ironing, I'd have to do it all again tomorrow after Mam had inspected it. Come through to the kitchen, though, just see the pile I've got to do! You'll just have to sit on that chair and watch me tonight. I warned you!"

"Can I talk?" I asked. "Is that allowed?"

"Well, I might let you talk! But no flattery!"

"You can't flatter perfection," I laughed.

"There you go. It won't get you anywhere tonight, though!"

"That sounds hopeful for other nights," I chuckled. "Am I allowed to look at you, then?"

"Don't be daft, but don't get any ideas," she said, putting the flat iron on the cooker hotplate to heat up. "Yes, Miss Speed. I'll sit in the corner, Miss Speed."

It was pleasant watching her ironing in her blue, short-sleeved, cotton frock, the thin material emphasising her bountiful curves. I knew that she had discarded her girdle - her shapely legs, as well as her cool, white arms, were bare. I was content for the time being to admire her young attractiveness and listen to her pleasant voice. I hadn't given up hope that some cuddling might be fitted in when she finished.

"What do you think of the news on the radio?" she asked, hanging a shirt on the rack.

"Maureen didn't have the wireless on. What was that?"

"Rommel's committed suicide, he was involved in that assassination attempt on Hitler apparently."

"Rommel! Fancy that," I said. "It must be two years since Monty defeated him at El Alamein."

"Perhaps the Nazis are creaking," she said. "The air raids have certainly stopped, touch wood. Those Baedeker raids were frightening, York was one of the targets, you know. We used to shelter in the ginnel between our house and next door. The worst night, the noise was terrible, bombs exploding, our guns firing. We wondered where the next bomb was going to land."

"It must have been scary for you. I remember hearing about those raids. In those days, of course, I didn't know my lass was in danger. I would have been worried sick."

"You're a daft 'ayporth, you know," she laughed. "Anyway, that night Dad was at work and Mam was afraid for my sister Liza and the bairns. We knew her husband, Patrick, was on night shift. If he'd been at home, he would probably have been drunk, anyroad. So I got some courage from somewhere and went round to Crichton Avenue in the middle of the raid."

"They'd be alright, weren't they?"

"They were scared out of their wits, their place had no shelter at all. So I brought them back to our house. By, I was petrified by the time we got home!"

"So, my girl was a bit of heroine! I wished I'd known at the time, I would have been proud of you! I've only had a few proud moments in my life. When we've an hour or two to spare I'll tell you about them!" I laughed.

With a neat flourish, she took the iron off the cooker and spat on it to test the heat. "That'll be thrilling! Anyroad, stop interrupting my tale. Next morning, we found a piece of shrapnel the size of a big tin of salmon on the pavement outside our house!"

"Why salmon?"

"Well, corned beef then," she giggled.

"You're making me feel hungry," I laughed.

Nevertheless, it was a sobering thought, I felt a needless qualm - what if Joan had been just another victim of the senseless bombing?

"You can listen to the radio if you like, Paul. I think Joe Loss is on tonight, I like his signature tune - 'In The Mood'. Zena and

I often danced to it when Bert Keech and his band played at the De Grey Rooms last winter."

"Did you now! Whom did you dance with?"

"Oh! Just lonely Poles and Canadians based at Sheriff Hutton. Zena was my chaperone, mind!"

I jumped up and grabbed her around the waist. "And Yanks and Free French I suppose as well! I hope they weren't free with you, precious," I said, nuzzling the nape of her neck.

She squirmed and shivered. "Oo! That does things to me," she laughed, "Get off! Or I'll burn you with the iron!"

I didn't want to get off, her waist and tummy felt deliciously soft and enticing.

"You're different tonight, Joan," I said, "sort of yielding!"

"Well, I'm not yielding to you, Paul Potts," she chuckled. "If you want to know, nosey pokes, I'm not wearing a girdle, it's too warm. I find it easier to work when I'm not restrained."

"What if I'm not restrained?" I asked, caressing her softness.

"Sorry, love, I must get this ironing done. I've still got my dad's thick railway overalls to iron, I hate doing them. Go and sit down again like a good lad."

"I'll sit down on one condition," I said.

"Oh, what's that?"

"That next time we're in the front room, you don't wear your girdle!" I laughed.

"O.K." she said, then added something in a quiet voice.

"I didn't catch that. What did you say, Joan?"

She laughed, "That's if you ever get in the front room again!"

"I better had!" I said. "And what's more, my love, promise you won't go out with Zena again, and get cornered by Poles and Canadians."

"That leaves me with Yanks, Australians, New Zealanders, even Eskimos?"

"No, not even Eskimos, I don't want you cornered by an Eskimo either!"

"Hang on, you can't be cornered by an Eskimo, not in their round igloos, anyway," she giggled.

The evening flew by - watching Joan iron was a lazy pleasure - she was perspiring, I was admiring. Much preferable to sitting with Maureen, Charlie and Fido, or reading alone in my room. Joan finished the ironing just moments before her mam and dad arrived home from the cinema. That was a body blow, hopes of delightful fondling that night now gone.

It was later that week in the office that Lance Corporal Bob Common came across to talk to Bill Dixon - the subject, the battalion soccer team. There was a crisis developing - they were a man short for Saturday, with key players on leave. Bill Dixon was secretary and centre-half for the team and Bob Common was captain and centre-forward.

"I've asked George Wilkins and Jack Thoms, but neither of them play football. What about your lad here?" Bob said.

I had been keeping my head down shuffling papers, but looked up then. I noticed that Joan was showing an interest too. (Visions of her lad scoring a hat trick?)

"'Ave thee played football, Paul?" asked Bill.

Joan looked across expectantly.

"Well," I said dubiously, "I've had one or two games." ('In the park,' I thought, 'or with Don and Cecil in the backyard.' I was good at shooties-in, headies, keepies-up and dribblies, with a tennis ball. I had a shrewd suspicion that was not the sort of soccer they were talking about.) "I'm no Stanley Matthews, mind!"

"Thee play on the reet wing, then, lad?"

"Yeah," I blustered." I was getting deeper in the mire. Why did I suggest that I was a right-winger, when I was left-footed? "The snag is I haven't played for a couple of years," I added.

"Oh," said Bill, disappointingly.

Why did Joan have to butt in then? She meant well, but I could have strangled her. In a nice sort of way, of course!

"Go on, Paul," she urged. "You could help them out!"

Soft me, couldn't ignore her entreaty. "If you're desperate, I'll play." Perhaps their standard of football wasn't high, after all Pay Corps wallahs were infantry rejects.

"Well, we are desperate!" said Bill, "Anyroad, I bet thee're O.K."

Thanks very much, they're desperate! I wonder what odds he would give for me being O.K. though?

That was when I thought of a lifeline!

"There's a snag, I haven't any football boots." I was grasping at straws now.

My hopes were quickly dashed.

"Don't worry about that," said Bob Lord, "what size do you take?"

"Eight," I said, wishing I took size thirteen or fourteen, that might have saved me from the fiasco I saw looming. As I expected - "We'll have you a pair for Saturday, there's plenty of spares," said Bob.

The instruction was - be at the sports pitch behind York City's ground in Bootham Crescent at two-thirty. Our opponents were Rowntrees reserves.

As Bill and Bob went off, either to discuss tactics and formations, or perhaps more likely, where they were going to have a pint that night, Joan piped up. "Fancy that, Paul! Dad can take me to see York City on Saturday, now that you won't be able to. We can see your ground from the back of the terraces. If City's game is no good, I can watch you instead."

"Gee, thanks!" 'Things are going from bad to worse', I thought. "You shouldn't bother watching me, I'll be a disaster!" I said dismally.

"Oh cheer up, Paul! You'll be a wow. Even if you're not, I'll still love you!" she promised magnanimously. That was no more than a crumb of comfort to me.

Nemesis was just two days away. In the dressing room, we changed into the team strip - predominately yellow to match my mood - ten sturdy athletic looking characters and me, the skinny one. I wasn't even sure how to lace my borrowed football boots. Such exotic items of sports equipment were alien to me.

We went out early for a five-minute kicky-in and a warm-up. I stood around in my flimsy strip, with a stomach full of butterflies, boots with slack laces, and a cold red nose. I watched my fellow athletes blasting the ball goalwards. A beetle-browed, stocky individual gave me a pass. This leather football was big and heavy. I found that out when I kicked it, it wasn't like a canny little bald tennis ball, my shot didn't whizz like those of my teammates. I was just thankful it reached the goalkeeper.

The referee called the teams into action, I took up a spot on the right wing.

The game started in ding-dong fashion, I wandered up and down the touchline - flinching second-hand at the crunching tackles, and in awe of the smart passing. The tackles were worrying. 'Someone could get hurt in this game,' I thought, 'and it might be me.'

About five minutes had gone by and the ball hadn't yet come in my direction - if it stayed that way for another eighty-five that would be just dandy. Sadly, miracles weren't on the agenda that day.

Blond, dashing Bob Common, playing at centre-forward, slipped the ball down the wing, I kicked it onwards and chased after it just as this big left-back came charging at me. I saw him out of the corner of my eye and had the presence of mind to stop in my tracks, avoiding what could have been a nasty collision. Oops! He went sailing on and landed in a heap over the touchline, allowing me ample time to foozle the ball to my inside-right and stop for breath. This running about wasn't doing me any good. The malevolent look their big left-back gave me didn't bode well for me either.

I was able to rest for a while after that bit of excitement. Our inside-left and left-winger were the stars of our team and the play was now concentrated on that side of the field. The pair won a corner and I trotted up to take up a position on the right.

I was alone behind the bustling throng, in and around the goalmouth; it was quiet out there. These Rowntrees fellows weren't marking me at all, probably thinking that I was no threat. Their attention was fully focused on our more dynamic players with orthodox legs. From the corner, I saw the ball coming sailing towards the back post. In theory, I knew what to do, meet it as it cleared the mob. At the last minute I shut my eyes, miraculously the ball hit my head with a thump and I dropped to the ground dazed. The next thing I knew, my teammates were pulling me up and slapping me on the back.

"Well done, lad!" said Bob Common, "Right in the roof of the net!"

'If the captain says I've scored, I must have done,' I thought.

That goal seemed to open the floodgates and by half-time we were five-one up. I played no further part in the avalanche - the ball came to me three or four times, but that big left-back robbed me with fierce tackles. Well, they seemed fierce to me.

To tell the truth, I was getting a bit tired with all this careering up and down the touchline.

Come half-time, I'd had enough, I was glad of the rest. No

oranges though, they were still in short supply. We had to make do with a drink of water.

The second half was a repetition of the first, except my legs were weaker and I received even fewer passes. I think Bob Common had decided I couldn't run, I couldn't beat a man, I couldn't pass. I wasn't good at tying shoelaces either - I tripped over them twice. With minutes to go, the score was nine-two in our favour, the chances were that we were going to win. Bob Common was almost through for another score, when their centre-half came to tackle him. Bob must have forgotten who was on the right wing, because as I toddled up breathlessly in support, he passed to me. I swung my useless right foot, the only one in the vicinity of the ball at the time, and somehow I connected. Their goalkeeper expecting a vicious shot from point blank range, fell backwards into the net. The ball trickled slowly forwards and eventually joined the custodian behind the goal line. My second goal!

This time the congratulations from the team were muted, they probably wondered how this caricature of a footballer had scored two goals. I wondered that myself. I didn't care, I had scored twice in my one and only appearance. For some peculiar reason I was never asked to play for the battalion again.

I had been invited to tea that evening by Joan, so after I changed back into khaki, I made my way along Burton Lane. Not before, very unexpectedly, Bob Common and Bill Dixon thanked me for filling in for them.

"We could see you weren't match fit," said Bill, "so we didn't give you much of the ball. At least you scored two goals!" he laughed.

Not match fit! That was a bit of a compliment!

Thankfully, it wasn't far from the ground to Joan's house. Just as well, I was done in, after jogging up and down that touchline for ninety minutes. My legs were all wobbly, and that was without playing proper football like the rest of the team.

Joan and her dad hadn't been home long when I arrived. "Cum in lad, thee clobbered them, didn't thee?" was the welcome I got from Joan's dad.

"There wasn't just me! There were ten others," I laughed.

I flopped into an armchair. "Yes, we won ten - two."

"We saw you score just before the end, you fooled the

goalkeeper alright," Joan said. "City had won by then, so we saw the last five minutes of your game. I saw other bits in between, mind."

"Fooled the goalkeeper! I nearly fooled myself!" I said. Nevertheless, I was pleased that she hadn't seen much of our match.

"You didn't see the first goal, then? I opened the scoring with a header." The way I put it, it sounded great. I hope I wasn't overdoing things. I also hoped she didn't have an in-depth analysis of the match with Bill Dixon on Monday.

"You scored two!" Joan looked surprised.

In a bout of honesty, I said, "I didn't do much else."

I didn't want her to get too carried away.

Joan started chuckling. "You know what Dad said when I pointed you out?"

Her dad butted in then. "Nay, Joan, doan't tell the lad that."

"He said, 'Ee lass, 'an't he got skinny legs!'"

Her dad laughed, embarrassedly, "Aye, Joan, but then Aa said they're athlete's legs, like Sidney Wooderson's!"

Her mam came into the parlour just then, with the usual pile of sustenance.

"Get stuck int' that, lad," said she. "You look whacked." She was a shrewd lady, was Joan's mum. I didn't need a second invitation. The fresh air had given me an appetite and I was hoping the nourishment would get down to my legs pretty quickly

Later in that cosy front room, Joan said, "I'm glad you didn't let me down, after I urged you to play."

Joan hadn't let me down either, I had already noticed her legs were bare, which surely meant she had discarded her girdle. It wasn't long before I confirmed that.

We settled down to a comfortable evening listening to the radio. I was feeling shattered and drowsy. Lazily, I cuddled and fondled her, feeling her warm softness through the thin material of her dress.

"I think you're tired after your exertions," laughed Joan.

"I am a little, but this is nice." I yawned, "Cuddling you and listening to the music."

I was in a euphoric mood, now that the worry of the match

was out of the way. I sensed I was drifting inexorably into what could be a long-term love affair. Did I mind? Not a bit!

Later, I struggled to my feet. "Well, darling, I'd better get moving, before I upset you and fall asleep! I'm sorry I haven't been a bundle of fun tonight."

"Don't worry, love, but you'd better be more awake next time!" she laughed.

'She's very understanding,' I thought.

There were more next times, thankfully, and Christmas was near too. We came to an arrangement - Joan and I would each spend Christmas with our respective families (I had leave due), then Joan would come up to Gateshead for two days at the New Year. Mam had grudgingly said that was alright if that's what I wanted.

So we parted on Christmas Eve with warm, yet doleful, kisses.

What a difference six months can make - Christmas in Gateshead was a bit of a comedown after our starry-eyed romancing. Mam and Rob's home wasn't as cosy as the Speeds' or even the Crows'. No bathroom of course, no hot water, no Joan, and I would be sleeping in the same room as Stephen. There were two beds in Stephen's room and when Joan came up for New Year, Cecil would also have to move in for a couple of nights.

Cecil, sixteen, was still working for the Boiled Sweet Company in Gateshead as a warehouse boy. Stephen was now nine. Don was in Normandy.

Rob was around of course but was never a father figure with us, more of a devil-may-care character. He had been gassed in the First World War and was just now suffering the ill effects, twenty-odd years later. He loved to go pub-crawling, a local sport, at weekends. Mam went with him at first, but soon got fed up of tripping from pub to pub.

I was concerned how Mam would receive Joan at New Year. I know that she was upset that I was getting seriously involved at nineteen years of age. Jealousy? Possessiveness? Who knows?

Chapter 15

NEW YEAR RESOLUTION

New Year's Eve was a long time coming, but at last, I was at Newcastle Central Station, waiting on the platform, with my penny ticket. A station platform was sacrosanct without a ticket, a penny to see the trains, a little more to travel. The London express carrying a precious cargo rumbled to a halt in a cloud of steam, piston rods clanking noisily. I looked at my brand new watch (a Christmas present from Joan) – quarter to five, the train was dead on time. Highly unusual.

As the steam cleared, I espied Joan alighting from a carriage, struggling with her suitcase. She was dressed as on our very first date - fawn jacket and yellow roll-necked sweater. The jacket was somewhat lightweight for December in the North East. Perhaps her thought was, that if the son liked her outfit, the mother would too.

She put her case down and, as I threaded my way through the hurrying crowds, held out her arms, her cheeks dimpling in a smile. We kissed as though we hadn't seen each other for six years, not six days.

"I've missed you, darling," I said, pausing for breath.

"I've longed to be with you, Paul," she said. I was oblivious to the bustle of the rushing crowds, aware only of the girl in my arms.

Hand in hand, we made our way to the exit. It was then that I remembered her suitcase. Quickly I dashed to recover it. It looked so incongruous - a lonely suitcase on a now deserted platform. I laughed with embarrassment.

"That would have been a disaster!" giggled Joan, "I would have had nothing to wear - and the shops shutting about now!"

"The only disaster, that I could see," I chuckled, "would be that you might have had nothing to wear, and no front room for me to make the most of the situation!"

"That's enough of that!" she warned. "We have to be on our best behaviour."

"Who says?" I asked, smiling.

"You want me to make a good impression, don't you?"

"You will!"

I could detect however, a hint of nervousness in her manner as we walked across the road to the Saltwell Park tram stop. How gratifying it was to see the streetlights beaming, though, now that the blackout restrictions had been lifted.

"Don't look so worried," I said.

"What if your mother doesn't like me?" she frowned.

"Why shouldn't she? Anyway it won't make any difference to us, whatever she thinks, will it?"

She gave a timorous smile.

Soon, the tram was rattling over the High Level Bridge across the Tyne. As we travelled along our family's old Saturday night shopping thoroughfare - Coatsworth Road - I said to myself, this is slightly better than Askew Road, particularly with most of the shops lit up now. I hoped that Joan thought so too.

"They clatter and sway a bit, these trams of yours. Not like our buses!"

"These double-deckers do rattle a bit," I said, "particularly when you're on the top deck."

"We should have gone upstairs then, for a bit of excitement," she laughed.

"That doesn't sound too promising, would that be the only thrill I'm likely to get during the next couple of days?"

"Paul," she said, in a grave voice, but with a twinkle in her eye, "I suspect you have a one track mind!"

As the tram approached our stop, the conductor rang the bell and we alighted. This time I remembered her case.

I decided to go into the house the back way. We had bare lino on the front stairs - no stair carpet - not a very auspicious entry. We didn't have carpet on the stone steps leading up to the back door either, but that would have been ostentatious.

"Watch your step, love, it's a bit dark," I said. Mam was in the large scullery. The term kitchen had still not percolated into our family's vocabulary.

"Hello, Mam, this is Joan," I said.

Mam appraised my girl for a minute or two, before offering her cheek. I knew she disapproved of our romance developing so strongly, at what she considered to be too young an age, but she couldn't fail to be impressed with Joan's appearance and manner.

"Pleased to meet you, Mrs Potts," said Joan. "Thanks for letting me come up for a couple of nights."

"Well, I couldn't say no to Dennis, but I may as well tell you that I think you are both too young for anything serious," said Mam, taking no time to make her point.

Joan laughed, nervously, "I can't agree there, Mrs Potts, I think we're both sensible."

'Good on you, Joan,' I thought, 'you stick up for yourself!'

"You know that I agree with Joan, Mam, so we'd best forget it," I said.

"I suppose so," said Mam, regretfully, "I'll show you the room, Joan, but first you'd better meet the family."

We went into the parlour. Rob was in an armchair, dead to the world, snoring. He'd finished work at noon and had been having a New Year's drink with his workmates. He was now sleeping it off. I introduced her to Stephen, still a quiet, nervous lad, and just then Cecil came in from work, so she met him too.

Cecil's room, which would be Joan's for the next couple of days, was not the most prepossessing, just bare lino on the floor. An old dresser, with the traditional water pitcher and washbowl, was the most important piece of furniture, apart from the bed and the chamber pot. I had purloined a clippy rug from the scullery to help give Joan a vague impression of opulence. For her to achieve that feeling, she would have to allow her imagination full reign! Mam spent most of the early evening preparing sandwiches, sausage rolls, cheese scones, for the New Year's Eve family party. She must have been saving some of the household's rations over the last few weeks to cater for Christmas and New Year celebrations. Joan for her part had brought half a dozen eggs, a piece of ham, plus half a bottle of gin and a bottle of tonic, all of which her mam had provided for the occasion.

I had bought Newcastle Brown Ale, a half bottle of whisky and lemonade at the local off-licence. Although liquor was not rationed, it was in short supply. I think my uniform might have helped my mission. Perhaps the assistant thought that my R.A.P.C. insignia stood for Royal Army Parachute Corps and that I was a hero of Arnhem. Joan had offered to help Mam with the catering, but had been politely refused, so she was chatting to Cecil and Stephen. She and Cecil seemed to get on like a house on fire. Not for the first time, I considered him to be a perceptive lad. They were discussing the relative merits of the centre-forwards of Newcastle United, Gateshead and York City, namely Albert Stubbins, McCormack and Winters. It was no contest when Cecil pointed out that Stubbins and McCormack were scoring about forty goals a season.

"I give in," she laughed.

"Did you know your brother was a footballer?" she asked Cecil.

It was then that Rob woke up. "Whee's a footbaaller?" staring puzzlingly at Joan.

"This is Joan, Rob," said Cecil, "you've been asleep hours."

He sat up then. "Gerraway, yer havin' me on, Cec. Hi, lass, pleased to meet ye," he said, yawning.

"Likewise," said Joan. "I was just saying Den was a footballer now!" She remembered to call me Den, it was very confusing for her. I hope she liked Den as much as she liked Paul.

Rob laughed, "In the backyard?"

"No," she laughed, "he played for the battalion, he scored two goals, would you believe?!"

"Wonders'll never cease, lass!" said Rob.

Later, the party got under way. Milly, Rob's daughter-in-law, arrived. She was a rather serious, fair-haired girl. She had something to be serious about - her husband was a prisoner of war, incarcerated in a Stalag in Germany. He had been captured in Crete, together with the rest of his unit, at the time that our troops on that island had succumbed to the Nazi invasion.

The dining table was soon laden with food, and drinks started flowing. Joan tried the famous Newcastle Brown Ale and found it quite palatable, sufficiently so, to have one or two more glasses during the course of the evening.

As we became merry, we played silly party games, 'Charades', 'Simon Says' (Stephen's favourite), before the whole thing degenerated into a singsong.

It was generally agreed that it was a pity that Robby (who apparently had a good singing voice) and Don (who thought he had) weren't present. We had to make do with a makeshift cast of songsters.

I think it was the first time (but not the last), that Cecil and I performed our infamous impression of Flanagan and Allen, singing 'Underneath the Arches'. We followed that with 'Hometown' as an encore. I have a hazy recollection that the shouts of encore came from Cecil and me.

Rob, now quietly drunk, gave us a maudlin rendering of 'Mother MacCree'.

"Oh, I love the dear sil-ver that shines in your hair,
And the brow that's all fur-rowed and wrink-led with care. . ."

I do believe Mam had tears in her eyes.

I countered swiftly, before anyone else could hog the floor, with that golden oldie - 'Yours'. Joan joined in and as she sang, her eyes were bright with love - or was it the brown ale effect?

It was about then that I thought Mam seemed a little put out. She looked at the clock.

"Rob," she said," it's nearly twelve o'clock! You'd better grab that piece of coal and the bottle of whisky and get outside to first foot!"

"You're right, pet!" he said and he was soon clattering unsteadily down the stairs and out the front door.

Joan was a bit puzzled by the whole performance, such happenings didn't occur much in York on New Year's Eve in those days. I explained that Tynesiders took New Year seriously - almost as seriously as the Scots.

"We've all got to stand and sing 'Auld Lang Syne' when Rob comes back in," I said.

"Why?" she asked, shaking her head in wonderment, probably asking herself, 'What have I let myself in for with this lot?'

"It's tradition, you see, love. It's just tradition." From the radio, came the sound of Big Ben chiming midnight, followed by the noise of Rob, staggering up the stairs, still singing 'Mother MacCree'. With the help of that brown ale, Joan, a quick learner, entered into the spirit of things. She mastered the words and clasped hands in time honoured fashion, thus humouring the natives.

She even flung herself into the kissing and handshaking rituals.

Shortly afterwards, Milly said she must get home, so Joan and I offered to escort her.

We went down Dunsmuir Grove and on to Saltwell Road.

"It was a good night," Milly said, "I hope that Robby is home for next New Year."

"He will," I said, "y'can, y'can y'can bank on that. The war's spinning out of Hitler's grasp."

'Almost as much as the spinning in my head,' I thought.

"Have you heard from Robby recently?" Joan asked.

"Not for a couple of months," Milly said, "it's awful waiting for a card. Reading between the lines, they're not getting much to eat. Let's hope you're right, Den, that the war will soon be over."

Wandering back up the hill, arms around each other, Joan said, "That was a fun, funny night. The drink's gone to my head a bit. I don't think your mam, hic, likes me, mind."

"Will you stop sur-surmising, darling," I said, unconvincingly, giving her a warm kiss.

"Listen," I said, "we'll go around by the back lane, then we can go to the net, hic, to the net, to the lav on the way in. I'm sorry we haven't an indoor toilet like you have."

"Don't worry, Paul Dennis," she laughed, "I understand. We had an outdoor lav, hic, when I was little and we lived in Ald, in Aldwark."

I chuckled, "When we win the war, everyone will have indoor toilets and bath-bathrooms and hot and cold water. Those, hic, hee hee, those may be our secret war aims!"

"Plus everyone would have a front room!" Joan added. Joan went to the lav first, I sang 'Underneath the Arches' again, so she wouldn't be embarrassed if she made a bit of a noise. She did, mind.

When she came out, I asked, "What are you going to, going to sing, eh?"

"I'll hum Handel's, hoo, hoo, whoops, 'Water Music'," she

giggled, and was soon in kinks of laughter. "Just wait, wait, till I come out," I threatened, "I'll give you 'Whoops, Water Music'!"

When I did emerge into the semi-darkness, she had disappeared into the lane, attempting to curb her giggles and not cause a disturbance in the backyard.

I went into the back lane to find her, locating her by her whoops. I stopped her laughter eventually, discovering that my kisses, given time, changed her disposition from humour to ardour. I liked both those facets of her personality.

We didn't linger too long, it was a cold night and time was getting on, Mam might send out a search party.

Everyone was ready for bed when we got back into the flat, and so were we. It had been a tiring, unusual and emotional day.

New Year's Day itself was an anti-climax. Everyone was up late, of course, and after a couple of aspirins and a midday snack, Joan and I went for a walk in Saltwell Park. I was able to demonstrate that Gateshead had some very pleasant parts. The park was probably the largest and finest public park in the area. Although attractive even in the winter, I told her that spring, summer and autumn were the three best seasons for colour and variety. Even so, I believe Joan was impressed with so much greenery in a grey town.

We went to the Honeysuckle pub with Rob and Mam that night, Rob wandered off for an hour to explore other hostelries. Perhaps checking that they hadn't disappeared since yesterday lunchtime. Mam had worked as a barmaid at the Honeysuckle for a period and knew most of the staff and customers. We were left to ourselves a lot of the time, which didn't displease us. We kind of liked each other's company!

Next day, after saying our goodbyes to the family, we set off on our journey to York.

The train was late, we waited half an hour on the draughty platform before it steamed in from Edinburgh. Strangely though, it wasn't too crowded and we found seats quite easily.

The coach didn't have the usual compartments, but, instead, was an open one. Tables seating four on one side, just two on the other. We grabbed two seats facing each other on a smaller table, pleased that we'd have some privacy for our two-hour journey.

The train was soon rattling over the Tyne on the King Edward Bridge, next stop Durham.

"Thanks for coming up, Joan," I said. "Now you know the worst about my home and family!"

She laughed, "Oh, it wasn't so bad, Paul. I can call you Paul, again, can't I? Your mother didn't quite bite me. I liked Cecil, mind, he seems a nice lad."

"He really is," I agreed. "Stephen's very quiet, though. He seems to have a lot of thoughts he keeps to himself."

As the train pulled into Durham Station, the panorama of the Cathedral and Castle came into view. Joan was appreciating the grandeur of the scene. I was simply admiring her attractive profile. 'How lucky I am, I mustn't lose this girl,' I thought.

As the new influx of passengers was moving along the coach looking for seats, I suddenly knew what I was going to do.

"Joan," I murmured, "give me your hand."

She looked puzzled, "Pardon, what for?"

"I've a reason," I said earnestly. "It's not just that I like to hold your hand, which I do, mind. It's something else."

Across the table, she put her hand in mine. "There you are," she laughed, squeezing with affection. "My, you do look serious."

Her warm brown eyes were enquiring.

"Joan, will you marry me?"

It was only then that I realised how possible it was that she could say no. In her heart she might believe that we were too young to make such a commitment.

She looked taken aback at first and said nothing for what seemed an age. Finally she spoke, teasingly, "What did you say, Paul? Say it again."

The train was rattling along now, I almost had to shout. "Will you be my wife?" I said, "Will you marry me?"

"Ssh," she said, looking around, "we don't want the world to know! I don't believe it!" She smiled, her eyes were sparkling now, that cheered me up no end. "Are you really proposing to me on a crowded train?"

Out of the corner of my eye, I saw a couple opposite looking at us interestingly. I had noticed them before, he a corporal in the Black Watch Regiment, her in A.T.S. uniform. They appeared to be in their early twenties. Obviously, either coming back from, or going, on leave. Probably coming back from Scotland, after celebrating Hogmanay, the lad being in a Scottish unit.

"That's the idea," I said. "Seeing you now, the way you look, the way you are, it just hit me, how much I want to be with you always, darling. I don't want us to be separated for six whole days again. Sorry, but I couldn't wait until York to ask. I have to know your answer now. Please say you will."

She clutched my hand tightly, "The answer's yes, Paul Dennis! Does that put you out of your misery? I hope you haven't got any more surprises today!"

"Just this!" I said, leaning with difficulty over the table and finding her receptive lips.

Soon the train slowed down on its approach to Darlington station. The couple opposite stood up and collected their luggage. I guessed they were stationed at Catterick Camp. As the corporal passed by, he offered me his hand, a smile on his face.

"Congrats, laddie, ye've made a catch there, she's a belter!"

His girlfriend leaned across, then, "Cheers," she said, "I hope it's infectious!"

The lad laughed, "Not tonight, Josephine!"

Joan was blushing, we were both glad when they left the coach.

"That's the last time you'll propose to me on a train!" she laughed.

"I promise I won't do it again."

"I won't forget this journey in a hurry, Paul, you're a devil."

"I should hope you won't forget!" I smiled, "I hope you'll still remember when we're Darby and Joan in our rocking chairs!"

Joan turned serious at that point, "I said yes to you, Paul, but I don't think we should get married too soon. After all we're both still only nineteen. We've got to be sensible. Perhaps after you're demobbed and have a job. What do you think?"

I took her hand. "Look, love, you know I said I wouldn't do anything that you don't want me to do? Well that applies to this, as well. The question is, can you wait that long, can we wait that long?"

"I know you can! You've proved to me already that you can curb your ardour when I ask you to. I think I can too! I know it's difficult when we love each other so much. Anyroad, you said the war will be over soon, demob might not be too far away!"

"But you will marry me?"

She squeezed my hand. "I said so, didn't I?"

"Well, Joan, as long as I can see you often, hold you often, it won't be so bad. You shouldn't be so delicious, though."

"You are a romantic lad, Paul."

"Don't you like that?"

"Of course I do, you send shivers up my spine sometimes, the way you talk."

"Only when I talk?" I grinned.

"Let's stick to talk," she laughed.

The train ground to a halt. I looked out the window and saw a dim station sign - York. We had been so engrossed in our own world that we had almost forgotten that we were on a train. We grabbed our luggage quickly and exited the carriage.

As we walked out of the station, I said, "Did you notice the engine? It was a Gresley Pacific, named 'Pretty Polly'."

"I did as a matter of fact," she said, "I'm nearly sure that my dad has driven it. The name seems familiar. Why did you ask?"

"Oh, nothing really. Just a little story, I'll tell you about it sometime. Did your dad want to be an engine driver when he was a boy?"

"Funnily enough, no, he wanted to work in an office."

"That's strange, most of the office lads I knew wanted to be engine drivers when they were little!"

On the bus to Burton Lane, Joan said, "You know I'll want you to mention it to my dad, before we get officially engaged."

"Oh! Do I have to?" There were things involved in this marriage mullarkey that didn't seem necessary. 'A pity we can't just elope to a desert island,' I mused.

"Well, darling, I would like you to."

"Then I will then. What else?" I asked.

"Just the engagement ring. Can you afford it?" She mentioned an amount which didn't seem exorbitant when she said it quickly, but seemed a trifle outside the confines of my current financial status.

I surreptitiously fingered my slim wallet, "When would you want that, darling?" I asked, trying not to sound too anxious.

"Well, Paul, what about announcing our engagement at about the time Germany surrenders? Then we would wait for your demob, before we got married. Does that sound right?"

Suddenly, I had lost my enthusiasm for a quick German

defeat, not until I had got a bit more money in the Post Office Savings Bank anyway.

"Yeah," I said, I hoped this 'yeah' didn't sound as unconvincing to Joan as it did to me. "That would be grand, love. I'll speak to your dad nearer the time, then." She gave my arm a squeeze.

"What's it like to be my unofficial fiancée, darling?"

"Lovely," she smiled.

Chapter 16

VICTORY

During the first months of 1945 we were on a high. We held a secret. We had made a promise. We had made a pledge. We were to face the future together. It was to be 'we', always. The world after the war would offer new hope. A war that would surely be over before the year end. There was much to look forward to. Those were halcyon days. We continued to have the freedom of the front room, her mam and even her dad, seemed to have complete trust in Joan. And me? Perhaps they also had their fingers crossed. If they wanted to speak to Joan, they would always knock on the room door or give her a shout. Often, when this happened, she would have to disentangle herself from my embrace, or straighten her dress before going through to the parlour. Fortunately, those interruptions were few and far between.

How did we resist the ultimate temptation? The reason? We agreed that we wanted our marriage to start on an even keel, no snags. "Willpower, love," Joan would say. Most of my reserves of willpower were needed in that front room.

We had disagreements, generally on important issues, such as who was the better football team, York City or Gateshead? Or, who was the better crooner, Frank Sinatra or Bing Crosby? One Sunday, there was a more serious discussion (if that were possible). We walked on the City walls near Lendal Bridge, admiring that well known view of the Minster.

Pointing to the church in its shadow, Joan said. "Isn't that the church you went to this morning? The Catholic church?"

"Yes," I said.

She stood looking at the scene for a few moments. "Have you thought that if we get married we have a problem?" she said.

"You said if, then! You meant when, surely!"

Her laugh was muted, "When, then."

I put my hand on her shoulder. "What's the problem, love?"

"You're Catholic, I'm C. of E."

"So, darling?"

She put her hand on mine. "We're going to have children, aren't we?"

"That's what we said."

"Well," she looked serious, "you'll want them brought up in the Catholic faith?"

"Mm, I haven't given it much thought, but I suppose so."

"There's your problem, Paul."

"Look, darling," I said pulling her close, "let's not try to cross our bridges before we come to them." I knew I was procrastinating. "We've agreed that any decisions we make about anything serious would be a joint one, haven't we? One thing I know, love, nothing is going to stop me being with you for the rest of my life. Unless one of these days, even before we're married, you give me a heart attack in the front room," I laughed. "We'll talk about it when the time comes, eh?"

Joan sighed, "What I've seen of this sort of situation worries me. My sister Liza's husband, Patrick, is a Catholic. He's a drunkard and now he's a wife beater."

"A wife beater? He isn't!"

"He is! She came across to our house yesterday, with bruises on her face and arms."

"Has he hit her before?" I asked.

"Apparently, yes. The first we knew about it, though, was yesterday."

"She should leave him, or get the police involved," I said.

"She won't. She says that when he's not drunk, he's a different man."

I shook my head, "He'll not change. Liza's a fool!"

"I know, we've told her that, but she's stubborn. Yesterday, she said that he had called her a heathen and that the children had to go to a Catholic school."

I squeezed her neck, fondly. "So that's why you brought this Catholic thing up. You don't think I'll ever be a wife beater, Joan?"

She laughed, kissing me on the cheek. "Of course not, more a wife pesterer, I should imagine."

"That could be me!" I laughed. "This man of hers must have a warped mind, and be a coward, to hit a woman, all the same, Joan."

"There's not much we can do, though, is there?"

"Not really, if Liza won't do anything herself," I said.

"Talking about religion, did you know my dad was brought up as a Catholic?" Joan said.

"No!"

"He lapsed, but I don't know whether he's renounced the faith completely, I just found out recently. My mam told me. Just think, I could have been a Catholic."

"Well, you're not. Anyway, Joan, don't worry any more about us. There won't be a problem that we can't sort out. Don't you think we are too sensible?"

"Are we?" she said dubiously. "I hope so."

In that spring, her brother Philip was discharged from the Guards. He returned to civvy life and work in the York office of Northern Breweries. He was a tall well-built lad, proud of his Guards service, but his leg wound was far from right, with still a possibility of the need for amputation. The wound was continually weeping through the dressings, which were still needed. He hadn't been home long before he was courting seriously - a girl called Doris. Fortunately, he didn't need 'our' front room, but spent most of his spare time at Doris's house. In that same spring, I was moved from Joan's section and transferred upstairs to join the Income Tax Department of the Pay Corps. Sergeant Jim Donaldson, who in civvy life was a Tax Collector (working in Edinburgh), was my new section leader. Including myself, he had a staff of three. The Inland Revenue delegated their responsibilities for Income Tax assessment to the Pay Corps. The tax affairs of army personnel up to the rank of Warrant Officer were in our hands. Army privates didn't figure much in our calculations, our meagre pay left us out of the tax net. My new job proved interesting, the drawback, of course, was that I was no longer working with Joan. Our love affair was far from secret amongst the staff of Electricity House and our segregation was the subject of ribald comments.

"You'd better watch out, Joan, there's some smashing A.T.S. girls upstairs!" said Bill Dixon.

"You won't be able to keep your eye on him now!" added Bob Lord.

"Don't believe any of it, Joan," I said. "Don't look so worried!"

I had obtained a second-hand bicycle at a knockdown price early that year, and on Sundays we would cycle around the countryside. Luckily, the area around York was flat. Even so, for the first few weeks I found great difficulty keeping upsides with Joan, who, having cycled for years, had leg muscles attuned to the task. Mine had not had much practice since that notorious football match. Riding along, she would turn her head and laugh, "Come on slow coach, or we'll not even get back for supper!"

We always did better than that. I made sure we got back for tea, never mind supper and a piece of crumpet afterwards.

One day, my bicycle, or at least me on my bicycle, caused a mini crisis in our burgeoning romance. That morning, Joan had discovered that her bike had a flat tyre. With no time to mend the puncture, she caught the bus into work. So, that evening, she had left the office in good time and hurried to the Exhibition Square bus stop.

Not in any such dash, I collected my bike from the cellar, just as Morag MacKenzie, an A.T.S. lance corporal, was pushing hers up the stairs. Morag worked also worked on the first floor, but in another section. A native of the Orkneys, I had thought her a pleasant girl, blonde, nice looking, always smiling. Probably one of Bill Dixon's 'smashers'.

I knew she was billeted in Burton Lane, so we rode part of the way together, chatting. We cycled into Exhibition Square, where I would then turn off along Gillygate and Morag would carry on up Bootham. I was surprised to see Joan still at the bus stop (evidently her bus was late). I gave her a wave, but I was flabbergasted when she turned her head away and stared into the distance. My front wheel wobbled, I nearly fell off. Shouting cheerio to Morag, I continued on my way, puzzled. Was there a problem? Surely not. But yes! Was it yesterday in the office that Joan saw us coming downstairs together and was Morag chuckling at one of my feeble jokes? Now today there we were laughing and chatting as we cycled along. Had Joan put two and two together, to make five?

I hadn't arranged to see Joan that night, and after my usual inadequate meal with Maureen, Charlie, Len and Fido, I went up to my room. Tense and uneasy, I was unable to settle. I tried to read a book, but concentration had gone, the words weren't registering. A mental picture of Joan at the bus stop ignoring my wave, wouldn't disappear. I knew what I had to do. I grabbed my jacket and hurried downstairs.

"I'm going round to Joan's, Maureen."

"Oh, right, Paul. Will you be late?"

"I'm not sure, but I've got the key." I was around at Burton Lane in about five minutes flat. I had to put things right with my girl. Joan answered the door to my knock. "Oh, it's you!" she said disdainfully. "What do you want?"

I was disconcerted. "I want to see you, Joan"

"Me! I thought you would be going around to Morag MacKenzie's! You seem to like her company." Her manner was cool, her eyes were red. Had she been crying? My heart filled with compassion, she seemed so upset.

"Don't be daft! Aren't you going to let me in?"

"Why should I?" she asked. "If you must, you must. You'd better go into the front room." She stepped aside to let me through.

"Well?" she asked. "Why are you here?"

I took her hand, she didn't pull it away, which I thought was promising. "You're being silly, darling."

"Why? First I see you laughing with her, then you both come cycling past, gaily chatting. Her with her nose in the air and all. She didn't even look at me. Bill Dixon was right. You've got all those so called smashers upstairs!" She sounded very distressed. I didn't think she could be like this. I tried to understand her viewpoint.

"Joan!" I cried grabbing her by the shoulders, "Don't be so silly, she means nothing to me, none of those A.T.S. girls mean anything to me. I want nobody but you. You know that in your heart. Haven't we vowed to be together always?"

Her eyes were bright with tears now. "I didn't know what to think. You both looked so absorbed in each other."

I pulled her to me and kissed her tenderly. "Shall we forget all this nonsense, love? You had me worried when you ignored me at the bus stop. I had to see you tonight."

"Well," she murmured, "You don't care for her? You think I've been silly, don't you?"

"I've said I care for you, haven't I? I wish you wouldn't be daft, darling."

Later, on the settee, in the front room, after a rather pleasant and fond reconciliation, happily eating one of her mam's suppers, I turned to her. "I'm glad I came around tonight, Joan." She snuggled up to me. "Tell me again, Paul, why is that?"

I laughed, "I wouldn't have got this lovely ham sandwich, if I'd stayed in the digs!"

When she put two hands around my throat to strangle me, I knew that everything was back to normal.

During late spring, the war in Europe was moving rapidly to a victorious conclusion. As Allied troops moved into Germany the horrors of the concentration camps were exposed. Newsreels showed the dreadful treatment meted out to the Jews.

Suddenly, the announcement came. The following day, May 8th, was to be VE Day - a holiday to celebrate victory in Europe. Early on the afternoon of the eighth, I cycled around to Joan's.

"Victory over Germany day, Joan!" I said, as she greeted me with a kiss. "You know what that means?"

"Of course!" she laughed. "It means we've won the war!"

"Yeah, we know that, but what else?"

"I can't imagine. You tell me!"

"You are a tease. Tell me, is your Dad in?"

"Well, he is as a matter of fact. He's not on holiday, though. He's on late shift. He'll tell you that engine drivers don't get public holidays. Why are you asking that?" she chuckled.

"You know darn well. Go and get him," I demanded, sternly.

"He's upstairs. Mam's in the garden, do you want her too?"

"Go on, then, the more the merrier. Why not get your uncles and your aunts as well? Mind you, it won't make any difference even if your dad says no!"

"Difference to what? No, to what?" she asked, trying to look puzzled.

Just before I could grab her, her dad came downstairs into the room, followed by her mam, in from the garden.

"Dad, Paul wants a word you with you about something."

"Oh, aye, lad," said her dad, "Aa' 'ope its more good news!"

"Well I think it is, Mr Speed, but my confident mood was beginning to evaporate. "It's like this. Joan and I want to get married when I get demobbed, and we agreed to get engaged when Germany was defeated. Joan said that you ought to be the first to know." It didn't sound like the way they did it in most of the books I had read. Perhaps I should have said - 'Sir, I am asking for the hand of your daughter in marriage,' but that sort of approach didn't seem the right one to make to an engine driver in a council house in York. That was my best shot, he'd have to take it or leave it. After all, I hadn't done this sort of thing before, surely he'd make allowances?

Her dad's reaction to my little speech was blunt. "Oh, so that's it, lad! What if Aa' doan't think it's good news?" he said, "What then?" It wasn't often he looked so stern.

Joan butted in then. "Come on Dad, you like Paul!"

Then her mam spoke up. "Ye'r trying t'be a clever clogs, George. By gum tha' knows tha' lass and yon lad think t'world of each other."

Joan's dad burst out laughing then, "Aa' was nobbut larkin' with 'im, Ida. Anyroad, lad, ye shud have asked Ida, tha' knows, she's t'gaffer in this house."

"And mind ye doan't forget that, George, ye barmpot!" laughed her mam.

'Well,' I thought, 'I'm glad that's over. It wasn't so bad after all!'

Joan thought it wasn't so good either. I could tell that, when she spoke to me afterwards.

"There wasn't much asking for permission in that little speech you made, Paul Dennis," she said in mock annoyance, but with a mischievous sparkle in her eye.

"Oh, I don't know," I laughed, "I think I hinted that we would like his approval! By the way did we get it?"

"You know darn well we did," she chuckled. "You're not going to get out of buying me a ring as easy as that!"

After a bite of tea, a big bite! Joan and I set off to join the celebrations in Exhibition Square. We knew the buses would be jam-packed with people streaming into town, so we walked in, hand in hand. I was happy in the knowledge that at last her mam and dad knew of our intentions, I didn't care if the whole world knew now. People in our own little world would all know soon, anyway. With the exception of my family. I decided I wouldn't tell my mam until my next leave. It would be a fait accompli, but I wanted to see her reaction to the news, face to face. Or was I just delaying that tricky moment?

Massive crowds were already in the square. Temporary staging had been erected and Bert Keech was on the podium, and his Band was belting out popular music to singing and cheering from the happy throng. 'White Cliffs of Dover', 'There'll Always Be An England', 'Roll Out The Barrel', and many more.

In spite of the general merriment, some of the women were wiping away tears with their hankies. Many probably recalling husbands, fathers, boyfriends, killed or maimed in that long six years of war. Others no doubt wondering how much longer they were going to have to wait for their men to come home. Some of those men, of course, were still in action in the Far East. Some, like stepbrother Robby, were prisoners of war, awaiting repatriation. A military band took over from the dance band and the stirring sound of martial music echoed around the city's old streets.

The music heralded a march past of some of the forces stationed in the area. They were mainly airmen, but it was a unit from the King's Own Yorkshire Light Infantry (the Koyli's) that raised the biggest cheer. There were detachments from the Royal Canadian Air Force, the American Air Force, the Free French.

"You'll recognise a lot of these, Joan," I chuckled.

She dug me in the ribs, "Don't be cheeky! Although to be honest, I think I saw a couple of Canadians I knew from last year!"

"You're having me on!" I said.

Bert Keech returned to the platform and his musicians were soon playing some of the big band tunes heard so much during the war years. The crowd were spilling over the square, dancing and jitterbugging to classics made famous by the late Glenn Miller. Was it just a few months since the news had come through that the American bandleader was missing, believed dead? Now, it was just the local band playing his tunes - 'In the Mood', 'Chattanooga Choo Choo', 'Girl in Kalamazoo'. The mood of the music changed again and soon couples were smooching to the slower beat of more romantic melodies, 'You'll Never Know', 'People Will Say We're In Love', and many others, during the next hour or so.

This kind of music was more up my street. Not the dancing, but the crooning certainly; being close to Joan, definitely. Fondly I warbled in her ear.

"People will say we're in love."

I confess I was never destined to be a dancer, but I shuffled along in the crowd holding Joan close to me on that fine May evening. Somehow I avoided stepping on her toes, which was some sort of a feather in my cap.

"You know what, Paul?" she said, as we swayed cheek to cheek.

"No, I don't know what, love - what, love?"

"You're a soppy lad!"

"Don't you like me to be soppy?"

"Well, you bring me out in a muck lather, sometimes!"

"Muck lather? What does that mean?"

She laughed, "I don't rightly know. I don't know all the meanings of Yorkshire expressions, but I get the feeling it suggests being sort of, you know, being a bit wobbly at the knees."

"You mean like me after that football match?"

She laughed, "Not quite!" As I walked her home that night, she asked, "What do you think of it all? Do you think things will be any better now we've beaten Germany?"

"I don't know, love, but we might have an election soon. I think Labour will get in, don't you? They can't be any worse than the Tories were before the war."

"Do you think they would win an election?"

"Well, I think a lot of the Forces will be voting for them, a lot of young people everywhere. If Labour carry out all their promises, we'll have a free health service, the railways, the mines will be nationalised, just think, they'll be owned by the people!"

"Yes, I know all that, Paul, they make it sound like Utopia, I'll believe it when I see it!"

"Anyway, love, it'll be a new dawn for us. What do you say to the idea that I take you for your ring on your birthday, the twelfth? It's four days away, that means I'll have another pay day before then!"

"You're not as broke as that, surely! Are you saying that I won't get a birthday present, just a ring?" she laughed.

"What do you mean? Just a ring! Anyway, that's an idea, no birthday present, I wish I'd thought of that!"

"Why? Have you already got my present?" she asked.

"I'm not saying," I said. "I don't have to say, Joan."

"You're a proper spoilsport, Paul. Seriously, can you afford to buy the ring?"

"Well," I said, "if ten pounds will cover it, I can!"

"Oh! That should be ample, love. I don't want the crown jewels! I just want to wear your ring. You must have been saving up, though!"

"You know I'd already been saving, Joan. That was before I popped the question, but I had to step it up, after that fateful day," I laughed.

"Paul Dennis! You make it sound awful." Then came that dig in the ribs again.

"Oh! It's been terrible," I joked, "I've only been able to take you to the pictures twice a week, lately. Still there have been compensations, a picture show replaced by an extra night in the front room with you!"

On her birthday, her twentieth, we went to the jeweller's during our lunch break. Joan told the assistant the price range we were interested in and soon she was perusing trays of rings. I couldn't see any difference between them, but then I wasn't a member of the jewellery cognoscenti. Joan must have been, because she selected a ring, which this highly trained assistant said was easily the best in the entire display. Surprise, surprise.

Anyway, if Joan liked it, I liked it. I know Joan was happy - she gave me a smashing kiss, even before I had paid for the ring. And right in front of the assistant! I was certainly happy, I would have some change from the transaction.

That night, after tea at Joan's, we cycled up to the Bumper Castle pub, out in the country, but just a mile or so up Wigginton Road. We sat at a table outside and basked in the evening sun, happy and contented, supping our drinks - me with a pint of John Smith's bitter and Joan with a gin and tonic.

Joan kept glancing down at her ring, smiling to herself.

"Do you like it?" she asked.

"I do," I said, "even more, I like what it represents."

Chapter 17

PEACE BREAKS OUT

Joan also liked the ring's message, that was obvious from the way she was admiring it the night we walked by the River Ouse on Clifton Ings. The Ings was a pleasant stretch of grassland and a favourite lovers' rendezvous, the agreeable sound of the flowing water never far away. We stopped and looked across the river.

"Look, Joan." I pointed, "Quack quacks."

"I can't see any quack quacks," she laughed, "they're mallards, you barmy lad."

"Well, mallards are quack quacks, aren't they?"

She ruffled my hair. "What have you got in that brain box? What sort of a cracker am I going to marry?"

"Just someone who's head-over-heels in love with another cracker," I laughed. "Changing the subject from ducks, ducks, you've been quiet this last half hour. It's as though you were plotting something."

"No, love, not a plot, really."

"Ee, I think we'd better sit down, this sounds serious. Here's a nice bit of grass, I'll let you sit on my blouse."

"I wish you wouldn't call that jacket a blouse, Paul."

"Well it is - 'blouse, battle, for the use of', that's what I signed for. Len always calls it that, anyway."

"I rest my case, then," she said, plumping down beside me.

"Right, Paul, now that we're engaged, what say I broaden your education? Get something into that daft head of yours."

"Oo!" I laughed, "That sounds promising! You've taught me a

lot already. F'r instance, I know a lot more about geography than I did when I first met you. *Your* geography in particular!"

"Do you know, Paul, I'm starting to worry about you? Just pay attention to your tutor!"

"Yes, ma'am."

"What do you know about Shakespeare?"

"Isn't he that centre-forward of Crewe Alexandra?"

"No he's not, you barmpot! You know darn well who he is. Even you must have learned something about him at school."

I lay back on the grass and watched fleecy clouds moving lazily across the sky. I ran a finger up her spine.

"Oh yes, Joan, now I know who you're talking about."

"Will you stop that?!"

"Why, don't you like it?"

"I do. That's why I want you to stop it. I want to talk. Have you heard of Gilbert and Sullivan, then?"

"Let me think," I said. "They sound like opening batsmen, but for which county they play, I can't remember."

"Are you really that gormless?" she laughed. "I bet you know of Murray and Mooney, though?"

"Now you're talking, they're just about my favourite comedians. I always listen to them on the wireless."

"My point's made," Joan chuckled, "you see how low down the scale you are as a connoisseur of the arts!"

"I lie here humbled, darling, a mere plebeian compared to you! I'm better than you on clouds though." I pointed upwards. "Look! They're cirrocumulus."

"Never mind clouds." She punched me gently in the belly. "I think you're having me on. You're not as stupid as you act. Anyway I've got a plan for the next few weeks, right?"

"I've got a plan for now," I laughed pulling her down and finding a ticklish spot. "Is your plan better than mine?"

"Will you stop it, you nutcase!" she laughed.

She tried to look stern, as stern as anyone can when lying on a riverbank and being tickled. "Don't interrupt me when I'm talking to you. I've bought two tickets for the Empire this week. Murray and Mooney are on, Nat Gonnella and his band and Issy Bonn. What do you think of that for your first lesson?"

"That's smashing!" I said, "But *I'll* pay, you can't pay for my enjoyment. I'm the man."

"Sometimes I'm not so sure. I wonder if you've grown up," she laughed. "I'm paying anyroad, I like music halls as well, you know. This is my treat."

"O.K., Joan, don't shout, love. Do you know, in my whole life I've only been two or three times to a show? Once I went to the Theatre Royal, Newcastle. My mother took me to see a pantomime - that's where I saw Len Wright's double."

I leaned over and found her smiling lips. "That's a thank you kiss, darling."

"O.K., O.K. That's enough of that, there's people about," she said sitting up again.

"You don't say, Joan! I don't think they're paying *us* much attention."

"Paul."

"Yes, love?

"Paul, I've also got tickets for Gilbert and Sullivan's 'The Gondoliers' at *our* Theatre Royal, but I don't want a thank you kiss at the minute. Save it for later," she said. "It's in two weeks time. You've not heard of 'The Gondoliers', I suppose?"

"There's a tune that goes something like this in it, isn't there?" Simulating a fine tenor voice I burst into song.

"Take a pair of sparkling eyes
Dara da da and anon
Dara da da o-of a kiss
Do not heed then my surprise
Having crossed the rubicon
Take a pair of rosy lips..."

"That song is almost a description of you, darling!"

"Don't come your blarney with me, you beggar. You've been having me on!"

I laughed, shielding my face from a punch on the nose.

"My dad had all the Doyly Carte records. 'Pirates of Penzance', 'H.M.S. Pinafore'. You name them, we had them! You're talking to an aficionado, my sweetie pie. It's very good of you all the same, I'm going to like this education course."

"You double beggar," she leaned up on one elbow. "What about this, then? You might not like this! *You're* going to treat *me* to see

'Hamlet' at the Theatre Royal, the week after we see 'The Gondoliers'. There's a surprise for you."

"You can say that again! You've been doing some research on the quiet, but there was no need to go as highbrow as Shakespeare, Joan. Don't you think you're covering too broad a spectrum, love, especially for an ignoramus like me? Shakespeare! 'Hamlet'! Come to think of it that's history. Don't you think a bit of local geography might have been better?"

"No, I don't, there's too many people abo-"

The rest of her sentence was lost in the enchantment of a kiss.

Joan's education course proved quite entertaining all the same. We laughed at Murray and Mooney, we enjoyed Issy Bonn's ballads - 'My Yiddisher Mama', 'Shanty Town' - all very sentimental, to please a sentimental couple of lovebirds. Then there was Nat Gonnella's swing band and of course the mandatory juggler and the contortionist, amid other turns.

'The Gondoliers' was another big hit with me. I knew the songs and the music, but the costumes and the comedy acting were something new for me.

"'Hamlet', however was a bit heavy. I had to concentrate on that.

"Well," said Joan, as we walked home along Burton Lane, "what do you think to the theatre, now?"

"Very good. Live theatre takes a bit of beating, but I think I should have *read* 'Hamlet' first, I might have understood it better! 'Brevity is the soul of wit'. Was it Polonius who said that in the play? Shakespeare didn't think brevity was the soul of some of *his* plays, if 'Hamlet' was an example!"

"You have been paying attention, love. Who was Polonius, anyway?" she chuckled.

Seeing a Shakespeare play was a first for me. Another first was a trip to the races - York Races. "It's t'biggest race meetin' int' North for yeers," said Joan's dad.

Her dad and her uncles had been talking about the big meeting for weeks beforehand. Joan suggested we go and find out what all the fuss was about.

We were in the front room when she came out with the idea.

"Come off it, Joan, that's not the real reason. I think this race-going lark is in the blood of all the Speed family. It's been passed down from generation to generation. Now you've got the bug!"

It was that innocent remark that prompted Joan to hit me with a cushion. That gave me an excuse to grapple with her, thus postponing the subject of horse racing for a while.

Anyway, there we were on the famous Knavesmire, "It's t'Ascot of t'North," I had been informed earlier. The crowds fascinated me - before each race, there were columns of punters waiting to place bets. After the horses flashed past the post, the queues collecting winnings were much smaller. There was, surely, a lesson to be learned from that, a lesson that Joan and I, together with almost everyone else, apparently ignored. We were more intent on enjoying the day.

As a team, the pair of us started well, I had beginner's luck, backing a horse called High Stakes. *My* stakes weren't high, just a shilling to win. Not only did it win, but some kind bookie gave me 10 to 1. I was over the moon when I discovered its starting price was only eights. Jingling eleven shillings in my pocket, I was thinking that perhaps this racing game *was* the thing for me.

Joan backed the winning favourite in the next race, but then our luck petered out. We came across Joan's dad after that second race.

Joan spied him first. "Look, there's Dad, and he's with Uncle Jack. Jack's really keen on the gee-gees. Even more than Dad."

"Well, he's a Speed isn't he?"

She dug her sharp fingernails into my arm.

"Ouch!" I cried.

"Well, don't be impudent!"

There the pair were, in front of a row of bookies. I noted that their shirt collars were unbuttoned, ties absent, a signal that they were on a day out. Her dad was studying his 'Sporting Life'. We watched him; one minute absorbed in the racegoers' bible and with a pencil stub marking his fancies, the next peering over his specs and surveying the line of 'turf accountants' chalking up the odds. Decision made, he pulled a couple of silver coins out of his pocket and marched confidently up to place his bet. Coming back to his spot, he carefully put his ticket into his breast pocket. The odds were that he would tear it up later, adding to the litter on the grass.

So preoccupied were they, they weren't aware of our

approach. It was apparent to all that they were brothers; Jack was just a younger version of Joan's dad, but with hair. "Hello, Dad. Fancy seeing you in this crowd. Hello, Uncle Jack."

"Hi, Joan. So this is thy Paul, then. Pleased to meet thee, lad. Hads't 'ad any luck?"

"I backed the first winner," I said.

"By 'eck, thee didn't, Paul! Aa fancied that one me'sen. Aa neerly backed it."

Joan's dad didn't add much to the conversation that day. Assessing the form and watching the ever-changing prices on the boards took every ounce of his concentration. Jack was much more chatty.

"Aa fancy 'thisun' int' next race, Joan, Aa really do," he said pointing to the name of a horse on the racecard, "but A'am goin' t'ave a plunge on t'favourite. It's a gud'n, and Aa got a strong tip for it this mornin'. Not only that, Gordon Richards is on its back. Mind, Aa still fancy 'thisun'."

The favourite got beat. 'Thisun' won.

We wandered away from the crowds and sat down on the grass for a while. Here, the atmosphere was more expansive. Families were picnicking, youngsters were playing with kites and bats and balls, mothers were feeding babies.

"Is your uncle always like that?" I asked

Joan laughed, "Yes, that's Uncle Jack all over. He always *nearly* backs the winner. He *has* been known to back a winner, mind. Way back in the Middle Ages."

In spite of our failure to capitalise on our first two bets, we enjoyed the day. The boisterous crowds, the bookies' shouts, the jockey's colours. The crowd at the rails was so dense that we didn't see much action. Just a blur of horses and jockeys as they flashed past us straining their utmost on that last furlong to the winning post.

Work in the Income Tax Department was more interesting than filing. Just as well - upstairs, Joan's presence was missing. Sergeant Jim Donaldson, although seeming austere, was a good boss and had a dry sense of humour. He was an excellent mentor and soon I was well versed in the functions of income tax assessment.

One day, he pulled a folder out of his drawer.

"You haven't seen my collection, Paul - letters from N.C.O.s, warrant officers, that I've gathered over the last couple of years."

For the next half hour or so, I browsed through them, chuckling. Some were side splitting:

'Please send authority for my increase in family allotment as my wife has fallen into errors with our landlord.'

'In accordance with your instructions, I confirm that my wife has given birth to twins, which I have enclosed in a big envelope.'

'My wife is worried about money; I think that's why she has been in bed under the doctor for three weeks now. She is not getting any satisfaction with his old fashioned ways, though. She thinks she would be better under a younger doctor but I told her that the taxman might be the answer. That's why I'm giving you the chance to help.'

"They're good!" I said. "You'll be publishing them next!"

The sergeant laughed, "I'm thinking about it, if *I* don't, somebody will!"

The promised General Election took place in July. Although we were too young to vote, Joan and I were hoping for a Labour victory. In the event it wasn't just a victory, it was a landslide - in the region of a two hundred seat majority. Clement Attlee was to be our new Prime Minister - Winston Churchill, snubbed by the people.

Was this really to be a new beginning? Two credulous young lovers hoped so - time would tell.

Within days of the election, the news broke of a more portentous event in world history - the dropping of the first atom bomb on Hiroshima, with unimagined devastation and high death toll. It was difficult to comprehend the scale and power of this weapon, but most people accepted that at least it would shorten the war against Japan.

The second atom bomb on Nagasaki was the final blow and Japan surrendered on the 15th August 1945. World War II was finally over.

Joan and I were delighted; surely demob couldn't be too far away. Paradoxically, sombre feelings were also present, as we thought of the sadness and suffering that the war had brought to so many people.

That September, I was given seven days leave.

"I'll have to go home, Joan, for part of my leave at least. Are you taking any time off?"

"Well, I don't particularly want to go up to Gateshead until you've broken the news to your mam. You haven't told her we're engaged yet, have you?"

"I see your point, darling. What if I go up for three or four days, then I spend time with you. Could you get say, three days off?"

"I think so."

That was agreed and off home I went. Mam seemed pleased to see me, but disappointed when I told her my leave in Gateshead was so short.

"You don't seem to get much leave, Den."

"Well, there's a lot of work in the Income Tax Department you know, Mam. I've got news for you, though. I hope you'll be pleased at it."

She frowned, "What is it? You'd better just tell me."

"Joan and I have got engaged, we're going to get married when I'm demobbed."

"No," she said, shaking her head in dismay, "you're much too young!"

"Come off it, Mam! I'm twenty in a couple of months, I'll probably be twenty-two before I'm demobbed."

I didn't believe that, I was hoping to be discharged within the year, but Mam needn't know that - yet!

"I haven't asked you this before, Den, I was hoping it wouldn't get so serious, but is she a Catholic?"

"Well no, she isn't as a matter of fact."

At last the news was out. Sooner than I wanted. Let's try to lessen the blow.

"We've discussed everything, Mam, we're going to sort it out. It'll be no problem. Leave it to us."

"The only way it'll be no problem for me, is that she converts, or at least that any grandchildren of mine are brought up in the Catholic faith!"

"As I say, leave it to me Mam, and please don't bring it up next time you see Joan, Just leave it to Joan and me, will you?"

How the problem was going to be solved, I hadn't a clue. I supposed I hoped that with time, Joan would get used to the idea that any children we had could be given a Catholic education. I was positive about one thing - I wasn't going to lose Joan, no matter what.

There was no doubt that Joan and I wanted children eventually. We had made plans, as most star-crossed lovers do.

Guess what? We wanted one boy and one girl, in any order, but not in the first few years of marriage. Not much to ask for! Would it happen?

I could tell Mam wasn't happy with the situation. 'The top and bottom of the whole affair,' I thought, 'is that she isn't reconciled to my leaving home for years, if ever.' However, thankfully, she didn't raise the issue again during the rest of my short stay.

I say short stay, but it couldn't be brief enough for me. I was still in a state of enchantment over Joan, my first girl and my only girl. To me the personification of everything I wished for - classical beauty? No, just bonny. Shapely? More than that, curvaceous, cuddlesome, but surpassing all her physical charms, was her straightforward, honest manner, her playful humour, her pleasing voice, her enticing laughter, her devotion.

I had been home a matter of hours, and here I was already wishing to be back in York. Why? Simply because Joan was there.

My feelings had changed quickly. Until a little over a year ago, I was reasonably happy with my life at home. Now, when I returned to Gateshead without Joan I was a restless mortal.

Of course, I was pleased to see everyone, particularly Cecil and Stephen. Cecil was shooting up, six foot tall, an inch taller than me now. Stephen, now nine years old, was still a very quiet lad, it was difficult to say whether his lameness affected his personality. He often seemed to be miles away, before coming back to earth with a bump.

Don was now in Germany, also waiting for demob after journeying through France, Belgium and Holland, manning makeshift airfields as the R.A.F. strike force moved onwards.

One night, I took Stephen to see Walt Disney's 'Dumbo' at the Palladium, our nearest picture house. Stephen, because of his lameness, couldn't walk too far, limping badly, even with his built up shoe. He seemed to enjoy 'Dumbo'; perhaps he felt affinity with the little elephant - the odd one out.

One afternoon on that leave, I met Robbie, Rob's son. He was now back in Gateshead and reunited with his wife, Milly, after traumatic years as a prisoner of war. Apparently he had lost a lot of weight. He was awaiting the formalities of his army discharge, before going back to his old job.

My visit, at last, came to an end and I was off - back to York, and three full days with Joan!

My landlady, Maureen, had pestered me during that summer to ask Joan to come around for Sunday tea. It was the end of September before Joan agreed to go. She wasn't keen on the idea, but admitted she was curious to meet Len, whom she knew only by sight.

Maureen had gone to town to produce a fine spread - a Sunday tea far removed from her usual parsimonious affairs. She was determined to demonstrate to Joan how well she looked after me.

I introduced Joan to everyone, except Fido; I thought that she would work that one out for herself. I suppose she would also have discerned which was Charlie and which was Len pretty quickly too, even if she hadn't already known Len by sight. Certainly she would as soon as Len spoke.

"So you're the famous Joan, our Paul has picked as a companion! My you're a lucky girl, Paul's a nice young man. Don't you think so, ducks?" he simpered, as he gave her a juicy kiss on the cheek.

Len's behaviour wasn't a culture shock; she had been well forewarned. But I hoped she wouldn't start giggling.

"He's nice to *me*, Len," she said.

Len patted a chair, "Come and sit down beside me, sweetie. We've probably got a lot in common, you know."

'You haven't got *me* in common,' I muttered under my breath.

Maureen brought in the teapot, we gathered around the table. Joan had Len on her left, and Fido on her right, an interesting trio! Joan gave me a black look, this wasn't like the Joan I had come to know and love. It wasn't me that had planted her between two queer tablemates. I gave her a wink, but that didn't seem to impress her one wit.

"What do you think to Fido, Joan?" asked Maureen.

I hoped that she wouldn't answer that question truthfully. She didn't like lap dogs.

"He has a lot of hair, Maureen," she said tactfully. "Does Fido go to the hairdressers?"

"Oh yes! You go to our doggie hairdresser, don't you, Fido?"

Fido didn't confirm or deny her statement; I didn't expect him to. He had other things on his mind. His eye was on a cream cake that Maureen was waving about.

Len butted in then, "You know, Joan, that's something I hate about the army, I used to go to a lovely hairdresser who styled my hair exactly the way I wanted it. Archie, that's my friend in Middlesbrough, said I had a lovely head of hair and it always looked really nice. Nowadays, I might as well be bald! I worry that Archie might have gone off me, me being away so much. I hope not, he's a lovely man! We've had some fabulous times together."

Maureen seemed determined that Fido was not going to be left out of the conversation for long. She wasn't too happy that Len was diverting Joan's attention from her little bedmate.

"Fido would die if he was in the army, with short hair," she laughed. "Here Fido, show Joan how you eat cream cakes!"

Fido would have displayed his prowess to Joan ages ago if Maureen hadn't been waving the cake out of reach of his little jaws.

I thought Joan's laugh was rather forced. "He likes the good things."

"I make sure that he lives off the fat of the land, Joan," said Maureen.

'You can say that again!' I thought.

"He's a precious little dog," piped up Len, then changed the subject. "Oh, Paul, I haven't seen much of you this weekend to ask whether you've seen the details of our demobilisation. Cur officer explained the system that's going to be used, although he waited until it was almost time to go home on Friday; he's a nasty man. Have you been told?"

"No, it might be because Lieutenant Young wasn't in on Friday."

"Well, it's not good news, Paul, I think we all knew that it was going to be based on age and length of service. But you know what?! Would you believe it?! Marital status is now going to be taken into account! From what I can gather there're something like eighty groupings. Number one group is almost immediate demob, eighty could be two years hence, or more!"

"Have the groupings been announced, Len?"

"Yes, I saw the list, do you know? I'm group forty-six, me with three years service! If I'd been married my group would have been twenty-eight! You wouldn't believe how desolate I was when I saw that. Do you know, I actually thought of marriage! That's how desperate I felt! But that wouldn't suit me at all! I'm not cut out for that sort of thing. You know me!"

I tried to sound sympathetic. "No, Len, you don't seem to be the marrying kind to me either. Don't you think it's awful, Joan, that poor fellows like Len are penalised?"

Joan gave me a look that I interpreted as 'don't put me on the spot'. Then said in false commiseration, "I think it's terrible! Did you find out Paul's group number, Len?"

"As a matter of fact, I did, pet. I thought to myself, 'That's bad.'"

"What was it?" I asked, impatiently.

"It was sixty-one, Paul, there are sixty groups to be demobbed before you! Ooh, it could be a couple of years at least!"

Joan looked a bit downcast.

"Cheer up, love, as long as I'm here in York with you it won't be so bad. Anyway, if they discharge one group every week I'll be out in just over a year."

For about the first time, Charlie spoke. "Well," he said, "you're welcome here as long as it takes, Paul, isn't he Maureen?"

"Why, of course he is, Charlie."

'She must be thinking of that thirty bob a week,' I thought.

Later, walking Joan back home, I said, "Well, that's over. What did you think to it all, darling?"

Shaking her head, she uttered one word. "Weird!" Then said, "What do you think about your demob, though?"

"Not much, Joan. But we can't do anything about it, can we?"

Chapter 18

DEMOB?

There was nothing we could do to influence my demob date, except get married. Neither of us thought that was an option after we had agreed to wait.

Demobilisation proceeded slowly. Only a few groups had been discharged by Christmas, 1945.

Over the holiday period, we followed the pattern of the previous year, which meant parting for a few days. The New Year party now included Robbie, as well as Milly. Robbie was in full voice, outshining even Cecil and me with our Flanagan and Allen routine. Mother MacCree was there again, however, and probably stole the show.

Mam and Joan got along reasonably well, although Mam was still unhappy about the situation. There was always that reserve between the two of them. I was hoping that time would bring them closer together. First day back at work, I was called into Lieutenant Young's office.

"Sir."

He was seemingly engrossed reading a vital document. I wondered what was going on, it wasn't very often a humble private entered his sanctum. Was I in trouble? Or was it to be promotion? A first stripe on my sleeve, a first step on the ladder?

I stood waiting. He was giving me plenty of time to ponder. At last he looked up, his plump face inscrutable. He beckoned me to sit. "Now, Potts, not to beat about the bush, you're going to India."

Was this a joke? Clem Attlee had promised India independence as soon as possible.

"India, sir?"

"Yes, India, Potts. Don't look surprised; there are still troops to be paid out there. There are four men from the battalion going. You're the only one from my platoon, thank God. I won't need a big reorganisation in my office."

"India, sir?" I was getting repetitive. "How long will I be over there, sir?"

He gave a smug laugh, "As long as it lasts, I suppose. I'll be sorry to lose you, Potts, all the same. I had you groomed for Donaldson's job when he's demobbed, but you don't argue with orders. You'll be leaving before the end of the month. Basically, that's all, you'll get the details in due course."

I was back at my desk. Oh, great, oh, good. He was grooming me. That was nice to know! India! I was in a bit of a daze. Why me? Why not Mad Jack or Little George? Because someone had stuck a pin in a list of names?

Concentration was impossible now. Sergeant Donaldson took me to one side.

"You'd better get downstairs and tell Joan, before she finds out from someone else."

On the ground floor, I beckoned to Joan to come down to the basement.

"What's up, Paul, is there something wrong?"

"I've got some bad news, darling." I blurted it out, "I'm being sent to India at the end of the month".

"What," she gasped, "they can't!"

"Unfortunately they can, Joan. We're going to be separated, I'm afraid."

"What am I going to do without you? What am I going to do? I'll be lost. Say that it's not true. Tell me I'm dreaming." She pulled me close and put her head on my shoulder.

I stroked her soft hair. "What you've got to do is wait for me, love. You will won't you?"

She looked at me, there were tears in her eyes, "Of course I will Paul, of course I will," she said, breaking into a sob.

We made the most of our last precious days together for what in our eyes, could be a long time apart. Remorselessly, those days passed over much too quickly. The last evening arrived, all too soon. I was to lose my soulmate for what could be years.

We sat in the front room - the last time together for many,

many months. Discussing plans, promising to write, hoping the time would soon pass.

We kissed and caressed and hugged, making the most of each precious minute as the night flew by.

There was a knock on the room door. We were snuggling up and talking earnestly about our future marriage. "Joan," shouted her dad.

"Come in, Dad," said Joan, straightening her skirt and sitting up.

Her mam and dad came into the room. "We're going t'bed."

"Now, luv," said her mam. "Yor dad and me just wanted to wish thee a safe journey, Paul. Mek sure y'cum home soon, m'lad, else our Joan will pine away." She gave me a kiss and a hug.

Then her dad shook my hand, "Aye, lad, we'll look forrard t'seein' thee before the year's out. We were just gettin' used t'thee!" he laughed. "I'll look after thy lass! So don't fret on that score."

"Our Joan," added her mam, "you must both be nithered int' front room, it's so caad outside. T'electric fire dosn't help much this weather. Why doan't thee go int' parlour for an hour? The fire's still on thaa' knows. Thee cans't say thaa' fond farewells int' warmth!"

It sounded like a good idea to me, so we transferred our activities to the cosy parlour. When Joan switched off the light we sat on the small settee, arms around each other, and gazed at the dancing flames of the coal fire.

"Do you have to go, Paul? I don't want you to. I want us to stay like this, always. It's romantic in the firelight, isn't it?" she said, snuggling up to me.

"I see a bright future for us, darling, when I come back from India."

"Where?" she murmured

"It's all there in the fire," I said, one hand stealing over her bosom, feeling the softness of a breast, then straying to a bare thigh.

"I'll miss your stupid jokes," she whispered. "By the way, what are you doing down there?"

"Waiting for my geography lesson again, darling."

"I've an idea Paul, I think you might like it! Just stay here, whilst I go upstairs!"

"You won't be long?" I was getting quite worked up, not for the first time when Joan was around.

"I'll be as quick as I can."

The fire was dying now, but the fire in me was still alive. I poked the embers and dancing flames sprung up, casting flickering light around the cosy room. Joan soon returned, closing the parlour quietly behind her. My heart gave a leap, all she seemed to be wearing was a white silky dressing gown tied loosely at the waist. "Ooh! You've been poking the fire, I didn't want it to be as light as this!" she murmured. She bent down to give me a kiss, the gown parted and the glowing firelight gave me a memorable impression of hitherto hidden delights, delights which seemed to be inviting my attention.

Sitting down beside me, her dressing gown fell away from her bare thighs. I stroked the soft whiteness.

"Honeybunch," I whispered my tongue teasing her ear.

Her limbs parting to my caress, the inside of a warm thigh, inviting, enticing. "This is lovely, I knew you were sweet but not as sweet as this, darling. Is it going to be open day at the geography class?"

"No, darling, we've got to be sensible. Promise you will be sensible. This is just a farewell treat."

Her dressing gown had fallen away from her, the belt now unfastened as Joan slid down onto the hearthrug.

The flames of the fire revealed all her girlish charms to my gaze. "Slip out of your things and let us be close, Paul," she whispered, "I want you to remember me as I am tonight. Waiting for your return," she said. Her eyes were bright. "Do you like me like this?"

"You're incredible, darling. Are you all mine?" I asked, as I slid down beside her

"Always," she whispered, as I caressed, reverently.

"And you? I want every bit of you, darling. Am I asking too much of you? I know I've tantalised you. I know!"

"I know you know," I said hotly, stirred by her nearness. "I'll just see if we fit darling, can I? We have to know, don't we? Please. I won't overstay my welcome, promise!"

Her eyes sparkled in the firelight, "That's one way to put it, see if we fit! Careful then, ooh, careful," she cried out.

For a tantalising moment I was lost in her luxuriousness,

then, reluctantly, breathlessly, respecting her pleas, I brought an end to out brief merging. Our loving, however, continued unabated until we had assuaged our desire and lay fondly cherishing our closeness.

"That was a wonderful thing you've just done, Paul," Joan murmured breathlessly. "Thank you, thank you, darling."

"You mean it was a wonderful thing that I didn't do, Joan!" Strangely I felt satisfied and content and with an easy conscience. There would be a time for more, but not now.

"I suppose that's right, a wonderful thing you didn't do, darling," she whispered. "Seriously though, we won't have to worry now about anything happening to me when you're in India, I'll worry about you, though! Especially with those pretty Indian girls!"

We lay in each other's arms, savouring those last moments, not wanting to break the spell. I heard a movement; Joan raised her head. "What's that noise?"

"What noise, darling?" Then I heard footsteps.

"It's Dad, he's on the landing. He's coming downstairs. My God!" He was. She grabbed her dressing gown.

A voice sounded from outside the door. "Are you alright, Joan?"

Joan took a deep breath to steady herself. "Yes, Dad. Paul's going in a minute or to, I'm alright."

"Right, love, I just wondered. I'm going to sleep now. It's just that I thought I heard you shout, luv."

"Yes, I got too near the fire, Dad,"

"Goodnight then."

"Goodnight, Mr Speed," I shouted, struggling into my underpants.

The footsteps disappeared up the stairs.

"Phew!" Joan said, "That was a narrow squeak!"

"That's two narrow squeaks you've had tonight, darling!" I said, laughing quietly, still trying to calm down.

We didn't want to part but I had to go. Reluctantly, I got dressed and soon I was at the front door giving her a long farewell kiss. My heart was aching, more than ever now that I knew of the heady delights we could share in the future. But when? How long would we have to wait before I returned?

Chapter 19

OVER THE SEA

The journey to Southampton seemed never ending. In my melancholy mood, sitting or standing in a crowded train corridor to King's Cross, catching a tube across London to Waterloo, and joining another jam-packed train to Southampton, was all misery. Between trains, we lugged our kitbags along draughty platforms. Every mile of the journey was another mile further away from my girl.

There were four of us travelling from York – down-to-earth Bill Kennedy, seriously studious, bespectacled Jack Dalton and laid-back Gordon Todd. I discovered that Bill hailed from Salford, Jack from Gateshead and Gordon from Sheffield.

Alighting from the train in Southampton, we soon linked up with our reception committee. This consisted of a weary looking sergeant and a lethargic lance corporal. These N.C.O.s had already assembled a dozen or so Pay Corps privates from other parts. We four were the laggards - I sensed that from the way that watches were being scrutinised.

"Dalton, Kennedy, Potts, Todd?" asked the weary sergeant.

"Yes, Sarge, that's us," said Gordon.

"You're late, we thought you had deserted," he remarked, sarcastically. I ignored that snide remark, working on the premise that you don't answer back to a sergeant until you get to know him. We bundled into an army truck driven by the lethargic lance corporal and before we knew it, were clambering out again at what appeared to be the dockside. It was a dark night and the lighting was poor, but my surmise was confirmed when I looked up and saw a ship.

"Wait here," said the sergeant, "while I find out whether you can board this hulk tonight."

I shuddered to think what would happen if we didn't. Surely we wouldn't have to sleep on the dockside? On a cold January night? As he disappeared, Jack and I wandered along the dock and in the dim light made out a name on the side of the boat - 'Llangibby Castle'. "It isn't the Queen Mary!" I said.

"It's named after a castle, probably in Wales," said Jack.

I hadn't spoken much to Jack yet. On the trains he had slept most of the time. Perhaps getting to know him might be fun. "You could be right," I said, admiringly. The sergeant returned.

"O.K.," he said, "grab your kitbags and get on board. They might've have been kidding but they say you'll be welcomed with open arms! So-long fellas, have a good holiday!"

That was that then, we were leaving dry land.

We didn't go far for a couple of days, in fact we didn't go anywhere - other units were still arriving. "This delay gives us a chance to find our sea legs," remarked Jack.

My glance was quizzical, but he seemed to be serious, and yes, there was a distinct and perceptible movement. That was the odd time a big liner passed by.

The wait to weigh anchor, however, did give us a chance to explore the amenities at our disposal over the next three weeks. There was a fairly well-stocked library, four sets of deck quoits. (At one set between two or three hundred troops we might get a game before we got to Bombay.) Also apparently, when we got into warmer waters, there would be wild nights playing tombola and watching films on the open deck. Plus a daily sweepstake called 'Guess the Sea Miles We'll Travel Today'. The potential for giddy enjoyment seemed endless!

If those diversions were to be the upside of our voyage, they were more than outweighed by the downside. The sleeping arrangements below decks were simply hammocks. Kitbags were stored on each side of the deck, and that was that. Except for the bouquet of hundreds of bodies in the confined space - an aroma that was already strong even before we left port. As I remember it, sleeping three in a bed was preferable to this - there were only two pairs of sweaty feet to contend with. Then there were the latrines - 'bogs'. Two rows of facing doorless stalls where one could either observe the performances of fellow visitors, or shut one's eyes and concentrate on the business in hand.

The meals, too, were basic affairs. I wondered whether it was possible to go down with scurvy in just three weeks.

We departed Southampton on our third day on board. Hundreds of young men lined the ship's rails as we moved off. There was a scattering of dockside workers waving us Godspeed. Someone beside me started singing 'We'll Meet Again' and almost all of us joined in as we edged slowly towards the open sea.

For me, it was a poignant moment - how long would it be before I was reunited with Joan? When would I, again, have a night to match that last one in York? I recalled the breathless wonder of our closeness, but then the tearful parting. I knew more than ever now the meaning of a heavy heart.

The ship moved down Southampton Water and into the Solent, with the Isle of Wight on our port side. (No 'left' and 'right' now.) Before darkness descended we passed The Needles and headed into the English Channel.

Over the next few days, Jack, Gordon, Bill and I settled into a routine. 'Below decks' was only for sleeping. The stench of the multitude was becoming stronger with each passing night. During the day we would find some sheltered corner on the open decks above the confined 'dormitory' and brave the raw wind and cold. There, we read, or played cards, or just talked. The ship's library was a godsend. I was in there most days. It was one day early in the voyage that I came out of the library engrossed in a book on troopships and bumped into him.

"Sorry," I said, "I should look where I'm going." I knew I'd seen him before, this bearded crewmember; then I remembered. It was in the galley - he'd been wearing an apology for a chef's hat. That he was a chef of some description was confirmed for me when I saw that the volume in his hand was a cookbook. My first guess was that he was looking for a recipe for 'Bubble and Squeak' or some other intriguing meal, 'Beans on Toast', perhaps? Was he trying to improve the fare of the hungry troops, or could he be a trainee learning the job at our cost?

"You were too wrapped up in that troopship book," he laughed. "There's no mention of 'Elsie' in it, mind," he added.

"Elsie?" I queried.

"'Llangibby Castle' - L.C.!" he laughed. "That's its nickname with the crew. No, that book you have was printed before 'Elsie' made her mark. My name's Tom, by the way."

"Paul," I said. I sensed a story looming.

"Yes, 'Elsie' has a history, though, 1942 was a hair-raising year."

"Were you a cook in those days, Tom?" I asked. "Sorry, I didn't mean it the way it sounded!" (Not much!)

He smiled, "No, I joined as a seaman, Paul. This is my first voyage as a cook. I preferred to be on the open deck when torpedoes were likely to hit us!"

"Your first voyage as cook! Is that why you've got that book?"

"You should be so lucky, no, these exotic recipes are for my private use!" he said, tapping the book.

"What happened in 1942, anyway?"

"Well, we were heading for the Med in a big convoy - cargo ships, troopships, tankers. That was the plan but sailing south off Portugal, making for Gibraltar, the convoy was attacked by U-boats.

"Elsie was unlucky. We were hit by a torpedo, which damaged the rudder. I would have hated to have been in the galley when that thing exploded."

He went on to recount how, with the rudder useless, the ship was steered using the engines, comparable to a paddleboat on a park lake. It was slow going and they were ordered to make for the Azores without escort, a destroyer couldn't be spared from the convoy. The Llangibby Castle headed west, but was still within range of German bombers when it was attacked by a long-range Heinkel. The bomber missed its target on the first run - it didn't get a chance of a second. The troopship's anti-aircraft guns scored a hit, causing the plane to turn away with smoke pouring out of its fuselage.

"So this old ship was safe?" We had wandered to the ship's rail as we talked. I patted the handrail.

"Not quite," he laughed, "the Azores were Portuguese, neutral territory. We had to limp out again within the fortnight allowed by international law, or be impounded."

"All this time the troops were on board? What happened next?" I asked.

He went on to tell me that they left the Azores with an escort of three destroyers. Two U-boats were waiting like jackals just outside territorial waters intent on sinking the crippled ship, but turned away on sighting the escort. 'Elsie' reached Gibraltar safely and the troops were disembarked to await another convoy. The Llangibby Castle limped back to England for repair, still under escort and now with an ocean-going tugboat assisting.

Tom looked at his watch. "Is that the time? I'll have to get back to the galley and help get your suppers. It's 'Bubble and Squeak' tonight."

On the fifth day at sea, still in calm weather conditions, we sighted land, first on the port side, Spain, then on the starboard, as the Atlas Mountains of Morocco loomed large. Within hours, we were passing through the Straits of Gibraltar and the famous rock became visible.

Our gang of four were lining the port rail.

"Well," I said, "we're in the Med now, we should get some sunshine and warmth all the way to Bombay."

Bill Kennedy spoke up. "I don't know," he said, "my dad was in the Med in the first war. He said it could be very rough."

I pooh-poohed the idea. "I bet it's calm from here to Egypt." I was still acting the sage.

How wrong could I be? The next morning came a warning on the tannoy.

"Pay attention, everyone. We're running into a heavy storm in the next few hours. Will all personnel ensure that their kit is stowed away and securely fastened? Everyone must take extreme care when going up on deck and doors and hatches must not be left open."

Bill laughed and looked at me. "What did you say yesterday, Paul?"

"It'll be nothing," I said. "They're just trying to frighten us landlubbers!"

Why did I open my big mouth? I wouldn't mind, it wasn't like me.

It was less than an hour before the storm hit us, first the sea began to heave, and then the wind arrived. We found our sheltered spot up on deck, but on that day there was no refuge. The ship plunged and rolled violently, the wind howled and soon we were engulfed in a mini typhoon. One moment we were looking down at the sea, the next at the turbulent waves above us, washing over the deck.

"Lord help the sailors on a day like this!" I shouted above the roaring wind. It was the last joke I made that day.

As a youngster I had never fancied riding on fairground figure-eights and suchlike whirling devices, even if I'd had thruppence to spare. I knew why now. This was like being on a non-stop roller coaster with no possibility of getting off. First, I felt queasy and thought I would stand up, then I decided it would be better to sit down again. The word vertigo spun around in my mind.

My pals were suffering too. With the exception of Jack, one after the other we were all violently sick. The ship was groaning and squealing under the onslaught of the tempest. Cold and shivery, three of us decided to head below.

"I'll stay on deck here," said Jack, "I'm enjoying this."

I think we would have thrown him overboard if we'd had the strength.

Just at that moment, I dizzily watched as a huge wave swept over the deck causing a soldier to aquaplane across the deck and crash into the ship's rails. He looked badly injured and Jack jumped up, struggling across to help. Crewmembers had seen the accident and soon arrived with a stretcher, carrying him away to the sick bay. We staggered below decks, Gordon and Bill looked ghastly; I felt the same. All through the long night, there was no respite from the storm. Not many men slung their hammocks, most of us were lying on the deck moaning and groaning, praying for some relief from our misery.

It came midway through the following morning when the storm abated. Within an hour, comparative calm returned to the sea, a calm gratefully welcomed.

It took longer for us to recover our equilibrium, but by the evening our fragile stomachs were accepting some sustenance. It was in the galley whilst we were picking at our food that another message came over the tannoy.

"Your attention, please."

'Oh, no,' I thought, 'not another typhoon!'

The crackly voice continued. "This is the Captain speaking. I have good news for you, not only have we weathered the storm, but conditions are now set fair for the rest of the leg through the

Mediterranean. Unfortunately there were two servicemen injured during the heavy seas. One suffered only bruises and is recovering in the sick bay. The other fellow has a leg fracture and will be dropped off at Port Said for medical attention and he'll eventually return to Blighty."

"Lucky sod," laughed Bill.

The captain continued, "The conditions we encountered yesterday were the worst I've experienced in the Med. The wind was registered at Storm Force Eleven on the Beaufort scale. I believe the old 'Llangibby Castle' stood up well to all the pounding. She has proved on more than one occasion that she's a tough nut. There was some sad news, however, a couple of Spanish fishing boats that were within our area yesterday are missing believed lost. That is all, thank you."

It took a day or two to recover completely from the debilitating seasickness but I suggested to my pals that we should sleep on the open deck now that the weather had calmed, a few soldiers were already doing that. Comfort on the hard deck was non-existent, but at least we escaped the foul stench in the sleeping quarters.

Nights in the open became all the rage, particularly when we entered the Suez Canal and approached the Red Sea. So popular that we had to stake claims to our spaces straight after evening meal.

Those warm starry nights were spent in conversation on any and every topic. Politics, films, sport, of course, inevitably girls. Amazingly, (or perhaps not, at that time), my pals were all innocents and envious of my tales of courtship, notably, my last night with Joan.

"It must be great to have a steady girlfriend like that!" said Gordon Todd.

"It is, or it was!" I said regretfully. "That's what makes this posting to India seem so terrible."

"I wish I'd had a girl like yours seems to be," said Bill Kennedy. "That front room must be great!"

"It's only a front room," I laughed, "I suppose it's the girl that makes the difference."

"Probably," said Jack. "I had a girl once who took me to church twice a week, she wouldn't go to the pictures. Church isn't the same. You can't smooch with a girl there for one thing. It was cheaper than the pictures, mind."

Jack's logic was sometimes difficult to follow.

Now that the weather was calm and warm, the ship's entertainment programme really swung into top gear. Tombola every afternoon; a film on deck after dark. There were problems with the projector at times, which caused breaks in the show, provoking the inevitable jeers and catcalls. The main drawback - there seemed to be only three films available. 'Laura', starring Dana Andrews and Gene Tierney, was shown five times. The other two were 'Jane Eyre' with Orson Welles and Joan Fontaine, and 'For Whom the Bell Tolls'. The latter brought back poignant memories of my first date.

Those who, compulsively, watched the picture show every night, got to know the dialogue in 'Laura' by heart. After a couple of showings, some of the fellows began operating as prompters, ensuring the stars didn't forget their lines. Bill was one of those - "I love you," they would scream in a high falsetto, "I love you," Gene Tierney would say seconds later. "I love you, too," they would shout in a deep baritone. "I love you, too," Dana Andrews would confirm in a grave voice. The general consensus was that this was hilarious, but it must have been very off-putting for any stray soldier (if there were any), who hadn't yet seen the film.

Through the Suez Canal and the Gulf of Suez we sailed, with the Sinai Desert on our port side and the Eastern Desert on the starboard. Then on into the Red Sea. The daytime heat was intense, although now we were wearing our newly issued khaki drill, which did offer some relief. What a display of white knees there was when we wore our shorts for the first time. Some knees were fat, most were sturdy; then there were mine and those of a few other scarecrows.

After three full days sailing through the stifling calm of the Red Sea, it was a relief to reach the Indian Ocean and to feel a breeze again, albeit a hot breeze. The last few days of our journey passed quietly. Glimpses of flying fish and sightings of dolphins relieved the boredom, before at last we approached Bombay.

Chapter 20

INDIA

The dockside was strange - the ground didn't move or sway. This was terra firma; this was not a pitching, rolling troopship. Circumspectly, kitbag on my shoulder, I traversed the few yards of motionless ground to one of the waiting trucks and climbed aboard. Once seated I felt more at ease, welcoming the jolting of the truck as it bounced over dockside railway lines and out into the city. After three weeks of wide horizons and clear air, Bombay was a different world.

The heat, the smells, the bustle of traffic – horse-drawn or ox-drawn wagons, a few lorries or cars, but a multitude of rickshaws and carts. The latter pushed or pulled by scrawny, dhoti-clad Indians, these either on foot or peddling cycle contraptions. Then there were the tongas with bony ponies between their shafts and the streets alive with zigzagging cyclists and scurrying throngs. The busy scenes befuddled my senses.

We headed for the railway station and soon were on a train heading out of the metropolis - destination Kalyan Transit Camp, a journey of a few miles. It was there we would await our final posting.

Alighting at Kalyan, the platform was packed with Tommies from an infantry regiment. We discovered that they were bound for Bombay, where they were to board ship. Not back to home soil, however, but onward to Malaysia as reinforcements for the jungle war - the British campaign against the Communist guerrillas.

Silently, I wished them all the best.

The transit camp was huge. We dozen or so Pay Corps

personnel from the ship were assigned to one hut, joining a few members of the corps already there. One of these earlier arrivals spoke up. "After tha's dumped tha' kit, A'll show thee's weer t'Naafi is lads. Thee can grab a cold drink. A'm Preston, by t'way. Smiler's m'Sunday name, doan't ask me why!" he said with a toothy grin.

Another of the 'old hands' spoke up. "Grumpy's more the word I would use for him."

Smiler, a big, broad-built fellow, was older than most of us, probably around thirty, his pal, about twenty-five. He must have been his mate, to call this big lump 'Grumpy' to his face.

That cold drink at the NAAFI was like nectar to me. Made from fresh oranges, the drink fulfilled the promise created by the tinkle of ice in the tall glass. Cool, thirst-quenching and unique. Fridges were non-existent in our humble kitchens at home, ice-cubes alien to our lifestyle. I remember that drink at Kalyan, not much else, except the intolerable heat. The stopover in that camp was more tedious than the voyage on the Llangibby Castle. We were relieved when we moved out on the third day, bound for our final destination - Meerut, Northern India - not far from New Delhi. It was to be a journey of a thousand miles travelling in wooden-benched coaches hauled by a giant steam locomotive. This monster boasted a high chimneystack and came complete with cowcatcher, giving the impression of having just steamed out of a Wild West film. As we puffed through the Northern fringe of the Ghats, the scenery, too, was remarkably like the Wild West. There were numerous halts on the way north, some for signals at danger, others at stations. Yet others were mysterious delays, which in the opinion of a weatherbeaten Royal Artillery sergeant in our coach, were simply caused by travellers pulling the communication cord and jumping off the train when they were near to home. "Saving on bus fares?" I suggested.

We were able to get drinks and snacks at the stations from refreshment wallahs. These fellows patrolled up and down the platforms shouting their wares, invariably followed by a cloud of flies. On every platform, too, were pitiful souls, all deformed in one way or another. Some with limbs missing, some sightless, others disfigured, each one with a begging bowl. At one station Bill Kennedy, stretching his legs on the platform, dropped an anna into a bowl. That was a mistake, as he soon discovered.

Within seconds, a crowd of these hapless beings were pushing and surging around him, causing him to beat a hasty retreat back into our carriage. Each time the train resumed its journey after a halt, we spent ten minutes killing dozens of flies with rolled-up newspapers. Then we would settle back to suffer more torpid travel. During the night, the clattering of the train and the hard benches made sleep difficult, but in our weary state, not impossible.

Complete with sore heads, we eventually arrived in Delhi, thirty hours after leaving Kalyan. The journey almost seemed to have taken longer than the one from Southampton to Bombay.

In Delhi, the local train was already in the station waiting to take us on our last leg - the short distance to Meerut. There were two Meerut stations, first the city station with the usual crowded platforms and flies, then the station for the military cantonment. What a difference here, the platforms were almost pristine. As we chugged to a stop, we could see a complex of what seemed to be large airy bungalows.

Stepping down off the train, we looked around - what was missing? Flies! Flies and beggars. "This looks alright to me!" said Bill Kennedy. "Not only that, it's cooler than Kalyan, the temperature's hardly seventy!"

"Don't be fooled by the temperature now, Bill," I said. "This is still February, wait until May and June."

"The voice of doom!" said Gordon Todd.

I didn't have time to respond, before trucks arrived to transport us to our billet. It wasn't far; we stopped outside a tall, large, one-storey building, with spacious verandahs and a number of lofty, arched doorways. It was part of a terrace of similar bungalows. Each bungalow was surrounded by extensive grass and trees.

There was an R.A.P.C. sergeant and a corporal standing in the main doorway. Near them were two char wallahs with their primitive stoves, and also half a dozen other Indians. The presence of the char wallahs looked promising. We were ready for a proper drink after only bottles of tepid water, or cups of so-called tea from those dubious vendors on the station platforms. We scrambled down and dragged our kitbags off the trucks. I looked around; this didn't look too bad.

The sergeant, a tall gangly fellow, spoke. "Right, lads, there's charpoys for you all inside. Put your kit at the end of a bed, grab yourself a mug of char, it's on the house today, then I'll give you the score."

We worked out that a charpoy and a bed were one and the same thing, and, as we had kept our mugs handy on the train journey, we were soon gathered around the two N.C.O.s, supping our tea.

"I'm Sar'nt Taylor, this is Corporal Brown; we'll each be living in an end room in this bungalow, Bungalow 39. Remember that and you won't get lost. The full address is on the notice board. I'll take you to the mess for Tiffin soon. First one or two things you should know.

"Number one. Malaria. Before dusk, change from shorts and short sleeves, into long trousers and long-sleeved shirts. It's also an order that you sleep under the mosquito nets provided. Failure to do so and you're on a charge.

"Number two. The water's safe to drink in the cantonment, but don't drink water in Meerut, certainly not in the bazaar.

"Number three. There's a shop, an eatery, a cinema, right here in the cantonment. Plenty of sports grounds, plus indoor games facilities. Meerut, in fact, is in the top tier of Indian army barracks.

"Number four. These fellas here are bearers. Each bearer will look after six of you. They'll clean your shoes, make your beds, take your dirty clothes to the dhobi wallah, that sort of thing. Every Friday, before you gamble away your pay you'll pay them two rupees a week, that's three bob in proper money. The union rate you would say in Blighty, no more, no less, right?

"Number five. More good news! Every serviceman in India gets Japanese Campaign Pay until the first anniversary of the Japs surrender. So you'll all get an extra shilling a day until August. What's more, as a bonus, in years to come, you can tell your grandchildren that you were involved in the fierce Japanese campaign! Just show them your Pay Book to prove it.

"Number six. You might not like this a lot - you have to work in an office in India for the next couple of years! That's if your demob group is higher than sixty. I don't think there's one of you here with a group number under sixty. Hands up if there is."

No hands were raised. Why did he have to knock the gilt of the gingerbread like that? Sadism, I suppose. Was it a prerequisite needed for promotion to sergeant? He didn't seem a bad stick overall, though.

"Has anyone any questions?" he asked.

Smiler raised his hand. "Will us get 'ome leave, Sarge?"

Sergeant Taylor, laughed. "Ho, a comedian. Well you might if you're here for three years!"

Jack Dalton raised his hand. "What are we doing in India, when we've promised them independence this year?"

"Wouldn't I like to know?" said the sergeant. "I can tell you the official line. There are a lot of men in India with long service. Like me for instance. It'll be our good fortune to be demobbed in the next few months. Guys like you are coming out to replace lucky sods like me. You see, the powers that be want a peaceful handover to the Indians.

"If you haven't had your head in the sand, you'll know that there's been unrest between Hindus and Moslems already. The British Army might well be required to help the civil police. The fresh troops still arriving in India need pay and that's why you're here.

"Of course, the other thing is, the Indians may turn against us British yet. Army and civilians. Some of you, not many, may know that's what happened just eighty-nine years ago in 1857. Right here in Meerut it started - the Indian Mutiny. British soldiers and civilians were massacred in this cantonment. For your information, at this very moment there is a naval mutiny in Bombay, so anything could happen.

"I think that's enough history for one day, let's go and have something to eat, eh?"

"Thanks, Sarge, for putting us in the picture," I said.

"Hear! Hear!" others shouted. We were a smarmy lot.

We soon settled in to life in Meerut. The weather was good, the big bungalow pleasant. I wondered, however, how long it would be before I could see Joan again. We wrote to each other every three or four days, pouring out words of affection. She told me the news from York, life in the Pay Office there continuing in the same old way. She was becoming increasingly friendly with her A.T.S. pal, Helen. Now that the war was over, they were planning to have a week's holiday in Dawlish, Devon, in the summer. I wasn't sure about Helen. There was something, something I couldn't put my finger on, I guessed it might be simply that she didn't like me.

Joan told me her brother Philip and his wife Doris were looking forward to the birth of their first child in August. Doris was from a Nonconformist family, whilst like Joan, Phil was vaguely C. of E. Philip and Doris seemed to dote on each other in those days. Any religious problems they might have would be insignificant compared to those of ours. I attended Mass every Sunday at the Catholic Church in the cantonment, but avoided commenting on religion in letters to Joan. Let sleeping dogs lie, my motto.

Instead, I told her of strict segregation in the Garrison Theatre (the camp cinema). Audiences were in three sections. The first, the front rows - all wooden benches - were occupied by Indian sepoys, bearers and char wallahs. The second group, the Other Ranks - mainly R.A.P.C. and King's Regiment personnel - sat in the leather-covered seats in the back stalls. The third section was reserved for officers who were regally ensconced in the Grand Circle with its plush velvet seats. Seeing films like 'Destry Rides Again' or 'In Which We Serve' was alright, except for two things - one, I had seen most of them in York already and two, Joan wasn't sitting in the dark beside me. I had no intention of holding hands with Jack or Bill. Not even Gordon, nice lad though he was!

Work-wise, I was posted to the Income Tax Dept., Officers' Accounts Branch, the powers that be surprising me by placing a round peg in a round hole for the second time. The office bungalow was only a quarter of a mile or so from ours. In the department we handled the income tax affairs of officers ranging from Second Lieutenants to Generals - even a Field Marshal when Auchinleck, the Commander-in-Chief, India, was promoted in 1946. As in York, the Pay Corps was an easy-going unit; it was allowable for example to wear shoes rather than boots, the only exception was when we were on the occasional guard duty.

Shoes triggered off our first jaunt down to the local bazaar. We sampled the atmosphere of the place and sought out a shoemaker. The unique smell of leather helped us to find one quickly and the four of us spent ten minutes or so haggling with the turbaned shopkeeper for bargains.

His shoes were made to measure and after we selected our styles the shoemaker checked our feet dimensions. I thought the poor fellow would pass out when he measured Jack's sweaty feet, the affliction exacerbated by the mile-long walk to the bazaar. I had been aware of the poor lad's problem when sleeping near him on the 'Llangibby Castle', so it was no accident - just good planning that his charpoy in the bungalow happened to be four places away from mine. We couldn't knock the shoemaker's service - all the shoes were ready by the following Saturday and gosh, they were comfortable. Mind you, Jack's pair did nothing to improve his pong.

In the bazaar I solved the puzzle of what to get Joan for her twenty-first birthday. Tucked away in a side street was a small stall selling nylon stockings. Nylons were like gold in Britain, these were obviously black market imports from the U.S.A. They looked genuine; fully-fashioned they were, the label said so. That meant top-rate, for top-rated legs. So three pairs were on their way to England. My regret? Sadly, I doubted whether I would ever see Joan's long limbs sheathed in them. Unless they were as hardwearing as the stallholder promised. I also bought a Persian Rug at a stall manned by a smiling, personable young Indian. He assured me that it was a genuine Persian Rug - his honest face clinched the deal. "Pukka rug, Sahib, first chop, very good bargain. Your memsahib will be pleased. I will tie it up. Make it easy to carry, Sahib. Special from Persia, Sahib."

To my untrained eye it did look exotic. Whether it would match a Geordie clippie rug was unlikely. Still, this carpet man had said that my memsahib would be pleased. That guarantee and the note I planned to enclose, swayed it for me. 'Dear Joan, I wish this was a Magic Persian Carpet, I would be on it, flying back to my future memsahib!' Surely, that message alone was worth all of the seven rupees.

The bazaar had another attraction for some of the men. 'Smiler' Preston, who had the charpoy next to mine, spoke up one Sunday afternoon. My pals were lying on their beds reading, I was writing a letter - my pen in full flow.

"Does't any of thee fancy goin' darn t'bazaar. There's a brothel, t'bearer, Ranjit, tells me. Aa'm missing t'old woman on Sunday afternoons. Aa am that. Dick's goan' with me."

"No thanks, Smiler," I said. Gordon and Bill also turned down the invitation. Jack, however, to my surprise, took up the offer.

"I'll come, just for curiosity, mind."

Smiler laughed, "Aa've heered that'n before!"

Off they went, the three of them, on their excursion.

"That's not my cup of tea," I said, "I don't think I could do it with anyone else."

"You're saving your body for Joan, you mean!" laughed Gordon. "I agree, though, the idea of paying for it just puts me right off!"

"Is it the money that puts you off, Gordon?" asked Bill, then dodged one of Gordon's new shoes. "O.K., I'm kidding, I know what you mean."

Just then there was a bit of a commotion as three Pay Corps privates came in carrying kitbags. They dumped them on empty charpoys at the far end of the bungalow and started to unpack. I was mildly curious, but not sufficiently so to get up off my charpoy, that would take up too much effort. Lazily I continued with my letter writing. I had nearly finished my epistle to Joan and idly considered adding a postscript. 'P.S. I've just been invited to go to a brothel.' Wisely, probably, I decided against it. Instead I flopped on my charpoy - after five pages of pouring my heart out and getting into an emotional state, I needed a bit of a rest. I think I may have nodded off, because next thing I knew, Taffy Evans was standing beside the bed.

"Those chaps that came in, lads, I bet you don't know who one of them is, look you!"

"No, and I don't know who the other two are, either," I said, sleepily.

Not to be put off, Taffy went on. "You'll never guess, not in a million years. Indeed to goodness, it was a surprise when I found out from one of his pals, indeed it was!"

"Look, Taffy," said Bill, "are you going to tell us who this bloody fellow is or not. I'm in the middle of a Sherlock Holmes mystery and I think I know who's done it. I want to find out if I'm right. So just spit it out. Who is he?"

"If you boyos are going to be like that, I've a good mind not to tell you."

"Oh, good, Taffy," I yawned.

"I will though, why should I let somebody else break the news. It's Ken Brown! What do you think of that, now?"

Bill looked puzzled. "Who the hell is Ken Brown, you red-headed oaf?"

"I know who it is, Bill," I laughed, "if it's the Ken Brown I'm thinking of!"

Bill groaned. "Will someone just say who he is?"

"It's Ken Brown, look you, the Arsenal left-back, he's tipped to play for England next season. He's hoping to be demobbed this summer. Mind you, playing for England is not as good as playing for Wales!"

"Don't be bloody daft," said Bill.

"Hey! We've got the Bungalow Cup matches coming up in the next couple of months," piped up Gordon. "We're sure to win that if he plays!"

"What about the other ten in the team?" I asked. "Apart from you, Bill, and you, Taffy, the Bryn Jones of Bungalow 39, who else is there?"

Our selection process was halted just then, as Jack Dalton came in and flopped on his charpoy.

"Well?" I asked, "What happened?"

Jack shuddered. "It was horrible, I came away."

"Was it that bad?" said Bill.

"There were about six Indian girls, but the shocking thing, I'm sure there wasn't one over twelve years old! They looked pathetic and frightened. I walked out and left Smiler and Dick. Never again!"

"That settles it for me," said Gordon laughing, "unless I happen to meet an officer's friendly wife!"

'It's no contest for me,' I mused. I was content with my dreams of Joan.

We didn't win the Meerut Bungalow Cup. In fact we got knocked out in the second round. Ken Brown played only one game at centre-half for Bungalow 39. I had the glory and fame of playing left-back beside him in defence. Not for one minute did I think I was keeping him out of his favourite position on merit, no, it was decided by Ken that he could control the game more from the centre of the field.

That was an understatement, in spite of his prowess, Ken was a modest lad. He scored two goals with headers from corner kicks and two from free kicks as we progressed to the second knockout round by seven goals to nil. "That was much easier than playing left-back against Stanley Matthews," he said.

Sadly, however, it was decreed by the sports officer, Lieutenant Black, that Ken would play no more for the bungalow, but would train on his own to avoid any possibility of injury. The battalion had three important rubber matches coming up against our mortal enemies the King's Regiment and Black wanted to keep Ken wrapped in cotton wool. The honour of the Pay Corps was at stake.

The battalion had another Football League player in the team, Thompson of Hull City, and then there was the Corps' own wizard dribbler, his name Riley - 'Paddy' Riley. Time and again our right-winger had their left-back trailing in his wake. I expected the defender to sing the old Irish refrain, 'Come Back, Paddy Riley', any minute.

With the talent at our disposal the Pay Corps won two and drew one of the three matches. Matches which were watched by crowds of a thousand or more. The respective personnel of the two army units turned out in force, and each team was also supported by their bearers, char wallahs, punkah wallahs and gardeners. For weeks afterwards, the battalion basked in the reflected glory of our triumph on the field of play.

May arrived, it was now much too hot to play football. 'Drink plenty of water' was the instruction. We filled our big earthenware chatties from the bungalow tap, which delivered hot 'cold' water. Within an hour or so that warm water had cooled enough to drink. As the month progressed, the Delhi-based New Statesman, our English speaking newspaper, indicated the temperatures - 100 degrees, then 105, finally soaring 110 and higher. Even with the big electric fans going at full blast in bungalow and office, the air was still stifling.

May ended, but June offered no respite from the heat until later in the month. Then, at last, the air gradually became more heavy and humid, the sun replaced by menacing, thick, dark clouds. The threat of rain was there every minute, but it was three days before it arrived. When it did, it came in a deluge, a massive thunderstorm lasting long into the night. We discovered, now, why the wide and deep monsoon trenches intersected the bungalows and flanked the cantonment roads. Next morning, we were surrounded by rivers; the trenches unable to cope.

The monsoon brought some relief from the scorching sun, but the temperature was still in the nineties and the air was stifling. Thundery downpours were interspersed with bright periods for day after day. Most of us were now suffering from prickly heat in the humid weather. A number of billet mates caught more serious ailments. Three or four contracted dysentery, and Gordon Todd, malaria. Too lethargic now to do anything energetic, I spent most of my spare time writing letters and reading the New Statesman.

Starting at the back page, as was my habit, there was news of the first cricket tour of England for seven years. Of Len Hutton, Denis Compton, Bill Edrich, great cricketers all. The touring team to England that year was the Indian side. If the threatened partition of India took place it could be the last time that the Indian sub-continent would be represented by one team. On the front page the Muslim leader, Jinnah, was demanding just that - a separate Muslim state.

There were riots in Bombay in July, and further afield I read of the attack by Jewish terrorists on the British Palestine Army Headquarters, with ninety-one killed. The British Army still seemed to be involved in many parts of the world, I wondered what effect this was going to mean to my demob prospects.

A more immediate concern surfaced in July - letters from Joan ceased to arrive. Every week she had written telling me of her thoughts and feelings and giving me the family news. Her last letter had told me she was going on holiday for a week at the end of June. As she had planned, to Dawlish in Devon, with Helen.

After two blank weeks with no letters, I became alarmed. What had happened? I was still writing as regularly, begging her to let me know what was the matter, why had her letters stopped? Over the last few weeks, in between snoozing, and unknown to my scoffy pals, I had put together a poem, a eulogy to her. My plan had been to send it on the second anniversary of our first meeting. The situation had changed, I couldn't wait until then. I was worried more than I would ever admit, even to Bill. If Joan forsook me, for whatsoever reason, my life would crumble. If she was having doubts I had to dispel them. I scribbled a hasty note. 'Dear Joan, I'm not sending an ordinary letter today, but a poem just for you. I may not be a Byron, but it expresses how I feel about you, darling. Remember, it was you who set my heart leaping, it was you who agreed to walk with me through life. Please let me know if you like it. Please, please, reply.

What is much more lovely
Than a sunset in the west?
Or a garden filled with roses
I know the answer best
More radiant, more beautiful
Than any precious stone
Are the eyes of the sweetest girl I know
Yours, my darling Joan
I love to hear the Inkspots
Or a ballad sung by Bing
The gentle murmur of a brook
Or a nightingale to sing
But I would turn my ear
If I could have my choice
And listen to the melody
That lingers in your voice
Your lovely charms I know so well
Your form, your smile, your touch
All in perfect harmony
I love you, oh so much
And though I'm now so far away
I know that you're my own
For now, tomorrow and each day
You'll always be my Joan.

All I could do now was wait and pray that I would hear from her.

Chapter 21

BLUE SKIES

Waiting, hoping, praying for a letter. I knew a reply from England could be expected in a week - but a week was a long time. The day-to-day pattern of life carried on regardless - trying to escape from the humid heat was at the forefront of our short-term ambitions. Showers helped the cooling down process during that hot summer. Instead of just a daily shower, most of us had two or three in the nearby communal shower block. This building was a square, bare, stone-floored affair with eight shower points and a few hooks to hang our towels. Before and after work, there was usually a procession of manly specimens walking to and from the showers, towels wrapped around their waists.

There could be as many as a dozen using the showers at any one time, which could mean having to share a tap with someone else. If that someone had been Joan, well, that would have been different. Even so, it was mildly interesting to observe the various shapes. There were thin ones, fat ones, long ones, short ones - and our physiques were all different too!

Extreme care was essential when we first turned the water on. Ostensibly the showers were cold, but if your tap hadn't been used for some time, the first burst of water was scalding, the metal pipe and the ambient temperature created this phenomenon. That first hot spurt of water could damage your libido if you weren't careful!

Those were the showers - then there were the latrines, top-hole ones and bum ones, the standard varied depending on their location in the cantonment. In the residential sectors these were furnished with water cisterns - pukka WCs. Those serving the offices, however, were primitive boxes, takeaway contraptions serviced by 'bog wallahs'. The failure to upgrade these could have been a ploy to keep us at our desks rather than suffer the putrid odours. The regimental barber visited each bungalow on a regular basis, thus ensuring that our hairstyles remained 'short back and sides'. One day that long week, however, I was moping on my charpoy when a strange Indian, wearing a white jacket, appeared by our beds. This fellow wasn't the barber - we'd had a visit from the man with the shears the day before. The newcomer triggered a vague illusion of a dusky Lew Ayres playing Dr Kildare in one of those films. I half expected Lionel Barrymore as Dr Gillespie to follow him in.

"Hey up," said Jack Dalton, languidly raising himself on his charpoy and peering over his specs to have a closer look. "Who's this fella?"

"He's coming to take you away, Jack," I said. The mysterious character approached us. I was still looking over his shoulder for his colleague.

"I give head massage, Sahibs. Awfully good. I use very best coconut oil, very pukka. I make you feel jolly nice. I have best references, sirs."

He showed us two or three tatty letters. I didn't read them but I thought that anything that might make me feel jolly nice would be worth a try.

"How much is it?" I asked.

"Eight annas, Sahib," he said.

It sounded reasonable, "I'll have one then."

I sat on my newly acquired cane chair as this fellow poured oil on my head. Then he started, not holding back. For the next ten minutes his powerful fingers were beavering away at my scalp. I was beginning to feel dizzy, when suddenly he stopped. Then, one hand on each side of my head, he jerked my skull, first one way then the other. For a moment, I thought that he had broken my neck. Gingerly I moved my head - to my surprise, it didn't drop off.

"That's finished, sir."

My scalp was tingling pleasantly, I felt a strange sense of well-being. In fact I would go so far as to say that I felt jolly nice.

"Will the massage stop me going bald?" I asked.

"No, Sahib, but it is very good for you."

He wasn't much of a salesman - he was honest though.

"Next week again, Sahib?" he said as I handed him eight annas. That was all of ninepence! I suppose it was worth it. I stood up, I felt taller somehow, after all that pressing down on my head.

"Right, next week then, O.K.?" I said.

Two or three other lads had a massage, but I was the only one in the bungalow to continue the 'treatment' for any length of time. There was a trace of masochism somewhere in my make-up because I dreaded the 'broken neck' finish. Each week I prepared myself for the coup de grâce, but with that finishing jerk, he always took me by surprise.

I was certainly in need of a fillip, the days went by and no letter from Joan. Bill Kennedy, probably my best pal, asked every time we received mail, "Anything from your girl?"

"No," I would say, "I can't understand it. I really can't." Although I was comforted in the knowledge that it was too early to have received a reply to my poetic plea.

"You'll have to buck up, Paul. It's getting to you, you know!"

He was right, I was a morbid individual to have as a pal. One day Bill collected the mail; I had just about given up hope, eight days had passed now. He came across to my bed.

"There's one for you here, I think it's from York."

I bounded up from my charpoy and grabbed the letter. The postmark was York. I studied it fearfully. '14802039 Pte P.D. Potts, L.B. 39, 83rd Bn R.A.P.C., Meerut Cantt., c/o G.H.Q. Post Office, New Delhi, India Command.' Yes, it was for me and yes it was in Joan's familiar hand. Never before had I opened a letter with fumbling fingers, was it going to be a goodbye missive? At last I pulled out the flimsy sheets and was soon reading the first page.

'My darling Paul,' my heart gave a leap. 'I'm very, very sorry that I haven't written to you for some weeks. Please bear with me if I don't tell you why in this letter, it's too difficult, but someday I'll explain. I've had a problem, darling, a problem concerning you and me. But not any more. Do you know what helped me solve it? Yes, your words, and your poem, it made me realise how much I love you. To me, it was wonderful. I'll treasure that poem all my life. Please write again soon and tell me you meant every word and that you'll forgive me. . . . . . '

Bill had been hovering around. At last he spoke "Well," he said, "What's the verdict?"

"If the second half of this letter is as good as the first I think it's alright," I laughed.

"What was wrong?" he asked

"She doesn't say, just that she had a problem."

"Does that mean you won't be moping around any more, lad?" he said. "Now the weather's starting to cool down a little bit, we should be knocking a ball about or something. We've been getting too lazy."

"All in good time, Bill," I laughed. "In the meantime, let me read my letter, will you?"

I didn't just read it. I pored over it, and not merely once or twice. I wondered what her problem had been. Another lad? If so, he was no longer in the running, Joan's letter convinced me of that. I thought for one mad moment that it might have been Jack Thoms, but realised that was too farcical. The main thing was that things were on an even keel once more. I was sure now that Joan and I had a future together, the sky was blue again.

I wrote back immediately forgiving her and within a week got a reply. It was a fifteen-page missive, had she a guilty conscience? What was amazing, was that with only a three-halfpenny stamp affixed, it arrived by airmail as usual, and so quickly.

'My dearest Paul,' she wrote. 'Thank you for being so tolerant with me for not writing for all those weeks. I promise it won't happen again, I love you so. What a lovely surprise when your parcel came last week. It's taken months to arrive. Your message about the magic carpet was lovely. What a pity it can't come true. I think the rug is a nice size to go in the toilet of our house, if and when we get one. A house I mean! Mind, I wouldn't put it in an outdoor netty, as you call a lav up in Geordieland. It's too good for that.'

'Faint praise indeed,' I thought, smiling ruefully to myself.

Her next paragraph was a big surprise to me. 'You won't believe this, Paul, but Len Wright was telling me that your ex-landlady Maureen Crow is expecting a baby! Len says she's getting so big that when she's in the scullery there's no room for anyone else! Trust him to say that.'

'Gosh,' I thought. 'Where was Fido when this happened?' It beggared belief!

She went on to tell me that her sister-in-law Doris had given birth to a blonde baby girl and that her brother Philip was over the moon. They were going to call her Clare. 'I wonder if and when we'll have a baby girl,' she added.

There was much more, so much more that she had to apologise for not enclosing the main sports page from the 'Sunday People'. She would send it with her next letter. What had happened to her sense of priorities?

That welcome letter seemed to stir me into action after those torpid weeks of idleness. The next day, I lay on my bed, pondering. "Shake yourself, Paul, you're going to be a husband, and hopefully, a father in the not too distant future. Will this cashier's job at your old firm be satisfactory enough for such responsibilities?"

Then my old irresolute self put in a word. "Rightly, it should be, it's quite a senior position."

But my new purposeful half was not to be denied. "Look here, Paul, what if the business should fold? Even now welding is taking over from riveting in the shipyards! You've got no qualifications for a job elsewhere."

"O.K., O.K. Point taken!"

Just then, Bill in the next charpoy, shouted across. "Are you talking to yourself, Paul?"

"What?" I awoke from my reverie. It was a pity, I was enjoying the byplay. "No, of course not. Anyway if I was, it could be more interesting than talking to you lot."

"I was thinking, though," I added. "It's alright for you, Bill. You're halfway to being a plumber with your apprenticeship, but I have no paper qualifications at all. I've just decided I'm going to study for this Forces Preliminary Exam that they're talking about. It's the equivalent of a School Certificate and recognised by the Civil Service Commissioners. That would give me another string to my bow if my job should pack up."

"Oh, suddenly you've woken up after moping this last month. That letter must have been good!"

I ignored his remark. "Not only that, Bill. You know the monthly magazine, the Monsoon?"

"Of course I know it, that Pay Corps rag. You're always saying you could write better stories than half of the yarns in there."

"Well, I'm going to try my hand at it. I might turn out to be another Graham Greene."

"Who's Graham Greene? Don't tell me - he's a writer. Anyway, what are you going to do in your spare time, then?"

"How about trying to organise a bungalow cricket team?" I laughed.

"Now you're talking," said Bill. "I'm with you on that. Two or three of the other bungalows have got teams, so why not us?"

My dilatory self had suddenly taken a back seat. What a difference a letter can make.

It was the middle of August, the monsoon was beginning to die out and the temperature was rising into the high nineties. Rain clouds were disappearing, to match my now upbeat mood.

On the political front, there were serious disagreements connected with the plans for Indian independence. Problems which could yet result in danger for the British in the sub-continent. The Muslim League were adamant in their demand for the partition of India and a separate Islamic state, despite Mahatma Gandhi's plea for one multi-religious country. The problem with partition was that the two religious groups were so intermixed. Notwithstanding that fact, Jinnah, the Muslim leader, had called for a massive demonstration in Calcutta to support their cause. This provoked counter protests triggering off bloody riots as supporters of each side rampaged through the city. The police and the army seemed to be powerless, as over twenty thousand deaths occurred in a just a few chaotic days.

Feelings were high in other parts of India. Isolated pockets of strife occurred in Meerut, where normally Hindus and Muslims lived in harmony. There was a high proportion of Muslims in the area. Partition here would cause problems.

Cantonment troops were put on full alert, even we Pay Corps servicemen were issued with rifles and bayonets. The last time I had handled a firearm was two years earlier during my training at Brancepeth. We were hurriedly given a one-day refresher course which, if trouble arose, would have to suffice. Nightly guard duties commenced in earnest. In the event, things settled down after a few days, as the authorities began to get a grip of the situation in Calcutta. Even in the seclusion of the cantonment however, we sensed a change in the attitude of the Muslim and Hindu servants towards each other.

As things became more normal, batches of men were sent on seven days leave to the hill stations as a relief from the scorching weather. It was in early September that most of us in Bungalow 39 were told the good news that we were going to Chaubatia in the foothills of the Himalayas.

It was quite an adventure for us lads. Chaubatia was around a hundred and fifty miles or so from Meerut, but it took a full day to reach our destination. The first stage was by train, then by rackety coaches to Nainital and its exquisite lake scenery, finally on the back of open lorries for the final few miles to Chaubatia.

The road sections were exhilarating as we twisted and turned ever higher into the hills. Hills! These hills were six or seven thousand feet in height. We crawled upwards zigzagging on badly surfaced roads with sheer drops of hundreds and sometimes thousands of feet in places. Strangely enough, despite my seasickness on the troopship, I was unaffected by the precipitous heights and the bouncing lorry. Instead I was enjoying the ever-changing vistas. Paradoxically it was Jack Dalton who fell victim to nausea. So much so, that he spent one vertiginous section leant over the back of the vehicle being physically sick.

As he was groaning in despair, head well over the tailgate, the truck almost came to a halt on a savage hairpin bend, at the same time hitting a huge pothole. The jerk flung Jack clean over the tailgate and he landed with a wallop on hands and knees on the dusty road.

Someone banged on the driver's cabin and the lorry stopped. Two or three of us scrambled out to help Jack to his feet. He didn't seem to be badly hurt, it was just his pride that was severely dented.

That night, after settling in to the pleasant billet, a gang of us were having a drink in the canteen. Jack was with us, having apparently recovered his equilibrium.

"Jack," I said, "I suppose some time in the future you'll be getting married?"

"Oh yes, Paul," he said, putting down his pint glass, "too true!"

"Will you invite me to your wedding?"

"If you're still living in Gateshead, probably, I suppose."

"What do you think your wife will say if I ask her where she got you?"

"What are you talking about, where she got me?" Jack looked puzzled.

Gordon butted in, "What will Jack's wife say, Paul?"

"She'll probably say, she'll probably say," I chortled.

"What the hell will she say?" demanded Jack.

"That, that," I was giggling now, possibly because of the drink, or more probably because of the look on Jack's face. "You fell off the back of a lorry!" Somehow, Jack was the only one who didn't see the funny side. I suppose that was par for the course.

Next morning, after breakfast, we went for a ramble in the hills. As we admired the views, our guide, one of the permanent camp staff, indicated points of interest. The air was fresh, the temperature in the sixties; a change from the plains, which were still visible at times in the hazy distance.

Cresting a hill we saw a marvellous panorama of the towering, snow-covered peaks of the Himalayas. Two stood out in particular.

"What are those, Charlie?" asked Bill of our guide, pointing at the imposing mountains.

"They're Nanda Devi and Nanda Parbat," Charlie said. "Nanda Devi, that's the highest mountain actually in India, about twenty-six thousand feet! Everest of course is in Tibet, Kanchenjunga in Sikkim, those two peaks are many hundreds of miles to the east of here.

"Tibet is a big country, though. The western part isn't so far away from this spot. Probably about forty miles," he added.

"Is there any possibility of going to Tibet, if it's that near?" asked Jack. "Would there be a coach trip or something?"

Charlie laughed. "Hardly, the terrain is practically impassable on foot. Unless you were an experienced mountaineer. A Mallory or an Irvine might do it, but look what happened to them. Mind you, there's plenty to see around here. If you were very lucky, you might see wild elephants, or a tiger, or even a leopard."

'Or unlucky, depending on which way you looked at it,' I thought. Still, it was interesting to hear Charlie talk about this India, so different from the India of the plains. We all enjoyed our hike, the clear and bracing air made such a change.

On the walk back, Charlie asked, "Who would like to go horse riding down to Ranhiket? It's a nice little town. It'll only cost you a rupee to hire a pony. We could go tomorrow."

Some of us, including me, looked doubtful.

"Horses?" I asked. "I'm not sure, I've never touched a horse, never mind ridden one!"

Some of the men turned the offer down altogether. The rest of us wanted to hear more.

"They're only docile ponies, and its only a few miles to Ranhiket, downhill there, uphill back. You could get your photos taken."

Photos? That's different. 'I could send one to Joan,' I thought. Me on a handsome steed would make a pretty picture.

"Right," I said, "I'm game!"

Next morning, there were seven or eight of us waiting outside the camp office when the horses arrived. That is if you could call these pathetic ponies by such a name. They were led by a groom, a pitiable fellow, an Indian lad in a ragged dhoti. He seemed to allocate the animals by matching the size of the rider to the size of the pony. Needless to say, I landed up with the scrawniest beast of the bunch. I noted the name on the pony's collar was 'Samson'. A misnomer if ever there was one.

We scrambled aboard our mounts and soon were proceeding down the road. Destination the famous hill station of Ranhiket. We didn't canter or trot, but more or less ambled on our way. I didn't mind the slow pace too much, to be truthful, I didn't mind it at all. "Good old Samson," I said, patting his neck in the approved manner. "Take your time." I was not finding it easy to hang on, my bony legs trying to grip the pony's skeletal frame. Despite this drawback, the funereal pace gave me time to admire the scenery as we approached the town.

Ranhiket was unlike the towns on the plains, much cleaner and greener with imposing residences scattered on the hillsides, summer abodes of the sahibs and memsahibs in the days of the Raj, no doubt. Days that were soon to end. The first priority was to have our photos taken, mounted on the ponies. It would be a couple of hours before we could pick the snaps up, so off we went to browse around the bazaar and have a bite to eat. Eggs and chips, that was the staple food of most of us in an Indian eating place. Eventually - us fed and watered, the ponies just watered - we set off for another amble back to the camp. We were more than halfway to base and the ponies were struggling up the steep inclines at a slow gait, when suddenly the tempo changed - certainly with my bedraggled steed. It must have registered with Samson that he was nearing his stables, perhaps he could smell the hay, because suddenly he lurched into a lopsided canter. He had found renewed strength from somewhere. "Whoa, old fellow," I cried rather anxiously.

That was a mistake. Perhaps 'whoa' in Urdu meant full speed ahead, that's what I got anyway. The canter changed without warning into a gallop and I was hanging on for dear life. In the kerfuffle, the reins went walkabout, Samson's straggly mane was the only thing I could get a grip on.

"Giddy up," I cried, hoping that would confuse him. He confused me instead. 'Giddy up' and 'whoa' seemed to mean the same thing to my nag. He interpreted both commands as 'Gallop your bloody fastest'. I had often read that when men are in mortal danger their past flashes across their minds. Not with me, it didn't, I was more concerned about my future, if I had one. At that instant, that seemed an unlikely scenario.

It had to happen. Just as we were approaching the camp, I lost my flimsy grip on the pony's mane and slithered to the ground, giving my head a crack.

I was in a daze for hours, just aware of being moved to a sick bay. Dozing fitfully, I awoke in the middle of the night with a throbbing head. In my drowsy condition, I was positive that I had a broken skull. If I survived, which was doubtful, I would soon be on a hospital ship heading for Blighty. In spite of my discomfort, a smile crept across my face and I dozed contentedly until aroused by someone shouting in my ear. It was an R.A.M.C. doctor, a wizened, sunburnt fellow who looked as though, after passing out of medical school, he had spent the last seventy years in India. He gave me a perfunctory examination and said I would be O.K. in a day or two. He must have had X-Ray eyes.

He was right of course. A couple of days later I was as fit as a fiddle. Ready for anything except a ride on a horse. 'These old doctors are wonderful,' I thought.

The worst thing about the whole affair was that, after the doctor had gone, and there I was with a throbbing headache, who should be my first visitor but Jack Dalton? Jack Dalton, with a huge smirk on his face!

Chapter 22

NOT YET

The stifling heat and the swarms of flies on the platform at Bareilly Junction signalled our return to the plains. Leave over, we were soon bedding down again under stuffy mosquito nets after those airy nights of slumber in the hills. Early one morning, shortly after our return to Meerut, Sergeant Taylor came into the bungalow.

"I want you all outside after breakfast, I've got something to tell you, be back here at 8.30 sharp."

In the mess, we found that the lads from other bungalows had received similar orders. There was a rumour that Wavell, the Viceroy of India was to pay us a visit. Ha ha.

"Right, are you all present?" The sergeant was counting heads. I was surprised to see the bearers, the char wallah and the gardener, also assembled.

"All very strange," said Gordon, "all very strange."

"Right lads, I'll put you in the picture. At very short notice, tomorrow in fact, the battalion's getting an important visitor, so we've all got work to do."

"It's the Viceroy!" said Bill.

"Shut up," I said. It wasn't the Viceroy, but Bill was not far wrong.

"Can I have a bit of hush? Tomorrow, the 83rd Battalion, Meerut, will have the honour of receiving a visit from Field Marshal Sir Claude Auchinleck, Commander-in-Chief, India Command. You've heard of Auchinleck, hero of the first Battle of Alamein?"

"Yes, Sarge," some of us shouted. It wasn't unanimous.

"Auchinleck?" somebody muttered under his breath, "Who's he?"

"Well, forget about General Montgomery, it was the Auk's Eighth Army that stopped the rot in the first place and halted Rommel's advance to Cairo and the Suez Canal.

"So it's going to be spit and polish today lads. Do any of you remember spit and polish?"

"Aye, Sarge, we 'ad that rubbish at trainin' camp," said Smiler. "We'ad t'smarten oop t'billet and smarten oop aarselves."

"I bet that took some doing," said the sergeant. "Anyway, it won't be the same here. Here, you'll go into the office and polish your desks and clean your inkwells. Get your pens and pencils arranged neatly. If the Auk comes in, pretend your working. Have a ledger on your desk, if you haven't got a ledger, borrow one. Make sure it's not tatty.

"If you have to go outside to another office in the cantonment, wear your cap and look on important business. Carry a folder neatly tucked under your left arm. Keep your right arm free for saluting purposes. Got that?"

"I think we've got the message, Sarge," said Taffy Evans, "but will he inspect our bungalows?"

"We've got plans for that, get your belongings into your lockers, the bearers will do the rest. You understand, bearers? Pukka job, Bearers, savvy? The Auk is a big nabob!"

"Yes, Sahib Sergeant," said Ranjit, my bearer. "Our Chief Commander Auk will find everything pukka. We will spit and polish all day. Spit and polish cap badges, spit and polish boots, make beds. It will be an honour, Sergeant Sahib. When Field Marshall Auk comes we will stand by the beds," Ranjit must have been a bearer with a spit and polish infantry regiment at some time.

"No need to stand by the charpoys, Ranjit. Savvy?"

"Nobody will stand by the beds, Sahib?" Ranjit looked crestfallen, denied his big chance of glory.

"No, Ranjit, and you, Mali, the grass must be pukka, savvy?"

The gardener spoke rapidly in Urdu, gesticulating with wide sweeps of his arms.

"What's the mali say, Ranjit?"

"He say he will cut every blade of grass on the lawn and sweep everything up tidy. It will all be spit and polish."

"Good, and bearers, this week, you will get an extra two rupees from every sahib. O.K.?"

There was a groan from the lads.

"Oh, thank you, Sahib," the servants chorused.

Next day, Auchinleck and his entourage did visit our office. Disappointingly though, the very clerk who handled his account - me - wasn't introduced to this important personage. Instead, Sir Claude was surrounded by a phalanx of senior Pay Corps officers fawning at his heels. We privates who did all the nitty gritty, kept our heads down, following our instructions. It was difficult however, to appear engrossed in our work with all the 'yes, sirs' and 'no, sirs' flying about.

As he left, he was followed closely by his retinue. I wondered if he had included our office in his tour of the cantonment just to check his Income Tax. It was strange that his folio had disappeared from my binder overnight.

After that welcome break in Chaubatia, and the visit of the Auk, it was back to the daily grind, and that included swotting to pass the Forces Preliminary Exam. The gateway to a successful career, read the bumph. Just up my street. Much of the course, organised by Cambridge University Correspondence College, involved postal teaching. However, part of the English curriculum was arranged in Meerut by the Education Officer. He introduced the class, nine of us, to our tutor, a Mrs George, wife of a captain in the R.A.P.C.

What a change to encounter a fragrantly scented Englishwoman, after putting up with smelly males for almost a year. 'Georgie' a raven-haired, pleasant lady, aged twenty-five or so, had a real enthusiasm for teaching. English Literature was my favourite subject. This could have been the reason why I became her star pupil. She used my essays as shining examples of class work, provoking the other students to call me teacher's pet. Jealous lot. Was it not obvious to them that with my prowess as a short story writer for the Pay Corps magazine, I would also excel as an essayist? Was I not the author of such gems as 'The Magical Toothpaste', or 'The Case of the Greyhound and the Grannie'? O.K. many of them could have also shone in class, if they had ceased dreaming of midnight trysts with 'Georgie'. Gosh! She was attractive. Besotted as I was with Joan, I still appreciated her presence. She was definitely off-limits though, so any thoughts of an amorous nature that the lads had were stifled at birth. Especially when they discovered that her officer husband was waiting outside the classroom after lessons to escort her home. About this time my application for a place in a Teacher Training College was turned down. I had been rejected by the Admissions Panel, blinkered so-and-sos.

That same day I heard from home, news of brother Don. Now discharged from the R.A.F. Regiment, he was existing on his demob pay, living a life of idleness. 'He'll have to get a job soon, he's thinking of working on the railway, or on the buses,' Mam wrote. 'He'd better translate thought into action before his money runs out.' There were no prospects of my demob yet, Group 38 had just left Meerut bound for Deolali Transit Camp and onward to Blighty. Twenty-three groups to go. It could be a year or more before I was back in England.

The weather was cooling down, the temperature in the eighties. "It's comfortable to move about now," Bill said. It was a Sunday afternoon; we were slouched in cane basket chairs, which we had plonked on the bungalow lawn.

"Moving about's O.K., but it's cushy just lolling about in these chairs, doing nothing, Bill," I yawned. Not that we were idle. Feeding peanuts to a family of frivolous chipmunks was keeping us busy. The little devils had appeared from nowhere at the first rustle of a packet. Fickle creatures, chipmunks, though. As the last peanut disappeared, so did they. All was peaceful again, we were left to our slouching.

I looked skywards, unusually there were fluffy white clouds in the blue, how pleasing they were. I closed my eyes.

"Hi! Paul!" Bill's shout impinged on my reverie.

"What?" I said, sitting up with a start.

"You've been asleep!"

"I have not, I was thinking," I said grumpily.

"So was I. You know what?"

"There you go with your you-know-whats. I know lots of whats, which what are you talking about?"

"What about this cricket team, Paul?"

"Oh, that what! We said we'd form one, didn't we?"

"But when? Do you know Bungalows 28 and 21 played each other yesterday. We won't organise a team lounging about like this. We're getting lazy."

"Don't worry, Bill. It's early days. Anyway, do you think we can raise a team? When you look around, excluding me and you and one or two others like Ken Brown who's due for demob in a couple of weeks anyway, we're not an athletic lot."

"Well, as you say, there's you and me, Ken Brown will play, Dixie Dean, Taffy, Lofty Bates, Dick. Then we can rope Gordon and Jack in. They couldn't refuse their pals."

"You're scraping the barrel now, Bill!"

"Hang on - Les Reynolds! He played for his school. That's ten," said Bill, counting on his fingers.

"That's enough for starters. We'll browbeat somebody else when we tell them the honour of the bungalow's at stake."

"You're a nutcase, Paul."

"Thanks, Bill. Right! We'll go to the Sports Officer tomorrow. See if we can scrounge some kit. If we get a couple of bats, two sets of stumps and a few pads, we'll have the lads falling over themselves for a game. What do you say?"

"I'll say you've got a vivid imagination," Bill laughed. "Now if you'd said we'd come back with a couple of brunettes and a set of blondes, well, then we might have been killed in the rush. Anyway, let's give it a go, then. I'll see you outside the Sports Office at Tiffin time."

That night we pinned a notice on the board - 'Anyone interested in playing cricket for the bungalow please meet at Bill Kennedy's charpoy at 19.00 hours Monday. Signed P. Potts, captain. W. Kennedy, vice-captain.'

"That should get them going," said optimistic me.

The appointed hour approached, we had set out the equipment on Bill's bed in a most inviting manner, bats asking to be swung, pads waiting to be buckled, stumps demanding to be skittled. Plus two cherry red cricket balls.

Jack and Gordon lay on their charpoys and waited with concealed interest for events to develop. Jack had said, "If you can find another seven stupid sods, we'll play."

Just then, Dixie Dean and Taffy sauntered across, followed by Lofty Bates and Les Reynolds.

"What's all this?" said Dixie superciliously.

"We're thinking of challenging Bungalow 28 to a game." said Bill. "They beat the 21 lads on Saturday."

"Well, you can count me in. Did you know I played a bit of cricket down Bethnal Green way?"

Did we know? Everybody knew. Just mention cricket to him and you would discover you were in the presence of an all-rounder of great potential.

"Who appointed you to be captain, anyway?" he added.

"It's simple, Dixie, they're our bats! Besides," I added, (he was a sucker for a bit of blarney), "you're our star, I want you concentrating on your batting and bowling."

The upshot was that half an hour later we had got a team together. What sort of team we would find out later.

"Right, chaps," I said, settling with ease into my new role as captain of cricket. "So that's agreed. We challenge Bungalow 28 to a game on Saturday?"

Unalloyed delight? No. Mutters of 'Aye, alright', 'Bang goes wor trip to the bazaar', 'Will we win in time for the flicks, eh?', 'Aa'll miss me arternoon on t'charpoy', were some of the comments heard. Eventually, however, Saturday was agreed.

Later, Ranjit collected our shoes for polishing.

"Oh, Ranjit, can you take this note to Bungalow 28 and give it to their cricket captain? He's a sahib called Grace. It's a challenge to a cricket match."

"Grace! Not W.G., the great English cricketer, Sahib?!"

"No, Ranjit. W.G. is dead. Like your Ranjitsinghi. Gone to a cricket heaven in the skies."

"Oh, I'm sorry to hear that, Sahib, but I will take your note, is this what you call a gauntlet? I will throw it at this imposter's feet, Sahib."

I was beginning to wish that I had taken the note myself. "No, just give it to him, then wait for a reply."

We had four short evenings of practice and what a shower we were. Dixie (with his spinners), Bill and Taffy could bowl a bit, Reynolds, me, and Ken Brown knew the right end of a bat. The rest were like the Keystone Cops. On the day, we discovered that Bungalow 28 were worse than us. Except for their secret weapon - Lieutenant Parker of Battalion H.Q. The riddle of how he had sneaked into their team was never solved. But there he was - a little fellow with a limp, legacy of botched-up surgery on a broken leg. He couldn't run, but he could bat and he could bowl.

Despite his skills (he took six wickets and knocked up

twenty), we won by nine runs, all out for 65 to their 56. Reynolds and I had opened and got the team off to a good start before Parker wiped up our tail. It was a long, long tail.

He limped up to me after the match and shook my hand.

"Well played, Potts," he said. "You know when I was standing at slip, I thought, why don't we form a battalion team? I could arrange a game with the Havildars. We could give them a run for their money, what? You, wicketkeeper again; those two bowler fellows, Kennedy and Dean; Reynolds."

"And you sir, all-rounder. You'd be worth two men!" If I kept this up promotion could beckon! "I'm all for it," I added. "You'll pick the team and arrange the date, sir?"

"Righto, Potts, I'll be in touch."

A few days later, the mini Test was on. Parker lost the toss and we struggled, the Havildar XI reached a massive 128 for 7 in thirty overs despite Parker taking five wickets. With our threadbare batting talent, I wrote off our chances. Unless our captain could pull it off single-handed.

I opened our innings with Reynolds and scoring off a surfeit of full tosses we soon had twenty-five on the board. Things were looking up, then Reynolds was bowled off the last ball of the over. Parker came in, but it was I to face. A new bowler now, a spinner. The wicketkeeper standing up to the stumps, a silly mid-off and silly mid-on hovering a few yards from the bat. A smell of garlic in the air. What a jolly looking bowler, what a cheery smile. He ambled up, the ball described a gentle arc. I moved to smother any break, I was deceived by the flight, hoaxed by the spin, and baffled by the fizz off the pitch. The ball snicked the shoulder of my bat, parted the wicketkeeper's hair and dropped in front of slip. The next ball was a googly, again snicking off the bat's shoulder, giving the 'keeper another parting. My good luck held and the next three balls shaved the stumps. The last ball of the over was overpitched. Nimbly I danced forward and drove it into the covers with a classical flourish. It rebounded off silly mid-off's shins.

"One," I shouted, hairing down the wicket.

Bamboozled by the bowling, I had forgotten that Parker was disabled. But game! Yes. Limping, he responded to my call and was run out yards from safety. Hey ho! Parker's innings was stillborn. So was my hope of promotion.

"Sorry, sir!" I shouted after the retreating figure. "My fault, sir!"

Did I hear him mutter, "Bloody fool."?

Whatever he had said under his breath, my concentration was ruined, I soon followed Parker back to the pavilion - cleaned bowled the next ball I faced. Out for sixteen.

Needless to say we lost that mini Test Match handsomely. I was still grovelling to Parker in the pavilion when our last wicket fell.

"Don't worry, Potts, I'm keeping a stiff upper lip, but I do think these havildar fellas are too good for us, by Jove."

That was his way of saying no more battalion games. Not unless Hutton and Compton were drafted to Meerut, anyway.

A more profound issue was exercising my thoughts around this time. Jack and I attended Mass every Sunday at the cantonment Catholic Church. Periodically I visited the Confessional and generally tried to behave like a good Catholic should.

For some time now however, I had experienced doubts about the dogmas of the Church and the formalities of worship. Looking around the congregation on a Sunday, I felt more and more that the routines of the service were carried out unthinkingly not only by the bulk of the worshippers, but also by the priest. The congregation, sitting, standing, kneeling, was just responding to each prompt automatically.

The panoply of the altar, the litany repeated almost in parrot fashion. The Holy Communion, where we accepted the body of Christ provided we hadn't had any breakfast. What about the solemn rites of other religions - the Muslim faith - the complicated structure of the Hindu religion - Jewish theology - Sikh beliefs - the many Protestant versions of Christianity? Worshippers in these varied religions convinced that their faith was the one and only true belief. If there was a God, which version was the true one?

Then, think of the strife and cruelty that had resulted from religious beliefs. Here and now in India, the horrific slaughter mainly inspired by conflicting dogmas.

Was there a God? The mystery of the Universe was an impenetrable enigma to me. In fact, the more my young mind tried to think it through, the more confused I became. Over a period of weeks I began to feel that this pomp was not for me. Yet I hoped, and yes, I still prayed that there was an omnipotent being.

One Sunday morning, instead of getting up, I turned over in my charpoy. I wasn't going to church, this morning, or any other morning. That was it. Back to sleep.

"Get up, Paul, you'll be late for Mass." It was Jack.

"Leave me, Jack. I'm not going."

"What's wrong, are you sick?"

"No, I'm just not going. I'm going to sleep, O.K."

"If that's how you feel, go to sleep, then." I couldn't sleep, though. My mind was trying to come to terms with my new philosophy. It was strange. 'Christianity and most of its precepts would continue to be the basis of my attitude to life,' I thought. The concept of right and wrong for example, but no longer would I be a practising Catholic.

What would be the ramifications resulting from my change of heart? Who would be concerned, whom would it affect? I could be certain that I would earn the disapproval of Mam. Imparting news of this kind to her would be put on hold. It would be delayed until I returned home. The easy way out for the time being. That appealed to me!

Notifying Joan however, would be a pleasant task, I would do that without delay. Now in fact! I jumped out of bed and slipped into my shorts, grabbing pen and paper

'My dearest Joan,

This is a special letter darling - are you ready for some news? Good news, I think. I've made a decision to cease being a Catholic. I think the pomp of the services is stupid and in some ways hypocritical. Don't panic, I still believe in Christian principles but the rigmarole to me now seems ridiculous. I suppose my view, now, also applies in many ways to the C of E, or what have you.

What this means to us darling, is that you can stop worrying about me being a Catholic. If and when, sorry, when, we have children, and you want them christened C of E, they can be. If you want us to get married in church, we can. I'll play a passive role in those decisions.

Just in case you're worried that I'm doing this for you and

that I may regret it, I can assure you that it's not so. On the other hand I'm pleased that it should help us to become even closer.'

Her reply soon arrived.

'My darling Paul,

Thank you for your letter with your surprising news. You could have knocked me down with a feather! Are you sure, absolutely sure that you're not doing this for me and that you won't regret it? I'll have to believe you, won't I? Mind it will certainly make things easier for both of us and I can see your view about the pomp of religion. All the same, although I seldom go to church, I do believe in God and I pray every night. I pray for all my family and last of all I save a special prayer for you before I go to sleep.

I do love you, you see, and you've made a big impression on my heart. I don't think you can see it, the impression I mean, but I might let you have a look when you come home!'

I must admit that I felt a tremendous load off my shoulders now I that I had cleared my mind and made my decision. Joan's letter had reinforced my new stance although, strangely, I had some regrets that my old solid reassuring faith was no more.

If I had still been going to confession in November, I would have had to tell the priest of my bout of drunkenness. My twenty-first birthday 'do' took place towards the end of the month. It wasn't much of a party, I had bought a couple of bottles of rum and there were a gang of about a dozen of us in the canteen. The beer flowed freely as, one after another, my pals bought rounds. A raucous singsong kept the night going, 'Roll Out the Barrel', 'Bless 'Em All'. I'm sure that tears were welling up in the eyes of some of my pals at the thought of a troopship leaving Bombay.

My turn for maudlin sentiment came with 'Lilli Marlene'. For Lilli Marlene transpose Joan Speed. What's in a name anyway?

The night seemed to fade into oblivion, I don't really remember staggering back to the bungalow. In fact the next thing I knew was someone shaking my shoulder in the light of morning.

"Wake up, Sahib. Char, Sahib."

I groaned, "Go away, char wallah, please!"

If this was what it felt like being a man, I wanted to be a lad again.

Christmas in Meerut was strange, the weather was beautiful, temperatures in the high sixties. The bearers presented everyone with garlands. We had a group photograph taken, me almost as skinny as ever. My thoughts were faraway with Joan. For the third Christmas, we were parted. Pray that this was the last.

Letter from Joan:

'Going to miss you at Christmas again, darling. Don't get drunk as you did on your birthday, I don't want you turning into an alcoholic. (I'm only kidding!)

I went to York Empire by myself last night. Peter Cavanagh, the impressionist, was on, he's good. Also there was a girl singer, a bit like Anne Shelton, who sang 'Always'. Do you remember when that girl sang it last year at the Empire, darling? 'I'll be loving you, always'. You turned to me and whispered that's very true. I thought of that last night.

I've kept all the letters you have written to me you know. I counted them last night - there were eighty-six, would you believe?!'

Letter to Joan:

'My dearest darling,

Thanks for the letter that you wrote just before Christmas. So, I have sent you eighty-six letters in a year? I must have been spoiling you! I've just counted your letters, I've kept every one too. Do you know there are only seventy-six? I'm winning easily, what have you been playing at? Neglecting your future husband like that. Mind you, there is still quite a pile, I'll have to throw some away before I come home, unfortunately. Unless I can hire a bearer to carry them, I certainly won't get them all in my kitbag!

I hope I don't receive many more letters from you.

Don't take that the wrong way, I mean I hope I'll be home soon. Then you won't have to write any more.'

There wasn't much new to tell Joan at the beginning of 1947. Mountbatten had been appointed Viceroy of India with a view to speeding up the independence talks and handing over power. He would take up his post in March. The stumbling block was still the rift between the Hindus and Muslims. I hoped that there would be a breakthrough so that we could look forward to my returning home. 'Not yet,' I thought.

Chapter 23

INDEPENDENCE

Up until now, most of the lads in our bungalow had escaped the ailments and diseases prevalent in India, faring better than many in the battalion. The previous autumn there had been an outbreak of dysentery, which had affected a half dozen or so, amongst whom were Jack and Gordon. Gordon was doubly unlucky, having just recovered from malaria. The men who contracted dysentery (probably picked up in the office privies), spent time in the cantonment hospital. There they received the appropriate treatment - starved of food and drowned with fluids. It was weeks before they were fully fit again. Gordon took longer than anyone to recover. Three other lads suffered from a virulent form of malaria, possibly as a result of neglecting anti-mosquito precautions. They could suffer a reoccurrence at any time. It was no surprise, however, to find that Smiler Preston had caught syphilis. His pal Dick had told me this 'on the quiet'. Smiler was no longer his old ebullient self, his toothy grin just a frail shadow of a smile now. Dick, too, was a much-chastened individual. The visits of the two of them to the brothel were now in the past.

Early in 1947, young Steve Reynolds (who had been my opening partner for the battalion cricket team), contracted typhoid. Our concern lessened when the word from the hospital indicated that he was progressing well - but then we heard that peritonitis had developed. It was a still a big shock when we were told that he had died. His death was the second in the battalion within the year. Reynolds had a girlfriend at home to whom he wrote often. He and I were known as the 'scribblers', because of our letter output. His sweetheart would be devastated.

The lads of Bungalow 39 attended his funeral en masse. Eight of us had been delegated to stand by his grave and were issued with rifles and blank cartridges. We fired the final salute as a trumpeter played the last post.

To a bunch of young lads it was a sombre reminder of the ephemeral nature of life.

Letters from Joan told me of the hardships being suffered at home during the severest winter in England for many years. There, it was bitterly cold with heavy snowfalls, whilst here in Meerut, we had pleasant temperatures and the warm sunshine of a northern Indian winter. The freak weather was one trial in Britain, a desperate lack of fuel was another. The shortage of coal, a shortage which seemed unbelievable after two years of peace, meant that a regimen of power cuts operated during daylight hours.

As Joan explained:

'We have been without light and heat in the office here in Grosvenor House all this week. The power cuts have lasted three quarters of the working day and it's been impossible to work properly what with the cold and the dim daylight. I wish you were here to keep me warm.

Apparently, we are getting oil stoves and candles next week, they will have to do instead!

The football fixtures are taking a hammering - as fast as volunteers clear the pitches of snow we have another fall and another game is postponed!

From the games that are taking place it looks as though Newcastle are going to miss out on promotion despite having bought Len Shackleton from Bradford. What do you think to him scoring seven goals against Newport on his debut? I expected something like that, after all he's a Yorkshireman!

By the way, darling, I've been thinking. I'm going to do something about my deficit of 76 to 86 in letter writing. You're in for a surprise!'

What did she mean by that? I asked myself. I soon found out. Two days later, four letters arrived together and every one in Joan's writing. What was more puzzling, they were numbered 1 to 4. I opened them in order. They were all one-page missives. The first one read:

'My darling Paul,

I love you very much. Your ever loving, Joan.'

The second one read:

'My dearest Paul,

I love you very, very much,

Your ever, ever loving Joan.'

The third one was in the same vein, but in triplicate, as was the fourth in quadruplicate. The last one had a postscript:

'What do you think to my plan? I can soon catch up, only another six letters to go!' I smiled to myself. The witch! Picking up pen and paper I wrote back without further ado:

'My darling vixen,

I bet you think you're clever! But you'd better stop, for two can play at that game! I'm warning you. If you keep that up I'll be spanking you when I see you again, instead of cuddling you! Let's just call it a draw, eh? I miscounted your letters anyway, I found some more from you, but I'm not telling you how many!'

Joan probably had a chuckle or two, but she didn't send any more one-page letters, perhaps thinking that she'd had her fun.

That spring brought new problems back home. Joan told me of the River Ouse at York bursting its banks as the snow in the hills finally started melting. Rowing boats, instead of buses, were operating around the bus station in Rougier Street. Many other streets were flooded, Grosvenor House was still above water however. Only just! With all the dismal weather, I hoped my news that I had passed my Forces Prelim Exam would cheer her up a bit.

As the heat returned to Meerut, so did unrest between Muslims, Hindus and Sikhs. Mountbatten was pressing for an early agreement and it seemed increasingly likely that partition would be the final solution. The mainly Hindu Congress Party, led by Pandit Nehru, would accept that only as a last resort.

Spasmodic riots were again taking place and guard duties were stepped up. I was part of the guard one sultry night, when the Muslims were celebrating noisily. Someone said it was Ramadan time. We could hear the chanting of the crowds in the nearby city drifting across the still night air. First reaching a crescendo, then dying away to an almost complete silence.

Theories were rife this night. Was their wrath switching from their Hindu fellow citizens to the British occupation forces? Were they silently approaching the cantonment to demonstrate?

Our hearing that black, cloudy, moonless night was magnified and our imaginations ran riot. The silences were eerie, so uncanny that we almost welcomed the return of the chanting. Even when we stood down, deep sleep was never a possibility.

I was dozing after my first spell on guard when a shot rang out. We lads in the guardroom jumped up and grabbed our rifles.

Bleary-eyed, I saw Sergeant Wright at the door, his rifle at the ready, peering into the blackness. "What's happening, Sarge?" I asked.

"I don't know yet, I've sent Hunt to investigate." Just then, Hunt returned with bespectacled young Les Dixon in tow. Les was just nineteen - one of the last intake from the U.K.

"This is the lad that fired his rifle, Sarge. He thought he'd heard a noise."

"Dixon, isn't it?" asked Wright.

"Yes, Sarge." The lad looked bewildered, frightened.

"What happened?"

"I was patrolling the perimeter and I thought I'd heard something."

"Did you make a challenge?"

"No, Sarge, I fired off a round to frighten them. I panicked, I suppose."

"You can suppose you'll be on a charge as well then, Dixon. There was nobody to frighten off, was there?"

"No, Sarge, but a charge?" Dixon looked as though he was going to cry.

"Yes, lad. You didn't issue a challenge, you didn't see anyone; you just fired a shot. You disobeyed orders!"

Stupidly, I butted in. "Sarge, make allowances, it was his first guard duty."

"Keep your mouth shut, Potts. I don't want any barrack-room lawyers around here. He fired a round; that has to be accounted for. He's on a charge and that's that."

Next morning, Dixon appeared before the Company Commander. He had no defence and so finished up in the brig, poor lad.

News came from Mam that Don was now working as a bus conductor, his demob pay must have run out. A thought of a Christmas past came to mind. Would he be walking up and down the aisle shouting "Fares please, fares please, room for six more upstairs?" Cecil wrote to me occasionally, the R.A.S.C. seemed to be full of busy, at least where he was stationed near Oxford. He told me he hadn't much leisure time. He had been home on leave however, and didn't seem to think much to Don's job. During Cecil's furlough, Don worked five consecutive shifts from four in the afternoon to midnight. 'Not my cup of tea,' Cecil wrote, 'but Don doesn't seem to mind. Perhaps he likes to be back in uniform! I don't think he likes change too much!'

Joan had settled down to writing proper letters again. She had not yet explained why she had not written for those weeks the previous summer. No doubt I would find out when I met her again. Whatever the cause, she was certainly back on song. Letter from Joan: 'Met Maureen Crow in town yesterday, with her baby. It's a bonny thing, a girl, much nicer than Fido! I asked after Fido and she said he hadn't been well! Perhaps he's suffering from jealousy. I didn't suggest that to Maureen, mind.

'Thanks for your latest snap of you on that horse. You still don't seem to have put on much weight. You look sturdier than the pony, mind. Perhaps it's all the exercise you get. I think I've lost a few pounds - and don't be cheeky and say I could spare a few! You might think I'm too thin when you get back anyway, you seemed to like me the way I was, didn't you?

So you're in the middle of the monsoon season again, at least it won't be so hot. I hope you get that leave in the cooler hills, they've promised you.

I'll close now darling. You know if sheer wishing could bring you back you would be in my arms right now!'

'Surely,' I thought, 'it can't be too long to demob now.' At last the date of Independence Day was announced - the 14th August 1947. There was to be partition, that meant that there would be a mass exodus of Hindus from the new territories of Pakistan to India, and countless Muslims making the reverse journey. Millions of people would be uprooted from their homes. Trouble and misery were inevitable.

On the fifteenth (the day after independence), a group of Pay

Corps men, including Bill, Jack, Gordon and myself, got leave at last. We commenced the long journey to Darjeeling, one of the best-known hill stations in India. Yes, Darjeeling! That word brought back memories of Uncle, giving me a piggyback when I was a little infant. "When I was in Darjeeling." Perhaps I would bore some great-nephew of mine in sixty years time with that same cry. With a bit of luck I might even recall what I was doing in Darjeeling, which in retrospect was more than Uncle could manage all those years ago.

Our old sergeant, Philips, had long since been demobbed so Sergeant Thomas was to travel with us and he explained what the journey entailed. First we would travel to Delhi, and there board a train for Calcutta. Thomas reckoned that with the security checks in force, it would take forty-eight hours to arrive there. Then a train to the railhead in Siliguri and finally the narrow gauge Mountain Railway to our destination.

It took longer. We travelled second class from Delhi and took turns to enjoy the comparative comfort of the few sleeping bunks. There was one bunk for every three of us. Wooden bench seats were the only other facility, except for a French-style toilet and a washbasin with a trickle of water.

The journey took us through the vast plain of the Ganges and progress was painfully slow. Stops were frequent and long lasting. Already, we were witnessing the beginning of the mass migrations as anxious families lined the platforms. Minorities seeking a way of quickly reaching what would be their new country - Pakistan for some, or a truncated India for others. Indian Army personnel manned every railway station trying desperately to maintain a semblance of order. They usually succeeded in preventing unauthorised entry to the British Army section of the train. If not, there was further delay until they had forcibly ejected the intruders.

One such incident occurred when a Muslim girl carrying a small baby somehow managed to get into our carriage. She looked bewildered and scared, probably making for East Pakistan, some distance beyond Calcutta. We weren't far away from that city now. I guessed the poor girl had become separated from her husband. I think if it had come down to a vote, the lads would have allowed her to stay, she looked so pathetic. Sergeant Thomas had other ideas, calling up an Indian sepoy to evict her.

I wondered how she would fare, just one of thousands in similar distress. I stuck my neck out again.

"Why didn't you let her stay, Sarge? We're not far from Calcutta now, surely?"

"Keep your nose out of this, Potts, my stripes were at stake there."

'Sorry I spoke,' I thought. We were tired and dishevelled by the time the train approached the environs of Calcutta. Sleep had been at a premium and in the chaos at each halt it had been difficult to obtain food or drink of any kind. Fortunately we had been provided with water and iron rations, in case such a problem arose. We stopped at yet another station, still not Calcutta! There were red-capped British Army Military Police on the platform. Sergeant Thomas alighted, pushed through a jostling, bewildered horde of Indian families and spoke to a Red Cap. It was then we saw that the M.P.s were holding signboards reading 'All British Army personnel detrain'. Thomas returned to the carriage. "Everybody off," he said. "We're not going into Calcutta today."

Instead we were soon bundled into trucks and travelling through streets of ramshackle houses. There was tension in the air, you could almost smell it. Bystanders were at every corner watching our progress. One or two waved as we went past. I thought that seemed a good sign. As we travelled through the town, an M.P. sergeant, who was accompanying us, explained the situation.

"You're in Barrackpore, we're fifteen miles out of Calcutta, and we're heading for the old East India Cantonment Barracks here. I gather you're from Meerut. Well, you won't find the bungalows here measure up to yours. These barracks are a bit run down, they're only used in emergencies these days."

Gordon Todd piped up. "Is this an emergency?" It was something we all wanted to know.

The M.P. laughed, "Well, it could be. From what we've been told, the Boundary Commission's findings have just been published, defining the exact partition line - how India and this Pakistan country are going to be divided. You can work out that could mean big trouble."

"What about Calcutta then, or Darjeeling, where we're supposed to be heading?" I asked.

"Well," the M.P. continued, "they'll both be in the new India. The problem is, will there be trouble in Calcutta on the same scale as last year? The riots took place at this time, remember. There've been demonstrations today already against the Muslims. That's why British H.Q. here didn't want unescorted and unarmed troops landing up in the city.

"The other thing," he went on, "Our G.H.Q. Delhi, have announced that British forces are to be evacuated from India without delay. Our role in India is finished. We should all be out within six months." That was great news. There wasn't any more that day.

The decision to block all army personnel from entering Calcutta had been taken just a few hours before. Hurried preparations to find us accommodation had been made. We soon had a meal and a mug of char and then were escorted to our billets for the night.

Our M.P. friend was right, Meerut it wasn't! There were charpoys, but there were no mattresses. Cooling fans were either non-existent or broken, mosquito nets the same. We were advised to sleep in our uniforms, smelly as they were.

Sleep we did, though; we were exhausted. No one stirred until the sound of reveille. Reveille! I had almost forgotten there was such a thing. It was a long time since initial training at Brancepeth. That wasn't all. Next thing, a damned sergeant came in rattling the beds and shouting at the top of his voice. Shades of Sergeant Bell!

"Rise and shine, you lot. You've got an hour to get a truck into Seeldah Station, Calcutta. Look at you! A scruffier lot I've never seen! I could smell you before I opened the door. And you've no time for a shower, either!" His laugh was malicious.

I looked around through sleep-filled eyes. I had to agree, we looked a crowd of layabouts, with our crumpled shirts and trousers and tousled hair. We followed him into the mess for a quick breakfast. It was then he relented.

"Right, you have fifteen minutes to have a shower and shave, on the double!"

Were we grateful! Even though the shower taps trickled with rusty water. Getting back into our smelly uniforms, however, was not so good.

Before we knew it, we were on our way in the muggy morning

air, travelling again in those ubiquitous hard trucks, with an escort of armed infantry men in the leading vehicle. Approaching the station, we observed men in groups and gangs, who looked hell-bent on trouble of some sort. Most ignored our small convoy as soon as they had identified us as British. Some even raised a cheer or waved a makeshift flag as we passed. Now that Mountbatten had 'severed the last links of Imperial Rule', any anti-British feeling that there might have been seemed to have gone. Our train was already in the station and within half an hour we were on our way, heading for Darjeeling. But first, Siliguri. Siliguri was at the base of the foothills, a three hundred mile slow journey from Calcutta, travelling seemed to be never ending. Again, we snatched sleep overnight, the train arriving in Siliguri in the early hours. Now for the last stage, a fifty-mile train ride to Darjeeling.

Chapter 24

GOODBYE DELHI I MUST LEAVE YOU

Sergeant Thomas had been given instructions at Barrackpore that we were to stay on the train when we reached Siliguri. We'd slept fitfully on the bench seats during the journey, but were all astir shortly after dawn making forlorn efforts to spruce ourselves up, although we knew there was no possibility of looking dapper in our crumpled, smelly, khaki drill. A couple of soldiers - a lieutenant and a havildar of the Indian Army - entered our coach. The officer sniffed the air and eyed us disdainfully.

"Right, you fellows, who is in charge?"

'Thomo' stood up and sprang to attention.

"I am, sir," he said.

"Jolly good. If you will all follow me we will go now and I will see you to your train. Remember once you are on the train it is necessary that you stay on until you get to Darjeeling. You see there is much unrest in India, although it is much quieter in the hills."

We followed the two Indians. They headed for a low platform at the far end of the station. There was a train there, a narrow gauge effort - for local commuters, perhaps? I looked around the airless station, where were the Indians leading us? Surely not to this toy? But they were. Our Indian friend gestured towards the train. "This is your transport, fellows".

I looked in amazement, the carriages were about four feet wide and about twelve feet long. In height from floor to roof not much above four feet either, it seemed. Were we actually going to travel fifty miles on this miniature train? Was it possible?

"This here is it, sir?" asked our sergeant. "I knew we were to travel on a smaller train, but can this get us to Darjeeling?"

The officer smiled, "This is your train alright. We call it the Toy Train," (I knew it!), "two-foot gauge, not the five foot six inches of the main line trains. A little bit narrower, eh? There are some tight bends, you see, and not much room in places."

"That sounds exciting," I muttered to myself. I looked at Jack, I had a feeling that he had turned ghastly white under his tan.

"How long will we be on this thing?" someone asked.

"It usually takes about eight hours if there are no landslides blocking the track. Those sort of things do happen, but mostly during the weeks of the monsoon. We're nearly at the end of the wet season now. With luck you will be alright. How do you say? Keep your fingers crossed?" he laughed.

"Eight hours for fifty miles!" I groaned.

"Don't forget, young fella, you will be going up to nearly seven thousand feet. Quite a height for a train. It comes down quicker," he laughed.

I shook my head, another eight hours before our journey would end!

Six of us, with our luggage, struggled into a coach marked 'Reserved'. I noticed there was a small washroom at one end. The rest of our party found seats in other coaches set aside for us. Our small group occupied half of the train, there weren't many coaches behind the diminutive locomotive. As we squirmed into our seats, a memory of playing a game of 'Sardines' one Christmas, when we piled into the gas meter cupboard under the stairs, sprang to mind. We sat on each side of the coach, our knees almost touching.

"What fun," said Bill Kennedy, "we're on a toy too-too!"

Jack gave a sigh, "I wish I wasn't on this bloody too-too. Why do these hill stations have to be in the hills?"

"It won't be so bad, Jack, at least we're on railway lines. We're not at the mercy of a reckless truck driver!" I said, trying to comfort the poor lad.

The journey was fascinating as we ascended, leaving the sultry plains behind us. The first section was one of gentle but steady ascent with some tight bends, bends much too sharp for a standard train. As we progressed however, the gradients got stiffer, the bends tighter. At times, the track looped around and over itself to gain height. The Lilliputian locomotive was now puffing madly, like an athlete in a hill race straining every sinew to keep up momentum.

Glimpses out of the windows showed us that the plains were now far below as we chugged ever higher. Every hour or so, the engine driver eased the train to a halt at sites where piles of logs were stacked.

The first time this happened, Gordon popped his head out of the window, which was quite a manoeuvre in itself.

"The train crew are restocking up with fuel," he said, keeping us informed. "They must go through some logs. Lads, you should see this drop where our carriage has stopped. We couldn't get out here if we wanted to, we would finish up in Siliguri!"

Jack moaned, "Come away from that window, Gordon, and don't talk about drops."

"It's all in the mind, Jack," I laughed.

"It'll be all over your lap if you two don't shut up! I'm warning you!"

"O.K., O.K.," I said hurriedly, as I suddenly perceived the dangers. "I'll say no more!"

That journey was undoubtedly an experience never to be forgotten, the loops, the shunts, the reversing, all to gain height in tight spaces on the hillsides. The views were breathtaking. Even so, after eight hours tightly packed as we were, sitting on hard wooden seats, I'd had enough.

How glad we were when at last we reached our final destination and were trucked off to our billets in Darjeeling.

Shattered and hungry, after a quick meal and a glorious shower, I, like most of us, flopped into bed. The charpoy, complete with mattress this time, gave me a dead-to-the-world sleep. Our ten-day leave was now reduced to eight because of the delays we had endured. The billet, not far out of the centre, was good, providing the best food I'd encountered from an army cookhouse. The weather was cloudy and cool much of the time with frequent bursts of rain, although there were pleasant sunny days.

Darjeeling was a town full of interest; the majority of the population were Ghurkhas, their religion Buddhism. There was a preponderance of women, as a high proportion of the men served in the Ghurkha Regiment. We had been told it was a tradition that the young men would join this famous regiment attached to the British Army, a regiment which had an impressive battle record over many years.

"Look at all these young girls without a lad!" said Gordon, "There must be a chance here!"

"Not for me," I laughed, "I've waited nearly two years, I might as well wait another month or two!"

"It's wishful thinking, anyway," said Bill, "they look much too well-behaved and religious to fall for a reprobate like you, Gordon. Not unless you convert to Buddhism!"

Bill was right, Gordon tried to chat one or two up, without success.

"No speak English," they said. I bet they did, all the same.

We spent most days walking into the surrounding countryside, countryside covered with tea plantations and had a view at every bend. When the weather was clear, our favourite walk was to Observatory Hill, with the fantastic panorama of the Himalayas. The towering, snow-covered Kanchenjunga, the world's third highest mountain, dominated the skyline.

One day, browsing through the central district of the town, we saw a sign. 'Trips to Tiger Hill, only seven miles, with views of Mount Everest. Enquire within'.

"Why don't we go?" asked Bill. "We could brag about seeing the highest mountain in the world, we'll never get the chance again!"

"It's an idea," I said.

Jack spoke up then, "I'm not going if there're sheer drops, it's not my cup of tea!"

Gordon was all for it, so the three of us went inside.

"Can you tell us about this Everest trip?" I asked the man behind a counter. 'This mountain air must be healthy,' I thought. He looked about a hundred and fifty years old, yet so alert. I had already noticed how many old-looking men here seemed so sprightly, as they walked up and down the steep streets. Was this place a kind of Shangri-la? Perhaps we might see Ronald Colman if we kept our eyes open.

The old fellow gave me a wizened smile, his eyes twinkling. "Yes, sir, it's a very good trip and the view of Everest very good! You leave at four o'clock."

"In the afternoon?" I was surprised, it seemed a late start. He cackled humorously, "No, sir, in the morning, sir. The morning sun, sir, on the mountain. Very pretty."

That was a bit early, we'd have to get up at three, I, for one, was having my doubts. Was Everest really worth it?

"Will the trucks come to our billet?" asked Bill.

He cackled again, we seem to be giving him fun. "No, no, sir, not trucks!"

"Do we have to walk? It's seven miles uphill!" I said.

"Oh no, sir," I was beginning to fear for his health as he collapsed into a paroxysm of chuckles. "Best horses, sir, you will all have good horses, good steeds."

I turned to Bill and Gordon. "Horses! That let's me out, I'm not going on another horse!"

Bill and Gordon were made of sterner stuff, they arranged to go on the trip the very next morning. Jack and I had chickened out for separate, but we thought, equally valid reasons.

We stay-at-homes had the last laugh. Brushing through trees on horseback in the early morning, Bill and Gordon had discovered leeches were attaching themselves unpleasantly to their neck and arms. It was then they discovered why their guide was chain-smoking. He touched each leech with the tip of his lighted cigarette, which caused them to drop off rather quickly. "Do not pull them off, Sahibs, you could get infection," their guide had said.

When they returned to the billet they showed us the marks on their skin; Jack and I fell about laughing, unfeeling characters that we were!

"What about the view of Everest?" I asked, just a wee bit concerned that I might have missed out on an unforgettable experience.

"There wasn't any bloody view, it was too cloudy!" shouted Bill.

Bill and Gordon were too tired to go far next day, their backsides too sore, their legs too stiff.

I had an idea. "Jack, why don't we go and see one of those gompas we heard about?"

"What gompas? What's a gompa?"

"If you'd been listening to that Entertainments Officer the other day, you would know. A gompa is a Tibetan Buddhist monastery. If you fancy a five-mile walk, put your boots on and we'll go now."

"Well, I'll come for a walk. There's not much else to do," he said resignedly.

As we tramped through the mountainous countryside, I studied a rough sketch map the officer had issued to those of us interested.

"We're heading for Bhutia Busta Gompa, it's the nearest," I said, showing him the route.

"Very interesting," he said, yawning. As we approached, even Jack admitted how very picturesque it was, framed in the mountain backdrop. As we stood admiring the quaint monastery, a procession of monks passed us and entered the gateway. Again, I was dumbfounded by the apparent age of so many of them.

When we returned to our hut, Bill and Gordon were still lying flat out on their bunks. We laid it on thick.

"We've just seen a marvellous Buddhist monastery!" said Jack.

"You've missed out, lads, you should have come, instead of staying here moaning and groaning. I bet that view you had of Everest wasn't a patch on this!" I added.

Bill threw a boot at me, before subsiding again on his charpoy.

The last night in Darjeeling we decided to go out for a slap-up meal. What the heck, our outings in Meerut usually finished up with two fried eggs and chips.

"There's a Chinese restaurant in Lloyd Road, that's supposed to very good," said Jack.

Gordon frowned, "Chinese restaurant, in India? I don't know about that."

I was dubious too, I didn't like Indian curries, I never had them in the mess - but Chinese!

"What about an English restaurant?" I asked. My experience of any eating-place living up to the title of restaurant was nil, but I thought I would feel more at home if it could be an English-type establishment.

Bill piped up, "Let's chance it. Mind, I haven't a clue what they'll have. My dad once had a Chinese meal in Hong Kong after the first war. He went on and on about the dish that he'd had that day."

Reluctantly, dragged along by Bill, that was where we ended up - the Chinese Restaurant. The waiter brought the menus.

"Drinks, sir?" he asked.

"Four beers," I said.

"Sorry, sir, no beers except ginger beer."

This was a good start. I looked at Bill, Bill looked at Jack, Jack looked at Gordon. Gordon looked at the ceiling.

"That's fine, that's great!" he said. "Whose idea was it to come here?" turning to give Bill an icy look. "What sort of a restaurant is this?"

It was a hypothetical question, but the waiter wasn't aware of the subtleties of the English language. "A teetotal restaurant, sir," he explained, politely.

I shrugged my shoulders resignedly, "O.K., bring four ginger beers."

I opened the menu, there seemed to be a hundred and twenty-three choices, providing there weren't any more listed on the reverse of the card.

"What's all this?" I asked. "Mixed giblets soup, ugh! Two rupees. Yang Chow fried rice, Chicken Fooyung, Rainapple Pie! What the hell are they talking about?"

Bill interrupted, "I know now what my dad had in Hong Kong. It was Shark Fins! It's here on the menu. Chicken Scramb Shark Fins or Yellow Fish with Shark Fins, eight rupees for four pers."

"What's pers? Does that mean four pairs of shark fins?" asked Jack.

"No, you daft so-and-so, it means for four persons."

"You three can have my share," I said, "I'm still looking."

"Right," said Bill, forcefully, "are you two game? We'll have Chicken Scramb Shark Fins, O.K.?"

Gordon and Jack shrugged their shoulders, Bill took that as agreement. I think they all had an idea what Shark Fins were, but Chicken Scramb? The mind boggled.

"Waiter," he called. "We want Chicken Scramb Shark Fins for four. For three," he added.

"Only for four," pointed out the Chinaman.

"Yes for four, for three," repeated Bill.

The waiter shook his head in bewilderment.

Gordon interrupted then, "Waiter, we want the Shark Fins for four, but him, him and me will eat it." He pointed to Bill, Jack and himself. "Savvy?"

"Aah!" I think he had got the hang of it. "Savvy, sir," his face was beaming, now the mini crisis was over. Then he frowned and looked at me. "You, sir?"

I was beaming now also; I had just espied a section hidden away in the middle of the menu. "I'll have Mixed Grill, waiter!"

"Bloody hell," shouted Gordon. "Mixed Grill! I didn't see that!"

"Shut up, Gordon, you're having Sharks Fins," I said. "Mixed grill for me, waiter."

"For one, sir?" he asked apprehensively, perhaps he thought I was going to throw a spanner in the works and say, 'No, for four, waiter.'

I nearly said, 'No, for two', because I was feeling peckish by now, after all the crosstalk, but took pity on him. "Just one, for me," I said.

"Ah, just for one," he smiled and went shuffling off to the kitchen, first counting on the fingers of one hand and then the other.

I don't know whether my pals enjoyed the Shark's Fin. It looked threadlike and transparent, but I couldn't see any sign of chicken, it must have scrammed. Bill now remembered that his dad had said that shark fin was a great delicacy so he couldn't say he didn't like it. Not in front of me, anyway, as I tucked into my mixed grill. I'm glad I hadn't ordered two helpings. There was steak, pork chop, sausage, bacon, tomato, mushrooms, two eggs, fried bread, chips. 'Probably worth the two rupees,' I thought.

It might have been imagination but I could have sworn my pals kept casting envious glances at my plate. Certainly Gordon did.

Anyway, I was quite pleased with my last night on leave.

Leave over, we now had to suffer that long journey back to Meerut. Luckily, the new Indian Government had the situation a little more under control and we got back to Bungalow 39 on schedule. Even so, we had been away over a fortnight.

Not long after our return, at the beginning of September, the news I was waiting for was announced. Group 61 were to proceed to Deolali Transit Camp near Bombay on the 15th of the month and await a troopship home. There was a strong possibility we would sail on the 21st September, but this couldn't be guaranteed. With the evacuation of British troops from the Indian subcontinent now being speeded up, troopship space was at a premium.

Things were moving at last, however. This was very good news to give Joan. I wrote to her without delay. 'Great news darling! As I write to you I keep looking at an official document lying on my charpoy. 'Soldier's Release Book 14802039 Pte P. D. Potts.' Yes, it's official! I'm on my way. Not only that 'Conduct exemplary,' it says. Not a stain on my character, ha ha!

'I bet my conduct won't be exemplary when I hold you in my arms again! I could be home as early as the 13th October! This means I won't be able to receive your letters after I leave Meerut in a few days time, so please write straight back and tell me whether you're pleased at the news.'

Inside a week came her reply. 'What do you mean am I pleased? I'm delirious with happiness. I was telling Mrs Dyer on our section. She said to me, you've got a sparkle in your eyes, you must care for him a lot. She has seen your photo and says you look nice. I shouldn't have told you that! I hope you don't get a big head!'

As if I would.

Deolali Transit Camp meant another long journey, twenty-four hour this time. It was one journey I was looking forward to - the first step on the journey home.

Gordon accompanied me, he also was a Group sixty-oner, but Jack and Bill, both Group 65, would have to wait a little longer. We had shaken hands with them both and wished them all the best. They had been good friends for nearly two years.

The transit camp was overflowing with Army personnel awaiting a ship. All permanent accommodation was full and tents had been erected on every available piece of ground. There were a dozen or so of us from the pay office in Meerut, handily, just the right number for one tent.

We didn't spend much time under canvas during the day; temperatures, over ninety in the open, were even higher in the tent. Every morning we would wander down to the camp office to scan the lists of units departing for Bombay.

The days went by with no sign of our names appearing on the board, it was not going to be the 21st, or the 28th, not even the beginning of October.

God! It was a boring period. Now I knew where the phrase 'Deolali tap' came from! The waiting was enough to make a man go crazy, particularly a man who knew someone was waiting impatiently for his return. There wasn't a lot to do. It was too hot for anything vigorous. Every evening, under the light of hurricane lamps we played moth-killing, cards, word squares, even 'I Spy'. Not that there was much to spy. The game usually developed something like this:

"I spy something beginning with T."

"Tent!"

"No, wrong, tent pole."

"Something else beginning with T."

"Tent, this time!"

"No, wrong again, troopship."

"You can't see a troopship in this tent!"

"I can spy one in my mind's eye."

"That's cheating!"

"Alright, something beginning with Y."

"Y? Nothing begins with Y."

"It does, what about the yardarm on the troopship?"

"Alright, yardarm."

"It's not yardarm anyway, it's all your yawns!"

Deolali tap, here we come! 'I Spy' usually degenerated into a scuffle anyway. Until we got too hot.

The one thing we were all scared of was catching malaria or some other ailment, which would prevent the unfortunate one catching the boat when it did become our turn to embark. Everyone of our group, myself excluded, had been in hospital with an illness at least once during our time in India. Was my luck going to hold?

Chapter 25

HOME

Was my luck going to hold? It did, but it was the twenty-second of October before we embarked from Bombay, ending five weeks of waiting. Our ship was the 'Empire Pride', marginally better appointed than the old 'Llangibby Castle' (the bogs had doors this time), but still not a luxury liner.

Wonderful it was to stand at the rail and see the Indian landscape slowly recede into the distance. For some time I viewed the hazy land on the horizon. It seemed to linger there. Puzzled, I sensed that our ship was steaming northwards, parallel to the coastline rather than in an westerly direction. That feeling was confirmed when an announcement came over the tannoy. Instead of heading directly across the Indian Ocean towards the Red Sea, we were first making for Karachi, the chief port of West Pakistan. There we were to pick up men from units who had been serving in what had been North West India. Logic would have indicated that these men should have travelled by rail to Deolali to await embarkation from Bombay, like the rest of us. Relations were so strained between India and Pakistan at that time, however, that inter-country travel was not a safe option. This diversion would add another two days to the duration of our voyage, yet a further unwanted delay.

Until we neared home, the rest of the journey was uneventful, more or less the outward voyage in reverse. We were all impatient to get back to Blighty, but even with no more hold ups, it would be still be over eight weeks since we had left Meerut. Meerut, where we had been ostensibly discharged.

Through the Suez Canal we passed, then the Med, and the

Straits of Gibraltar, making steady progress in calm weather. It was when we crossed the Bay of Biscay that gales sprung up. The ship was pounded day and night by the heavy seas. Conditions worsened as we headed north into the Irish Sea, making for our landfall - Liverpool.

The storm was more severe than the one suffered in the Med on the outward journey. Inevitably, many lads were seasick. Miraculously, this time, I wasn't affected. Perchance, fantasizing of my reunion with Joan dulled any feelings of nausea.

There was one last disappointment for us, the seas were now so wild that we it was deemed too dangerous to enter port. Instead, we had to heave-to in Liverpool Bay and await a lull in the storm. Another delay, a twenty-four hour one this time. So near, yet so far!

At last, the Empire Pride was able to dock during the night and early next morning we walked unsteadily down the gangway.

"It's great to be setting foot at last on England's shore. Who said that?" asked Gordon.

"You just did, you cracker. Before that, everybody!" I laughed. Cliché or not, it was how I felt too. Quickly, we were whipped off to Padgate Demob Centre, to swap our army uniforms for civilian issue.

This Padgate place was no bespoke gents outfitters. This emporium was almost run on a conveyor belt system. I was lucky to emerge at the other end wearing clothes that more or less fitted my angular frame. A herringbone-pattern, single-breasted suit, complete with waistcoat; braces, a shirt with three detachable collars, two cufflinks, and one collar stud. Then a tie, a pair of socks and a pair of Oxford shoes. My army underpants and vest were retained, the rest of my army issue was surrendered.

I tell a lie, I was wearing only one collar; the other two were in a big, brown-paper carrier bag issued to hold any personal odds and ends that we may have collected. For me - the pair of shoes I wore in Meerut, some of Joan's letters, some photographs. Memories of India I carried in my head. I was quite happy to discard my khaki, but it was with regret that I was parted from my kitbag. It had been a companion of mine on every journey for nigh on three years. Travelling without it would feel weird. What would I sit on in the corridor if the train was crowded? Near the exit of the kitting-out centre, I spied a full-length mirror. I stopped to marvel at my new image. My sunburnt reflection looked almost as pleased as I felt, giving a little smile and straightening its tie.

We weren't out of the army yet. Instead, we dispersed to various discharge centres. Gordon and I, with a few others, were off to Strensall Military Disposal Unit, outside York. On our train journey across Lancashire and Yorkshire (seats available), I marvelled at the lush green of the countryside, a contrast with the parched yellow vegetation of the Indian plains.

"England's green and pleasant land!" said Gordon.

"What's wrong with you, Gordon? Have you been reading Shakespeare under the bedclothes in India? I thought you were doing something else!"

"Ouch!" I cried. He packed a bit of a punch, did Gordon.

At Strensall, the final formalities were completed. Now, I was officially discharged and could pick up on my civilian life. First and foremost, for me, that meant to be reunited to my girl.

Joan had given me her office telephone number to ring and at Strensall, I tried and tried to get through. Frustratingly however, the line was continually engaged. An army truck was outside, engine running, waiting to take us to York Station. Hastily, I abandoned the useless phone, dashed from the office, and jumped aboard. In my pocket was a railway warrant for Newcastle, but there was no way I would be using that today.

I scrambled to the front of the truck and leant over to speak to the driver. "Do me a favour lad, can you drop me in Exhibition Square when you get into York?"

Gordon added his twopennorth. "He wants to see his girlfriend, the laddie does. He's been pining for her for two years!"

That caused general merriment, but I didn't care. I could stand the ribbing for a few miles. In York, the driver pulled up in the Square, outside the Theatre Royal. "There y'are mate," he said. I grabbed my carrier bag, shook hands with Gordon and one or two other lads and jumped down.

"Best of luck," shouted Gordon, "be careful, don't get carried away. Don't do anything I wouldn't do."

That could leave me plenty of scope.

I gave him a disdainful wave and hurried down Davygate, my

heart racing. I stopped outside Grosvenor House for a moment, gathering my thoughts.

'Here goes,' I thought, barging into the old office. I stood at the entrance, looking around for a minute, then spotted her. There she was, head down, immersed in her work. A couple of A.T.S. girls, whom I recognised, looked up.

"Hello, Paul," said one, "you're back at last!"

Just then Joan glanced across, she was bonnier than ever. At first it didn't register with her what was happening. Then she jumped up and scampered around the desks.

"Paul, you're here!"

"This is me," I laughed.

The whole office seemed to have cottoned on, even those who didn't know me. Everyone was standing up now, some clapping. We weren't embarrassed, we were too overjoyed at seeing each other. I grabbed her arm.

"Let's get out of here, love." I hurried her downstairs where I knew she kept her coat.

She grabbed it, eyes bright, as I led her out of the side door and into the street.

"I'll get the sack for this," she chuckled.

"Just blame your kidnapper! I'm sure that nice officer you keep writing about will understand."

We walked hand in hand towards the bus stop. We knew where we were going.

"You didn't ring."

"Your office phone was engaged, I wasn't going to hang about."

As we reached the stop, I dropped my carrier bag, and pulled her to me. "I haven't had a kiss yet."

That omission was soon remedied. Her lips were just as warm and inviting as I remembered them to be.

"Do you love me still?" I asked, looking into those honest, twinkling eyes.

She gasped, "My you're masterful, all of a sudden!"

"It's all that sun in India, it goes to your head, you know."

"Don't be daft."

"Hey, come on though, Joan, you haven't answered my question!"

"What was that?"

"You know!"

"Oh that one about love! I suppose so," she laughed.

"What do you mean, you suppose so?" (Trying to sound indignant.)

She hugged me close, "Of course I do, Paul."

"You'll still marry me then?"

For answer, she gave me her lips. Her hunger was apparent. I responded ardently. Two years was a long time.

There was a crowd at the bus stop now, we had been unaware of the queue forming behind us.

A homely looking middle-aged woman who had been observing our performance, spoke up.

"That's right lass, marry the lad, he looks t'ave the mekin's of a gradely husband. Gi'him a few Yorksheer puddins and thee'll soon build him oop."

We laughed, now almost as much embarrassed as the onlookers seemed amused.

Joan grabbed my arm, pulling me away from the stop. "I've changed my mind, love. We'll not get the bus. We'll walk."

"Now who's being masterful?" I asked. I gave the discerning woman at the bus stop a thumbs up, as we moved away. 'A gradely lad!' That sounded like me. I wasn't too sure of the build him up talk, though.

"Well, I'm not getting on that bus now, Paul, they might ask for an invitation to the wedding!"

That's how we came to be walking along Bootham, retracing our old path. I kept giving my lass admiring glances as we sauntered happily, hand in hand. I knew now why I had missed her, why I had yearned for her. She squeezed my hand and smiled, her cheeks dimpling.

A couple of Red Caps passed us, my hand went up to my head to check that I had my forage cap on, and then realised I was in civvies. The military policemen had gone by before I could stick my tongue out at them. Joan laughed at my antics.

"You don't know how much I've missed you, darling, How much I've wanted to be with you," I said.

"I do, you know, I've felt the same."

"Not as much as me, I bet."

"I bet I have, I've missed you every minute, Paul."

"There you are then, I've missed you every second," I laughed.

"You always have to have the last word, you rogue. You're a precious rogue all the same."

I put my arm around her waist. "You know something, Joan? I've often thought about that last night we spent in York, have you?"

She looked at me, eyes glowing, as a couple went by. "Don't embarrass me, darling."

"They won't know what I'm talking about."

"No, but I do. Anyway, what's in your carrier bag?"

"Oh, just a pair of shoes and a bundle of old letters from somebody I used to write to."

"Who was that?" she laughed.

"The nicest girl I know," I said earnestly.

"Do I know her?"

"I'm not saying, I don't want this lady to get a big head. Anyway, you're trying to change the subject. Let's get back to that night, Joan. That last night when we were nearly one. Almost one, but not quite. You were so exciting, it was lovely."

"It was wicked!"

"You don't mean that. I want us to be one, Joan. I've waited nearly two years, two long years."

She looked at me, cheeks flushed now. "You're meaning before we're married?"

"I mean soon, darling. Now! There's no other girl for me, I want you, it's as simple as that! Don't you feel the same?"

She didn't answer, although her arm stole around me as we walked down Grosvenor Terrace. She was deep in thought. It was still daylight, but I pulled her into an archway beneath the railway line.

"What are you doing?" she smiled. My lips on hers was the answer she wanted. A train rattled above our heads.

"Can you feel the earth move?" she laughed, coming up for breath.

"You see what happens when we get together, Joan!"

To sense her perfume was delight, to feel her lips yielding to mine was bliss, after those barren months without her.

"Do you remember what happened here, at this spot, three years ago sweetheart?"

"I know you nearly suffocated me with kisses, just as you're doing now, darling," she said breathlessly.

"You haven't forgotten, have you? This is where I first told you that I loved you."

"I do remember, love, I do remember."

It was then that three schoolboys came through the arch kicking a tennis ball.

"Soppy barmpots, soppy barmpots," one called.

I made to chase them and they disappeared around a corner.

"You see what you are," Joan laughed, "a soppy barmpot! But I still love you!"

We walked on, Joan quiet again, She stopped and turned to me.

"Are you staying in York tonight?"

"I was hoping so, then go home tomorrow, possibly."

"I suppose you'll have to go home," she said, disconsolately.

"I'll have to go into work sometime as well, to sort the job situation out. I'll come back down at the weekend if your Mam will have me, darling."

"Of course she will, we have a spare bedroom again, now that brother Philip's married. Wouldn't your Mam want you to go straight back today, though?"

"Ho'd thee hosses, lass," I kidded her, "you're my number one person. Don't you want me to stay?"

"Of course I do. I do, I do very much. But what you were saying before, when I changed the subject. Could you make this being one, as you so nicely put it, safe? I don't know a lot about the contrivances of the thing."

I couldn't help smiling. "That's a good way of describing it, Joan. You'll be saying contrivances for the contrivance, next!"

"Don't be rude."

"I have a plan," I said.

"Oh! I thought you would have everything worked out, you knave."

"There's a chemist in Crichton Avenue, we could go there before we go to your house."

"And who's going in? I'll tell you who's not! I'd be the talk of the neighbourhood! Anyway, what do you ask for? Do you know?"

"Do I know? Do I know? The truth is I don't, Joan," I confessed. "The lads talked about French letters - if I ask for them the chemist might send me around to the greengrocers."

"Ho ho, I get it French lettuce, on the other hand you might come back with a packet of envelopes. They won't be much good!" she laughed.

"I'll think of something," I said as we passed Joan's house and walked down to Crichton Avenue. "Leave it to me."

"I intend to, Paul," she said firmly. "I'll wait here on the corner, I hope nobody sees me, or sees you coming out of the chemist."

I peered into the pharmacy, there appeared to be no one in, no customer waiting for a prescription. Good. I opened the door to the sound of the bell and walked to the counter. A bespectacled blonde girl of about eighteen, possibly even younger, appeared from the back of the shop. I nearly walked out again. No, I decided, the reward for a successful mission was much too great. I steeled myself.

"Yes?" she smiled, looking at me expectantly.

"Er, Er, have you contraceptives, miss?" I stuttered, cursing the fact that I'd never found out from experienced Smiler Preston exactly what to ask for. I didn't fancy a discussion of what kind I wanted, what size, for instance, what width. Not with this seemingly nice, innocent girl.

"You want Durex?" she asked in a businesslike way.

"That's it, the name just slipped my tongue, pet. Yes, Durex," face feeling beetroot red.

Thankfully, she didn't ask what size, but she did ask, "How many? You know they come in threes?"

"Ah yes, three will do I think." Three seemed more than ample to me. For starters. I wasn't all that bigheaded.

She pulled open a drawer underneath the counter and handed me a small packet, wrapped in plain paper. I took the packet, I hoped this was right, shouldn't it possibly have been a longer parcel? The good thing was that she seemed to take the transaction in her stride.

"That's two and six," she said.

Two and sixpence, for three. Tenpence each. That seemed a cheap admission fee to paradise. Cheaper than going to the pictures!

Thankfully, I gave her a half-crown, slipped the packet into my trouser pocket and beat a hasty retreat into the street.

Joan was waiting nervously around the corner.

"Did you get them?" she asked, as we linked arms.

"I think so," I said happily, "Durex, the name. I think I've heard of them before, now I come to think of it. But aren't we ignorant?"

"I suppose it's good we are, Paul, in a way."

"We'll look at them later," I said, patting my pocket. I felt they were burning a hole down there, already.

"We'll check them out in the front room, tonight, eh?" she smiled. "Then later, perhaps! I'm not promising anything, mind. We have waited a long time though, darling."

By this time we had reached her house, I followed her in.

"Mam!" she called.

Her mam's voice came from the kitchen, "Is that thee, Joan? Wot's brought thee 'ome at this 'ower?"

She came into the parlour. Surprise, surprise, her hands were floury. She hadn't changed much, perhaps a little stouter. Her straight black hair, her cheery face. "My God," she said, "it's Paul! W'knew you were on thy way, but ye've got me flabbergasted, lad!"

She wiped her hands as best she could on her apron, then gave me a hug and kissed me fondly on the cheek.

"It's grand to s'thee, lad. By, tha's sunburnt, but by gum, you 'aven't filled out much, though. Thee looks grand in thy suit, mind. Doan't he, Joan?"

"That's a silly question to ask me, Mam."

She laughed, "I s'pose it is, lass! Tha' knows thee Dad'll be in soon. He'll be bowled over."

"Mam, can Paul stay the night. In the spare bedroom?"

"Doan't ask such silly questions, lass. He can'st stay t'week if he wants to."

"I'll have to go home tomorrow, Mrs Speed, I haven't been home yet, you see."

"Aye, Aa suppose your mam will want to s'thee. Anyroad, Aa'l finish these scones and get t'tea ready. Joan, thee can show Paul his room and he can dump his bag and his jacket and then thee can mek theesels comf'table. You can have fire int' front room after tea, it's ready to light."

Joan took me upstairs and opened a bedroom door.

"This is yours, Paul, just put your jacket and bag on the bed for now."

"Where will I find you tonight?" I said earnestly. "You want me now, don't you? Now you know I'm not dangerous."

She frowned, mischievously, "I don't know, I'll have to inspect the merchandise first. I mean the little parcel," she added, as I laughed. "Anyway, my bedroom's next door here." She pointed across the landing. "Whatever you do, don't open that door! That's Mam and Dad's room. If my Dad finds you wandering into bedrooms, he'll chase you out of the house! Another thing don't stand on this mat here. There's a creaky floorboard under it."

She opened her door. "This is my room. A double bed, see? Mind this dressing table, don't bump into it! I'll leave the door ajar as well, it squeaks a bit when you open it. There'll be a bit of light from the street lamp to help you."

"I'll be a bundle of nerves before I get into your bed, at this rate!" I laughed. "An irate father, creaky floorboards, squeaky doors, nobbly furniture. I'll be all deflated. Are you trying to put me off or something?"

"That'll be the day when you're deflated," she giggled. "You must have changed a lot if that sort of thing happens, that's all I can say."

My hands went around her throat in that old familiar way. "Get off," she cried, laughing, falling back on the bed.

I collapsed on top of her, the bed yielding springingly. "It's big and soft," I said.

She opened her eyes, looking startled, "Oh!" she chuckled, "That's half a disappointment!"

I pinned her down playfully, "I'm talking about the bed, you wretch." Biting an ear. It *was* shell-like.

I raised myself up and looked down on her, "But I love you!"

Just then, her mam came to the bottom of the stairs.

"Joan, your dad's here, luv."

"Right, Mam," she shouted, as I stood up and pulled my unfamiliar waistcoat down and straightened my tie.

Downstairs, Joan's dad had washed his hands and his coal-flecked face, his bald head shining. He was unrolling his shirtsleeves.

"Ee, it's grand to s'thee, lad," he said, shaking hands warmly. My, you look a proper man in that westcoat. Mind, y'avent put much flesh on, though!"

'If anyone else says that, I'll crown him,' I thought.

"Joan lass, ye'll have to mek a start and feed him up." He turned to me, "Was it rough owt there, Paul?"

"It was hot, Mr Speed."

"Aye, t'would be. It were 'ot int' Dardanelles in first war, mind."

"Did it get to a hundred and sixteen in the shade?"

"Ee, lad, Aa doan't know abowt that, but it were 'ot. Thee coulds't fry eggs in thy mess tin."

"Ye' teas are ready," said Mrs Speed, coming in with a tray and interrupting the conversation on cooking and the weather. "Aa've dun a fry up. Yer Uncle George kem this mornin' and browt sum duck eggs and a luvly piece o'gammon from t'farm."

"'Ee's a reet dip, is 'im. 'Ee didn't ask thee to loan 'im sum brass again, Aa 'ope, Ida?"

"No, George, not this time. Oh, Aa forgot, he browt a brace o' rabbits as well. Aa've just 'ad an idea, Paul. Ye could 'ave one for thy muther."

"Thanks very much, Mrs Speed." Trying to puzzle out how I could explain to Mam how I'd got a rabbit. I'd planned to pretend that I had come straight home, more or less, not staying the night in York. I might have to change my story. Even if they had rabbits in India, I'm sure it wouldn't have kept fresh all that way on the boat.

I was enjoying my tea, a thick slice of gammon was a novelty for me. So succulent and tasty.

Joan's dad seemed to be enjoying it too. He had just speared a nice piece on his fork when his wife spoke.

"Paul's stayin' t'neet, George."

George's fork stopped when it was halfway to his mouth.

"Oh, aye?" he said, frowning.

"Int' spare bedroom, George."

"Oh, aye," he smiled quietly, "'int' spare bedroom," popping the succulent morsel into his mouth. I gathered from his manner that the spare bedroom was alright. He'd spit that piece of gammon out if he knew our devilish plan.

The rest of the meal passed off uneventfully, Joan's dad was waxing lyrically about his favourite daughter.

"She's missed thee, Paul, tha' knows. She's spent many an hour writin' to thee."

"Well, he would know that, Dad. He got the letters!"

"Aye, of course, love," he laughed.

"Mam, I'll light the fire in the front room, O.K.?"

"You'll help your mam with the dishes first, lass."

"Nay, George. Let t'love boids go int' room. Aa'll manage well enough. Anyroad, they might want t'set t'date!"

Setting the date was the last thing on my mind.

Chapter 26

SLEEPWALKING?

It was the last thing on Joan's mind, too.

We snuggled lovingly on that comfortable settee and rediscovered many reasons why we had such affection for each other. We kissed, cuddled, chatted and listened to the radio, relishing our reunion. Dick Haymes was crooning 'A Million Dollar Baby'. I joined in, warbling in her ear.

"You're my million dollar baby, love. You know that?"

"I didn't work in a five and ten cent store, Paul." she said, snuggling up.

"But it was you I spied across the floor," I murmured, paraphrasing the words. "Do you want to hear any more?"

"If I must," she laughed, teasingly. My hands closed around her neck. "Get off," she cried, "I can't stand that. I'll lock my door tonight, if you don't stop. Sing some more instead. Sing that bit where I'm selling china."

"You weren't selling china, Dick Haymes sang that, you cracker. Let's be serious for a minute. Do you believe in fate, Joan? It's awesome to think of the combinations of 'ifs' that brought us together?"

"How do you mean?"

"Well, the things that could have happened to prevent us ever meeting. If I had been exempted from the army. If I'd been posted to the D.L.I. If I'd gone to another office."

"I'm sure we would have met, love. I'm sure we would."

"Can you feel a magic in the air tonight?" I asked.

"You are a romantic, Paul," she murmured. "Let's see what magic you've got in that parcel."

I unwrapped the brown paper and opening the small carton, I took out one of the little packets and handed it Joan. "My!" I said. "They're little."

"Don't be daft," she laughed, "they're rolled up."

"It seems a complicated affair. Do you think I'll manage it in the dark?"

She took one out and put it over two fingers and did a little demonstration.

"By the looks of it I'll have to wait until I'm ready, then."

"You'll be ready!" she said saucily.

"I don't know about that. All those hazards before I even get into your room. They might put me off."

"When you get into my bed you won't be put off. Don't forget, I won't be wearing a nightie. But don't you come out of your room with nothing on. If you're caught with your underpants on you can always say that you were sleepwalking."

'A likely story,' I thought, but I thrilled in anticipation - her words, "I won't be wearing a nightie!"

"How long should I wait, Joan?"

"I'd think about half an hour, sweetheart, mm?"

"We'd better synchronise our watches then. Another thing, how many should I bring?"

"Synchronise our watches, you're potty! Anyway let's settle for just the one, love," she laughed. "I don't want to tire you out. You'll just have to make it last!"

"That's going to be difficult. If you have nothing on, it could happen quick, don't you see?"

She giggled, bewitchingly. "Well, love. Just let it happen quickly if I'm going to be so irresistable! But in that case don't put it on, but don't trespass! Not until you're dressed for action. Then, it can happen again, properly!"

I breathed a contented sigh. "That's sounds feasible, that seems a likely scenario. Yes, I'll probably follow that idea."

I was still a touch concerned. "Another thing."

"Oh no," she chuckled, ruffling my hair as I nestled into her. "Not another thing!"

"I mustn't make a noise?"

"You certainly mustn't make a noise!"

"That's going to be difficult as well, I'll want to shout it from the rooftops! Do you know something, Joan? I'm all nervous, I bet going over the top in the trenches in the First War was something like this. The briefing, then the action."

"You wicked lad, I'm not as fearsome as German machine gunners, though, am I? You make me sound awful!"

"No," I laughed, "but I bet the action will be more exciting tonight, darling!"

She was cuddling me, stroking my hair, my head on her soft bosom. "What time is it, Joan?

"I make it half past nine."

"So do I, I thought my watch had stopped. I can hear your heart beating, mind. It seems to be beating faster than usual, love."

"I wouldn't be surprised."

"What time will your mam and dad go to bed?"

"About ten thirty I would think."

"Oh Lord!"

Just then her dad knocked on the door. "Are thee two cumin' for a bite o'supper?"

"Yes, Dad," she said, "we're coming."

"Do we have to, Joan? I'm not all that hungry somehow."

"We'd better though, Paul."

"We're goin' t'bed soon, Joan," said her mam, when we went through into the parlour. "Just tek pot luck, you two. There's a couple of Wright's tomato sausages and one o' their pork pies and a few sandwiches."

"I'll just have a sandwich, Paul, I won't have a sausage just now, I don't like them before I go to bed, they might repeat on me. You have them."

Did I detect a twinkle in her eye when she said that?

After supper, Joan said, "Paul's tired, Mam, he's had a hectic day, I think we'll go to bed now."

Good old Joan, she's speeding things up, I hope.

"Reet, luv," said her dad, "we're goin' as well. Aa'm up at six."

"If thee 'ears a noise int' neet, Paul, it's only fether goin' t't'toilet."

We all went upstairs together, Joan opened the spare bedroom door. "There you are, Paul. Have you got everything you need? I'm going to have a quick bath. It's twenty-five past ten."

I checked my watch, then patted my pocket, "Yes, I think so, Joan," giving her a chaste kiss. "See you in the morning."

"Goodneet, Paul," said the Speeds.

I closed the door and undressed to my underpants.

I looked at my watch again - 10.32.

I picked up my trousers, took a little packet out of the bigger packet and placed it on the bed. Mm, perhaps I'd better not take any sort of a packet into Joan's room. Her mam might find it, if it was lying about. I took the smooth thing out of the packet and put it on the bed. The empty packet I put back in my pocket. 'Packet in the pocket,' I sang to myself. 'Thingie' on the bed.' It was one way to pass the time.

I checked my watch again - 10.37. Eighteen minutes to kick-off.

I went to the window and peeped through the curtains. It was moonlight, I could see her dad's garden, there wasn't much growing now, not in November.

I closed the curtains, returned to the bed and checked that the 'thingie' was still there.

I peered at my watch again - 10.46. Nine minutes to go.

I went to the door and listened for a moment. No sound. Then suddenly I heard someone snoring. I hoped that wasn't Joan. It couldn't be Joan! I'd never forgive her. I breathed a sigh of relief. It was her dad. That was hopeful, he was out of the equation by the sound of it.

I went back to the window and peeped again at the garden. Still not much growing.

I tried unsuccessfully not to look at my watch. It was 10.52. Three minutes. I started counting to 180 but my mind wandered to thoughts of Joan minus her nightie and I lost count. Now it was 10.54. I watched the second hand slowly moving and picked up the count. Five, four, three, two, one,

zero.

Gently, I switched the light off, turned the door handle and stepped onto the landing. There was a hint of moonlight. There was also something missing - the 'thingie' was still on the bed. Carefully I retraced my steps not bothering to switch the light back on. I found the bed without much difficulty - I stubbed my toe on it. I groped around for the dratted thing and at last my hand closed on it. Success, but I was running late now.

Again I was on the landing, now trying to make up for lost time. I stood on the mat. 'Squeak'. Hastily I pushed open her bedroom door. 'Creak' it went, as I stubbed the other toe on the dressing table.

In the soft light of moonbeams and the street lamp, a nymph-like vision, of a kind that I'd dreamt about, arose sensually from the bed and gently closed the door. This vision was real alright, I knew for certain, for it brushed up against me and I felt bountiful femininity, soft and delicious.

"Where have you been?" the damsel whispered.

"I nearly forgot my thingie," I replied quietly.

Her hand wandered, "I don't think so, love." She took my hand and led me to the bed. There she slid gracefully on top of the covers, holding out welcoming arms. Hastily, I stepped out of my underpants, heard an intake of breath and fell into her arms.

I had imagined such a scene in wild dreams in India but the aura of that night was magical. Our hands caressed and explored as we kissed and whispered endearments. Luminous beams of moonlight enhancing the moment, gave me glimpses of her bountiful charms. Her eyes were bright with longing, a longing I shared and which would soon be mutually satisfied. Strangely, I found I could contain my ardour, sufficiently to whisper, "I think I'm alright, my darling, I'll put the thingie on."

I reached under the pillow and knelt up.

"Can you manage, love?"

"I think so, Joan," but I was struggling.

"Here let me do it, Paul."

Gratefully, I passed it to her and nimbly she fixed it in place.

"You're a wonder, Joan," I whispered. "I'll let you do that every time."

Our coming together transcended any emotion I had ever experienced. My desires, those months of longing, exploding in an exquisite togetherness unsurpassed.

I knew that Joan felt the same, whispering words of love and desire, urging me on.

At last we lay, spent and breathless. I stroked her cool yet moist forehead, a soft breast, a smooth flank, as she caressed my back, fingers playing down my spine. A long kiss was now a satisfied, tender, grateful expression of our fondness for each other.

We lay for some time, contented, then we heard a bedroom door open. Her mam spoke in a hoarse whisper.

"Doan't mek a noise George and wek Paul, he looked exhausted last neet."

"She should see me now, Joan," I whispered. "She would be really worried about me!"

This caused Joan to start giggling silently, which was almost impossible. Her shoulders started to shake, causing ripples in more interesting parts. I began to wish I had brought another 'thingie'. We heard her dad come back from the toilet and close the bedroom door. We waited a few minutes, then Joan whispered, "I'm sorry, Paul, but you'd better go back to bed while the coast's clear."

"Do I have to?"

"I'm afraid so, love."

"I wish we were married, though."

"So do I, we'll have to fix a date, mm, Paul?" I ran my hands over her alluring form one last time, pulled on my underpants and regretfully returned to my cold bed.

Next morning, after breakfast, we walked to Grosvenor House, and there, ruefully, I had to leave her.

"You'd better go, Paul, or you'll miss your train."

"Thanks for last night darling, you were a million dollars. Certainly more than tenpence!" I added, giving her a deep farewell kiss and grabbing her arms to stop a punch. Her last words, "See you on Friday." If only for a few days we were parting again.

Chapter 27

GOOD AND BAD

Up the backyard steps I went, into the scullery. Mam was cooking the dinner.

"I'm here, Mam."

She looked a little careworn, traces of grey in her auburn hair. Putting down her knife she gave me a hug.

"Well, hello, Den. We've been expecting you for days. Have you been in York instead of coming straight home?"

'Here we go,' I thought, and me hardly over the threshold.

"No, Mam. I haven't been staying for days. Just last night. The train got in late and we had to go to the discharge centre in York. So I stopped off, right? The boat was delayed as well."

"Alright, alright, Den."

"Anyway, Mam, I'm getting married soon, or had you forgotten? It's no surprise I wanted to see Joan, don't you think?"

"I suppose so, but why you want to get married at your age, I don't know."

"Well, I am, so just forget it, please. Oh, I've got a rabbit here from Joan's mam."

"That'll make a nice rabbit pie and help the rations. You'd better tell her thanks, when you see her."

"How's everybody, anyway? How are you?"

"So-so, there's always too much to do. Don's on early shift, he'll be in soon. Stephen's just the same as ever, Rob's not too good, it's his chest."

She made me a cup of tea and I had a couple of scones.

"I've made a plate pie for tea. We'll have that with potatoes and cabbage. I'll just have to make it go further. Oh, Den, I'll need your ration book if you're staying, rations are still small you know."

"Of course I'm staying, Mam, just now, until we get married."

"When will that be?"

"Soon, I think, if we can get a flat or something. Joan and me will try to sort something out when I go down at the weekend. Oh, by the way Mam, will Joan be able to come up here some weekends? We'll need to look around."

"I suppose so, Don'll have to go in with you and Stephen, and you'll have to go in Stephen's bed. It's a nuisance. How is Joan, by the way?"

I thought she'd never ask. "Fine, pleased to see me, of course."

"I should think so, a young lad with your prospects. I've brought you up, you know, and now you're leaving when you're just starting to earn some money."

"You'll get my board money until we're married, Mam."

"Oh, I know, I'm not complaining about that."

Stephen came limping up the front stairs just then and into the room. I shook hands and gave him a hug. He pushed me off, embarrassed.

"How's school?"

"Sometimes it's good and sometimes it's bad."

"A bit like you," Mam laughed, then turning to me, "he's still a bit of a dreamer."

Later in the afternoon, Don came home off his early shift. I couldn't believe it. When I had last seen him over two years before, he was a sturdy airman. Now, he was a plump bus conductor, he must have put on three stones at least.

"Gosh, what's happened to you, Don, what have you been eating?"

"I think my weight went up a bit when I was on demob leave, Den."

"He was lazing around for two months, living on his demob pay, before he got a job," said Mam. "Mind, he's always given me his keep and a bit more."

Don gave a smirk of satisfaction.

I didn't think Rob looked well when he came in from work, and after tea he was soon in his armchair, fast asleep. Mam settled down to read a book, Stephen a comic, and Don smoked his pipe and listened to the radio. The smoking thing was a habit he'd acquired in the R.A.F.

I picked up the Evening Chronicle, the night was off to a dull start, all in all things weren't very exciting. It got duller when Don struggled up from his chair and turned the radio down when a programme of classical music began. Minutes later I realised that he had cleared the decks for a bout of reminiscing.

"I'm glad I'm out of the R.A.F. Regiment, Den," he said, refilling his pipe with his Erinmore Pipe Tobacco, tamping it down, and then puffing it manfully. "We had some hairy experiences."

Mam looked up from her reading and peered over her glasses at him, at the same time keeping her finger on her place.

"Go on, tell him some of your tales, we've heard plenty of them. It's about time Den suffered."

Don had a wonderful capacity to ignore that kind of remark. It would take more than that to put him off his relentless stride.

"There was that time when I was stationed in Lossiemouth. A Wellington bomber returning from a raid missed the airfield and crash-landed. That was scary. Me and my mate were sent to guard it, it was cold, so we just sat in the cockpit all night."

"You've missed out the bit about the dead airmen under the plane, Don," piped up young Stephen. "Tell us about the dead airmen under the plane."

"I'm coming to that," he said, sending up another puff of smoke. "Guess what, Den?"

Mam broke in again, "There were dead airmen under the plane and your corporal didn't tell you until next morning."

Don carried on, unabashed, "And we didn't know until next morning. Aye, there were dead airmen under the plane."

"Mam," I said, "why don't you tell the story?"

"I could, I've heard it often enough."

Don took another puff, "Aye, there were dead men under the plane, Aye, there were."

I think I'd got the drift of the story by now.

"Why don't you go up to the Azure Blue, Don, and get a couple of bottles of brown ale to celebrate Den's return?" said Mam.

Mam was always ready for a celebration.

"Aye, I will," said Don, lost in a daydream under a cloud of smoke.

"When will that be?" she asked. "Next week?"

"Soon Mam, it's early yet. Den, you haven't heard the story about when I was stationed outside Berlin?"

"Tell me another time, Don. I'll tell you what, I'll save your legs. You must be tired walking up and down the bus all day. I'll go up to the Azure Blue."

"Right, Den, if you want."

I was glad to get out of the house, away from that tobacco smoke and into the fresh cold night, alone with my thoughts. Was it less than twenty-four hours since Joan and I had made love? When would it happen again? We had to fix a date for our wedding and get a place to live. That was priority number one.

Next morning, I decided to walk down and see my old boss, Mr Patterson, to check out the job situation. On the way, I started musing about the previous night.

When I had returned from the pub, Don said he would just have a glass of beer, Mam and Rob had a little more, propelling Mam into a loquacious mood.

"I'm suppose I'm lucky to have four boys," she said, to no one in particular, "I was hoping to have them all together at home for a while, though."

"Mam, we'll all be leaving home to get married, it's only natural. Don will be next."

"Don will stay, won't you, Don? You'll look after your old mother!"

What was this old mother talk for God's sake? She was only fifty. Mind, as far as I knew, Don had never had a girl, so she could be right about him staying at home.

Don was noncommittal. I could see that. At that precise moment he was content smoking his pipe and rehearsing his next trip down memory lane. What was it Cecil had said? He doesn't like change? Finding a girl and then the fuss of getting married could be just too big a departure from his routine.

With every minute, Mam seemed to be getting happier, thinking she could rely on Don. It could be a good time to break some news. "By the way, Mam, I've stopped going to Mass."

She nearly spilled her beer. "What do you mean, Den?

"Just what I say. Come to think about it, you haven't been for years!"

"That's different. I always go to Midnight Mass, anyway. I still believe."

"Once a year! Come off it, Mam. That's not enough."

"Wait a minute, Den, does that mean you're not going to get married in a Catholic Church? If that's so, I shan't be going to your wedding!"

"You've got to, Mam, anyway, I'm not sure yet, I'll think about it." That was me, one step at a time Paul.

"Let's not fall out," it was Don speaking. "It's Den's first night home."

(He had a good heart, the lad. Besides, he wanted a bit of peace and quiet for his storytelling.)

"I'll tell you that story about Berlin, Den, now we're settled.........."

That was last night. All of a sudden I found myself outside the entrance of the Caledonian Connectors Co. My mind had been mulling over the good and bad points of the family, the good and bad points of Mam.

This *was* the entrance to the old firm's general office, wasn't it? I didn't recognize the old place. The whole fascia, the doors, the reception area, had benefited from a sparkling coat of paint. Things must be looking up for Caledonian Connectors. Of course! Fool that I was, so many ships had been sunk during the war and were being replaced - and what were important components? Why, bolts, nuts and rivets.

I entered the general office without knocking this time and saw that it too had been spruced up. Old Miller hadn't been renovated; he was still in his grey overall, grey hair a little thinner.

He was at his desk shuffling his timecards as of old, almost as if playing patience.

"Hello, Paul, you look well," he smarmed, aware that soon I would move well above him in the hierarchy.

"Hello, Mr Miller. (They were all 'Misters' in the general office.) Except Sandra, the boss's secretary, and the office boy, Freddie. She was Sandra, he was Laddie.

"Is Mr Patterson in?"

"Yes, he's in, Paul. Just knock."

I was going to anyway. On his bright new door.

"Come in. Oh hello, Paul. Welcome back."

Patterson stood up and shook hands. He was a fearsome

looking individual, bushy black eyebrows, thin mouth, craggy chin, piercing blue eyes. A boss you would imagine could sack somebody on Christmas Eve and enjoy it. Until he smiled, which he did often, as he did then.

"Sit doun, Paul." He still had that trace of accent from over the border. "I suppose you're still wantin' to retur'rn here?"

"That's it, Mr Patterson. I'm looking forward to taking over from Mr Henderson."

"Ye will, Paul, ye will. Snag is, Norman wants to stay on until June."

Norman! Everybody knew him as Mr Jackson; he had a first name! Was I the first to know it? That piece of information was immaterial. Let me concentrate on this June business - June was a long way off.

"What does that mean to me?"

"Weel, ye'll have six months t'learn the job. Sad fact is, I canna' gi'ye Norman's rate of pay until you take over."

"So, what rate will I get until next June, Mr Patterson?"

"Weel, it'll be four pounds, ten shillings, but w'are paying bonny bonuses. There'll be one at Christmas, and me'be more next year."

Four pounds ten, this was a blow - it wasn't much more than Don's bus conductor's wage. Luckily, I had some weeks of demob pay in reserve, plus my post office savings.

"What will I get next June?"

"Oh, then ye'll be on six pounds ten shillings, Paul."

"You know I'm getting married soon, Mr Patterson? So I'll be able to tell my girl, Joan, that I'll be getting that wage come June?"

"That's right, ye can tell your lassie that, Paul. Ye'll be wanting to earn some money as soon as possible, then? Ye can start on Monday."

Back in York, in the front room, that Friday evening, I broke the news to Joan.

She looked disappointed, but gave a resigned smile.

"Never mind, you'll be earning a good salary in June, Paul."

"I suppose so. Will I be able to keep you in the style to which you're accustomed, though?" I laughed.

"Oh, I think so, Paul. You know, love, I've been thinking all week about being married to you. I've decided it's going to be wonderful."

"Does that mean I'm going to have to wait until then for another treat?"

"I think we should wait, really. There's still a risk. Also, I wouldn't like Mam and Dad to find out. Dad would be so upset - it happening in the next room, too. What do you think?"

"I know what you mean, I won't like it, but if that's what you want."

What was I saying? A little persuasion and I knew she'd succumb again. A warm glow of righteousness was little solace for missed enchantments. Saint Paul of Propriety, that was me.

"It's not that I don't like it. You know I loved it, it was fantastic, darling. It was the most marvellous thing."

"O.K., I believe you, and I understand," I said pulling her close.

Saturday afternoon, we were off to Bootham Crescent, to see York City play Gateshead. Fortunately, it ended in a draw, honours even. No fights. Saturday evening was film night to see 'The Jolson Story' at the Odeon. Saturday night, just fond goodnights and separate beds.

Sunday, after early tea, we spent a last hour in the front room before I left to catch my train. Back to work on Monday.

I couldn't go without raising something which had been niggling at the back of my mind for so long.

"Joan, tell me why you stopped writing to me, last year. You said you'd explain when I came home. I'm home. I've always wondered. It seemed so unlike you."

Over the months, in some ways I'd been dreading to hear her story, my imagination sometimes running riot. I realised, however, that I would never be settled in mind without knowing the truth.

A frown came over her face, "I'd rather not, Paul, it's over with now. We're together again and we're happy, aren't we?"

"Is it something you're ashamed of? No secrets, Joan, That's what we promised, to share everything."

She sat up, "Please don't ask me. You may get mad."

"Just tell me, Joan. I'll get madder still if you don't. You don't want me to think the worst of you?"

"Why don't we let sleeping dogs lie, Paul, eh?" She shifted uncomfortably on the sofa.

"Please; come on." I took her hand.

"Well, it happened when Helen and I went to Dawlish. We'd had a good time, the weather was nice, we went to the pictures or a show on a night. It was the Thursday when Helen suggested we go to a dance at a local hotel. Helen had gone for a walk that afternoon, I was happy reading a book on the sea front. Apparently, she met a couple of Royal Artillery men who had told her about the dance."

"So you went?" It was my turn to frown.

"Helen pestered me. I was looking forward to writing to you after dinner. I hadn't written to you since arriving, I felt guilty. Helen was a bit of a nuisance at times. I wish I hadn't gone, but I knew she'd be in a mood for the rest of the holiday, so I went. I gave into her again."

I listened, making no comment.

"They were there at the dance, Bill and Charley. Charley was a little whippersnapper. Helen fancied Bill, I could see. Bill fancied me, though. He hogged my company all night."

"You encouraged him, you danced with him!" I glowered.

"No, Paul, I wish you hadn't started this. I didn't encourage him, we had a dance. They walked us back to our hotel, well, boarding house I suppose you would call it."

"So, he started kissing you?"

"No, not that night,"

"Not that night!" I said.

"Listen, love, this isn't easy. We all went for a walk on our last night in Dawlish. If you must know he kissed me goodnight. He tasted of tobacco smoke, he smoked a pipe."

"So was that, that? Is that why you didn't write? It seems strange."

"Of course that wasn't the reason. I don't feel like going on with this, Paul. Please don't be nasty. I'm trying to explain."

She was looking upset, about as upset as I felt.

"He told me he wanted to see me again. He started praising me up to the skies. He had told me earlier that he had been to grammar school, he was going into the family business, he had marvellous prospects. I suppose he was too good to be true, really. Helen said he was a nice lad, I might do better with him than with you."

"And all this time you were engaged to me!" I cried.

"I know, I know, don't rub it in, Paul. When I got back to York, there were two letters from you, but also a letter from him. Helen must have given him my address. He bombarded me with letters.

"I wrote and told him I was engaged and to stop writing. I was bewildered. He said he would come to York on his next leave. Then he sent me two postcards each with his photo on. They were signed 'Your Bill' plastered with kisses. Helen said he was ideal for me."

"That bloody Helen," I shouted, every minute I was feeling more and more betrayed.

"I wrote again to him, telling him to stop. I suppose I was all mixed up. Every time I picked up my pen to write to you, the words wouldn't come. I did feel guilty.

"Then I got your letter with that lovely poem, I wrote back to you straightaway. My legs felt like jelly again when I read it. Just like that last night."

"So, if you hadn't got my poem?" My face was burning. "He was everything that I was not, grammar school, well-off!"

"Don't go on like that darling, I wanted you, deep down. Do you know, after I replied to you, the very next day, my dad took me to task? He had seen one of the postcards when he brought the mail in, and some of the letters in his handwriting. He had been mulling over what to say to me."

"What did he say?" I was almost shouting now - rage mixed with jealousy.

"He told me that I wasn't being fair to you. I had to tell Bill to forget me. Of course I already had. He wrote a couple of times more; I just returned his letters unopened. Will you forgive me?"

I stood up, "I don't know, Joan. I don't know. You've let me down. You promised to wait. You promised there'd be no one else. Could you do it again, could you get all bewildered again? You must have had some feelings for him for you to stop writing to me!"

She took my hand, I didn't respond. "Anyway, I'll have to go Joan, or I'll miss my train."

She stood up; I gave her a perfunctory kiss.

"You've upset me, I'm going to have to think about it."

On the way out, I shouted through to her mam.

"I'm dashing off now, Mrs Speed, or I'll miss my train," I said, storming out into the street, leaving a tearful Joan in my wake.

Letter from Joan.

'Darling Paul,

I couldn't sleep last night. I was worried sick, but I'm glad I got it off my chest even though it upset you. I know it was wrong, but I couldn't write to you in India until I'd sorted myself out. One thing I'm not is two-faced, darling. I couldn't write loving thoughts when I was twisted up inside. That Helen didn't help either. I'm writing now to tell you I'll never be twisted up inside again. I love you, and have only loved you. Please believe me. I know I was wrong. Please write and say I'm forgiven.'

I sent her a terse note:

'Dear Joan,

I'm not sure, I still feel let down after your promises before I went to India. I'll come down on Saturday afternoon (I'm working Saturday morning), and talk to you. Can you meet me at the station? The train is due into York at two thirty.'

Chapter 28

RING A DING

All that week thoughts jangled in my head. My dreams, when I did sleep, were weird and convoluted. One dream I do remember was of Joan on a station platform, a Gresley Pacific came to a halt in a cloud of steam. She walked into the mist. When it cleared she was gone.

Was I being stupidly jealous? Was I being unrealistic, was I overreacting? I couldn't forget her promise when I left for India. There'll be no one else for me, she'd said. Yet she must have had serious doubts not to write those long weeks.

On the train to York, I wasn't sure. Walking towards her on the station concourse, I wasn't sure. What had I decided? What was I doing here?

She smiled nervously as I approached. Smart as always, a neckerchief, soft yellow, gracefully hugging that white throat and contrasting with her russet jacket.

"Hello, sorry I'm late," I said. She expected a kiss; I took her arm instead. "Let's have a cup of tea in the refreshment room." I wasn't going to Burton Lane yet. I wanted to get things settled.

"O.K.," she said. She looked pale and tired.

When I returned with the two cups, her fingers were drumming on the table, nervously. Her head bowed.

She looked up at me; her eyes were brimming with tears.

I hadn't known what I was going to say to her. I did now.

I put my hand on hers. "I love you, Joan. I can't help it. I'm sorry for making such a fuss. You see I can't do without you."

She sighed, the tension suddenly gone. She smiled. It was like a shaft of sunlight in the dimly lit cafe. Her free hand pressed mine. "I love you, Paul."

"You look tired," I said. "You haven't slept."

"Neither have you, have you?" She looked more relaxed, but couldn't stop a tear escaping. "You see what you've done?"

I took my handkerchief and gently brushed the tear from her dimpled cheek.

"This fellow doesn't matter now, does he? Forgive me for being so nasty."

Her warm brown eyes gave an answer. "He never did, my darling, not really. I'm sorry I stopped writing, it must have been awful for you, you looked forward to my letters, didn't you?"

"Joan, I'm sorry I wrote that nasty letter on Thursday. We shouldn't quarrel, we should never quarrel. Just tell me once again that there was nothing between you."

"Nothing, nothing, nothing. He was just so insistent and Helen was no help. There was just that one kiss and then he sent those cards and letters. Do you know something? I'm glad I told you of him now."

"So am I, Joan. No secrets, eh?"

"We can put it behind us, my love. It sounds trite, but it's like a weight off my shoulders." She looked radiant now. Her old self again.

"Just one thing, Joan. Have you still got a photo of him?"

She looked at me quizzically, "I think I have."

"Can I see it? I just want to see what this might-have-been rival looks like. I won't get upset any more, love. Promise!"

"Well," she laughed, "if you won't be nasty to me again."

"Never, never, darling."

Hand in hand now, we walked to the bus stop, immersed in each other once more.

"We're too late to go to the match, now, Paul."

"Never mind, sweetheart, we're sorted out, that's more important than an old football match."

She laughed, "I never thought I'd ever hear you say that, Paul Potts, that anything was more important than a football match!"

"It's only York City, Joan."

She gave me a dig in the ribs.

"Are we going to the pictures tonight?" I asked, when I got my breath back. Her elbow was quite hard.

"Well, 'Brighton Rock' is on at the Odeon, Richard Attenborough is supposed to be good in it."

"That's a Graham Green novel. It's funny how we always end up 'seeing' books. We could go earlier, if we're not going to the match. That would give us a bit of time in the front room afterwards."

"You and the front room! No front room tonight."

"No front room! Come off it."

"How about my bedroom instead?"

"Your bedroom! What about your mum and dad?" We were nearly at the bus stop now, a couple of girls in the queue turned round inquisitively.

"Ssh, I'll tell you on the bus, if we can find a quiet seat." In the queue, "Did you have a good journey?" she asked. Good journey! I was more interested in this bedroom talk!

"Tittle to good journeys, Joan, I want to know what you mean."

"Just be patient, love, please."

Was I glad when the bus turned up? Was I even more glad when we found quiet seats on the top deck?

"Come on, then, what's it all about, then?"

"Well, there'll be no mam and dad tonight, they've gone to Sheffield to see Mam's sister Jane. They won't be back until tomorrow afternoon."

"What! Leaving you alone with me? That doesn't sound like your Dad."

"They didn't know you were coming."

"You didn't tell them?"

"I didn't know you were coming until I got that nice letter from you yesterday, by then I didn't want to worry them," she laughed.

"Nice letter! Don't be sarcastic. You're a minx, a lovely minx, mind. Why didn't you tell me this good news at the station?"

"I didn't tell you at the station, because I wasn't sure you would be coming back with me. I didn't want you to think I was throwing myself at you. By the way, have you got any thingies?" she asked cheekily.

"I've still got those two in the packet in my pocket. I haven't used them." This time the dig in the ribs really hurt.

"Shall I get some more at the chemist, do you think?" I asked, rubbing my chest.

"Let's not go overboard, darling!" she said.

A night to remember, it was. No worry this time about creaky doors and squeaky floorboards. No tiptoeing back to a cold bed. Instead, loving, lingering hours of love and sweet talk. And after, contented satisfied slumber in each other's arms.

Next morning, breakfast together, the two of us alone, just like a married couple. Even more so when I started washing the dishes. Joan came up behind me and held me tight.

"I'm sorry it's Sunday, Joan."

"Why, darling?" she whispered, "You don't want to leave me?"

"That as well," I laughed, "but the chemist's shut!"

"Getaway with you, you devil."

"Joan, what about the photo of this Bill fellow."

She withdrew her arms.

"I'd thought you would have forgotten. I have."

"I just want to see what this guy looks like, I won't get mad about him, especially now that I know how much you love me. You've still got his card?"

"I think so, I think it's in the wastepaper basket," she laughed.

"Come off it."

It didn't take her long to find it.

"Come here, here on the settee, love, and let's see it."

"He's not as good looking as you, Paul."

"Flannel," I laughed.

I was disappointed; you couldn't call him ugly. No, not ugly. But that pose!

"Who does he think he is, this Bill?"

"What do you mean, darling?"

"Well, just look at him, he thinks he's a Richard Greene, or a David Niven without the moustache. Or perhaps he's a Walter Mitty and thinks he's a fighter pilot. Look at the way he's holding that pipe, hand cuddling the bowl. And why has he got it stuck in his pretty mouth like that? Talk about fancying himself! He must have spent hours perfecting that pose!"

Joan burst out laughing, "Go on, pull him to pieces, I don't care. Tell me more."

"There'll be no tobacco in that pipe, anyway. It's all for show. You know something else? He's a mammy's boy!"

"Why do you say that, love? Tell me."

"Well, it stands to reason - men with pipes are like babies with dummies."

"Have you finished?" She was still chuckling. "Ee, it's a good job you wrote that poem and saved me for a lovely, honest, unassuming lad like you!"

"Can I tear this here photo into little pieces?"

"Don't do that, darling. Let me keep it as a reminder of what a narrow escape I had."

"Flannel again," I laughed, "I'll tell you what. We'll come to a compromise, I'll only tear it in half, right?"

Joan pursed her lips, "Go on then, if you must."

It gave me great satisfaction to tear his smug facedown the middle. I made sure I broke his pipe.

"You can do with it what you will now, Joan."

She laughed. "You can't do what you will with me, darling, you haven't got any thingies!"

"No, but I can go close, Joan." Pushing her back on the settee.

I left her early that afternoon, before her mam and dad came back from Sheffield, it would save Joan explanations. We had agreed that we would get married the following March, three months hence, providing we could find somewhere to live. Her mam had told Joan that we could have some of her spare furniture to get us started.

We had both agreed that living with my mam was a non-starter. There was no way that would work. I would search in earnest for a place after the Christmas and New Year holidays. If successful we would arrange for the banns to be read. Rather, Joan would arrange for the banns to be read. She would tell the parson that I was living at her brother's address and thus avoid me having to organise anything in Gateshead. She would get her wish; she would be married in church. Christmas, I spent in York; New Year, Joan came to Gateshead. Christmas in York was an experience. Joan's mam seemed to have a network of food suppliers in those austere days of rationing.

Weekly rations, then, consisted of twelve ounces of meat, an ounce and a half of cheese, six ounces of butter or margarine, one egg.

Compare that with Christmas in a certain house in Burton Lane. A Dickensian kind of Christmas. A goose, a leg of pork, plum pudding, Christmas cake, mince pies, ham sandwiches for supper. Joan's sister Liza was there with her two children. Brother Philip with wife Doris and little blonde baby girl Clare. Joan and I, her mam and dad.

One drawback, the front room was like Piccadilly Circus on a Saturday night. Smooching cancelled for the festive season.

Even so, it took me all the working days between Christmas and New Year to recover.

New Year at Mam's. Less food, more drink. Then tearful goodbyes as Joan returned to York.

My free time in January was spent searching for a house or flat to rent. Day after day frustrated. Any kind of unfurnished accommodation was difficult to get. The reason for the housing shortage of course was those long war years without any house building, just dwellings destroyed.

To help, Joan's mam came up on an early train one day in late January and went house hunting, visiting estate agents in Newcastle and Gateshead.

She turned up at our house about six in the evening. I had not long been home from work when I heard the knock at the front door. Guessing whom it was, I clattered down the bare lino staircase and opened the front door. She looked shattered, her usual pink, cheery face, white and drawn.

"'Ello, Paul," she said.

"Come in, I'll take that carrier bag, have you been carrying that around all day?"

She struggled up the stairs breathlessly and entered our parlour to be met by a sea of curious faces. Rob, Don, Cecil (home on leave), Stephen and Mam.

"This is Joan's mam," I said to one and all, then rapidly identified the family.

"Sit down, Mrs Speed, Den tells me you've been looking for flats, have you had any luck?"

Don shuffled along on the settee to make room for her. There was no room there now for anyone else.

"Not as y'could reetly say, Mrs Potts, Ida's m'name, by t'way."

"I'm Agnes. I thought you wouldn't have any success," said Mam pessimistically.

Joan's mam turned to me, "Aye, not much luck at all, Paul. Theer's one in Back Hammond Street int' Newcastle. Aa didn't see it, but nobbut basic by t'sownd of it. Thee and Joan cuds't 'ave a look at it. Oh Paul, give thee mam that carrier. There's a few sausages and 'alf a dozen eggs in it."

"That's kind of you, Ida, but you shouldn't have bothered. You won't have eaten anyway? I'll get you something."

"Aa 'ad a cup of tea int' the High Street. Is't any chance of stayin' the neet, Agnes? Aa cuds't look agin int' mornin'."

Mam's face was a picture. "I don't think so, Ida. What with Cecil home on leave we've got a full house, you see."

'Mam isn't going to make any effort here,' I thought.

"Den will go with you to the station after you've eaten. There'll be a train, won't there?"

Mrs Speed hid her disappointment well. "Aa think theer's one abowt eight o'clock. 'Appen Aa shud catch last bus in York. Oh, can Aa use your toilet?"

"I'll show you, Mrs Speed. Down the back steps, hang on to the banister. It's on the left there."

With a struggle, she negotiated her way in the darkness.

I returned to the parlour. "Is there no way Joan's mam can stay, Mam? It seems terrible she should go back at this time of night."

"There is no way, though, is there?"

"I suppose not," I said, feeling ashamed, after all the hospitality I'd received in York.

Joan's mam was soon eating a hastily prepared fry-up and chatting to the family. The sausages smelled nice.

"Thee were int' the R.A.F. Regiment, Don, weren't thee? Thee must 'ave 'ad sum hair raisin' 'appenin's."

"I did, Mrs Speed, one was in this country funnily enough. Well, in Scotland, Lossiemouth."

"Mrs Speed hasn't time to hear that one, Don, that's one of your long ones. Time's getting on," Mam said, looking at the clock. People missing trains were the last thing on Mam's evening agenda.

On the tram to the station.

"Aa wud 'ave liked to 'ave stayed and looked agin t'morrow. It's goin' t'be 'ard for thee and Joan."

"I'll keep looking, Mrs Speed, we'll find something."

Joan came up at the weekend, Cecil had now gone back off leave. We found Back Hammond Street. We wished we hadn't.

The street reminded me of the houses surrounding the dark Satanic mills depicted in films of Lancashire cotton barons, 'The Master of Bankdam' kind of thing.

Kids in raggy trousers and bare feet scurrying around piles of rubbish. Seedy-looking down-and-outs sitting on doorsteps. Windows boarded up, walls falling down. A putrid smell in the dank air.

We stopped outside the house - the hovel. 'To Let', the notice said on the cracked window. The door key didn't seem to fit. It didn't matter; I just pushed the door open. We took one look inside - a floorboard broken, wallpaper hanging off the wall. I pulled the door shut and took Joan's arm.

"Let's get out of here," I said.

Joan shuddered. "What estate agent would send anyone to look at that? What are we going to do, Paul?"

"It looks as though we may have to find rooms to start with, love," I said, stepping over the outstretched legs of a derelict. There was a smell of methylated spirits in the air.

"I suppose so, but it won't be the same as our own home. It would give us time to look around, though."

So we agreed on that option. Neither of us wanted to postpone our wedding.

With renewed energy and with a hint of desperation, I scanned the adverts in newsagents' windows, the 'Rooms to rent' column in the Evening Chronicle. At first, I followed up leads without success. Rooms were either already snapped up, too far away, or unsuitable.

Then, in the middle of February, I called at a house in Low Fell - Castle Avenue. A sitting room, bedroom attic, and use of kitchen at specified times, the advert said.

I discovered that the street was a quiet cul-de-sac, the house, a three-storied terraced with small garden, the district - Low Fell, the Jesmond of Gateshead. Say no more! A bespectacled, prim, serious-looking woman of about sixty welcomed me in, introducing me to her husband. He appeared to be more affable. Davidson was their name.

Mrs Davidson showed me the rooms. The sitting room with

coal fire and old-fashioned furniture, the bedroom a small attic, with a double bed.

She explained that we would be able to use the kitchen at specified times.

"How much, Mrs Davidson?"

"Thirty shillings a week." That seemed a big slice of my wage of four pounds ten shillings, but things were getting desperate. "I think that would be O.K., but I'd like to write to my fiancée (fiancée? I'd never called Joan that before. That was Low Fell talk, I was learning fast.) "I would like to get her agreement."

"When are you getting married? Before you move in, I hope?"

Gosh! She'd want to see our marriage certificate next!

"We're getting married the middle of March."

"Oh! You'd have to put a deposit down to secure the rooms then. That could be five weeks before you'd move in!"

"How much would that be?"

"Well, four pounds would secure the rooms for five weeks. There could be other people after them you see."

As the future man of the house, I made a decision there and then.

"Right then, Mrs Davidson." I counted out four one-pound notes. She took them carefully; I thought she was going to examine them for watermarks.

Joan welcomed my news. She could busy herself with the arrangements now.

March 20th, 1948, was to be the day. The banns could be read, she would be married in white, she could get the material for her wedding dress, her mother's dressmaker would be called into action. Borders Cafe, Coney Street, was to be the venue for the reception; her Dad was paying for the room and the beer - and the food?

Then there was the wedding cake, Joan's Mam's responsibility. She had a few black market sources, so the ingredients would be no problem. Some little woman with the apt name of Bessie Cook would make it. She had been making cakes for the Speeds and their ilk since time immemorial. We, the lucky couple, would supply the 'wine' - sherry and port - that was the only wine known to our strata of society in those early post war days. I checked my Post Office Savings Book, that wine could make a hole in my balance of £51 5s 11d, at nine and six a bottle.

"There's a lot to dooo!" I said, to Joan.

"Not for you, there isn't, you lucky so-and-so."

"Why don't we just elope, then, Joan?"

"You know I want a white wedding, love."

With all this turmoil, it seemed that there wouldn't be much time for smooching this side of the wedding. Then there was the guest list.

"Can you find out how many will be coming from Gateshead, Paul?"

That was a good question.

Chapter 29

DING A LING

Who was going to be on my guest list?

There was a little uncertainty here. With only weeks to go, the position had to be clarified.

"Mam, my wedding - you'll be coming down on the Saturday morning to York?"

"Don't jump the gun, Den. You know what I feel about your wedding."

"What do you mean?"

She frowned, "Well, to add to the fact that you're not getting married as a Catholic, you've gone the whole hog and are getting wed in a Protestant Church!"

"There's not much difference, Mam, is there? They're both Christian." I think that was the wrong thing to say.

"That's a laugh - not much difference! The things the Protestants did in Ireland in the eighteen hundreds. The potato famine, the cruelty. My dad went on for hours about the 'troubles' when I was little."

"That's ancient history, Mam."

"I'll never forget those stories. Then there were the Black and Tans! Far better that you get married in a Registry Office. Anyway, it's your funeral!"

"It's a wedding, Mam, not a funeral. Does that mean you won't be seeing your own son get married?"

I couldn't believe the religious thing was the whole explanation. She had never seemed so bigoted before. There must be another reason. Whatever it was, she wouldn't say, but she was adamant. "There's no way I can, Den. Tell Joan I don't blame her, mind."

"Oh, great. She'll be really chuffed at that. So you won't go. Is that final?"

"I can't, Den. You can ask Don, you'll need a best man. I'm sure he'll agree to go. I'll get him to go. I don't suppose Cecil will be able to get, he's just had leave."

"What about Aunt Sally then and Uncle Leslie?"

"I'm sure Aunt Sally will feel the same as me, she's an even more devout Catholic."

"This is marvellous. So Don just possibly might go!"

As it turned out, Don did agree to go. Good old steady Don.

That weekend, Joan met me off the train, giving me a hug. She looked a little wan; I thought the wedding preparations must be taking their toll. "I've missed you, Paul," she said, as we kissed. "I wish we were married now."

"So do I, love. It won't be long, just three weeks to go."

We made our way to the bus stop. There was a queue of Saturday afternoon shoppers. "Have you got your guest list, Paul?"

"As a matter of fact I have, Joan. It's a short one, mind."

"How many?"

"Not many, love."

"Just tell me - half a dozen?"

"Not quite, just the one as a matter of fact - Don."

"One! What about your Mam?"

"She won't go into a Protestant church at any price."

"You're joking! Why ever not for goodness sake?"

"Because of what the Protestants did to the Catholics in Ireland in the year dot. Mind she says she doesn't blame you."

"That's very kind of her. I wasn't even in Ireland in the year dot. What about your Aunt Sally?"

"Ditto, I'm afraid."

"Your other relations then?"

"Mam seems to have drifted away from them since she married Rob."

"So we've got Don, he'll be your best man?"

"He'll talk enough for twenty guests if you let him!" I laughed.

She smiled in spite of herself. "It's a good job you can laugh about it. It's not very nice for you though. Come to think about it, you'll be coming, I hope?"

"I wouldn't miss it for the world, love. How are things going?"

"O.K., I think. Mind, if I had known what was involved, I might have followed your idea and just eloped!" she laughed.

"It's a bit late now, love, isn't it?" I added resignedly.

"You bet it is," she said, squeezing my arm. "By the way, Paul, what about my wedding ring?"

"Crikey! I forgot about that."

"You're kidding!" she said.

I wasn't, but I didn't confess that to Joan. Instead, I suggested we chose one that afternoon, that would be one less worry for her.

Wedding day at last. Twentieth of March, 1948. I wasn't nervous; this was to be my day of destiny; I had decided that, over three years before. I wasn't going to have cold feet now. I had stayed overnight with her brother Philip and now we awaited best man, Don's arrival. Wedding to be at 11.30, taxi at 11.00.

Don arrived in good time and soon Philip and he were on the same wavelength recounting wartime exploits.

"Don, can I interrupt?" I said. "I'd better give you the ring. Put it in your waistcoat pocket, whatever you do don't lose it"

"Oh, right, Den."

Soon we were at the church, me in my new grey double-breasted suit, with carnation buttonhole, Don in sober navy blue. Walking down the aisle, I noticed the imbalance in the congregation between right and left. The left wing had it by a large majority although there was a goodly smattering on the right. Charlie and Maureen Crow were there, and a number of lads and lasses from the Pay Office. I spied Morag MacKenzie sitting in the third row, that was nice, but I hoped Joan didn't see her.

The organist burst into life, 'Here Comes The Bride' rang out.

Now we were at the altar together. Joan looked nervous, almost as though wondering whether she was doing the right thing. I was calm knowing I was. It all went without a hitch, nobody raised an impediment to the marriage and Don hadn't lost the ring

Photographs outside the church. I noticed bridesmaid, Helen.

Traitor! Everyone was saying how lovely Joan looked. I thought the opposite, she looked tense and tired.

Then to Borders Cafe, Coney Street. Joan and I and her parents welcomed the guests, I knew few of them, but guessed that two or three were Joan's dad's brothers, in various stages of hair loss, the family likeness so distinct.

Next the meal and then the port and sherry flowed. Her Dad, his bald head shining with perspiration, got to his feet and banged the table with his spectacle case.

"Ladies and gentlemen, let's 'ave a bit of 'ush."

I think he'd had a pint or two beforehand to give him a bit of Dutch courage.

"Woulds't thee all stand oop and toast the bride and bridegroom. Joan and Paul, may thee allus 'ave as much 'appiness as Ida and I 'ave 'ad."

He sat down to rapturous applause and wiped his brow and shiny pate with his hankie. Then it was my turn. "I would like to thank Joan's mam and dad for this wonderful reception and you for all your gifts. A brief check of the presents tells me that if we have an anniversary party we'll be able to invite all of you. I don't know about the food, but we'll have enough cutlery, anyway."

It was just a daft remark - I knew we'd got some cutlery, but the uneasy silence suggested a faux pas on my part - had they all bought knives, forks and spoons? It came into my mind that I'd better close this speech and quickly. "Anyway, thank you all. I believe my best man, brother Don, has a few words to say." Don ceased looking into his knife and stood up.

"I've never been so nervous, since a night I spent in Lossiemouth during the war."

"Stick to the script, Don," I whispered.

"Oh yes, my thanks to the wonderful bridesmaids. Also I've a couple of telegrams to read out. One from Den's, sorry, Paul's mother. 'Sorry I can't make it, but every happiness to you both...'"

"Gosh, that's something, Paul!" Joan murmured.

There were a couple of telegrams from my pals and then it was over. All that was left was to cut the cake. An hour later we made a quick dash by taxi to the station.

Our train was in the platform, we boarded it and I put our suitcases on the luggage rack.

Soon, the engine would get up steam and we would be off on

our blissful two-night honeymoon in a Scarborough boarding house in the windy month of March. Well, you can't have everything, can you? Plonking down on the seat, I took Joan's hand, closed my eyes and laid my head back. Was it only four years or so that I had asked myself when I would get a girl? Not until the cows come home? Well there must be a herd of the smelly animals milling about in our backyard at this very minute. Mam would be having a fit.

Printed in the United Kingdom
by Lightning Source UK Ltd.
104898UKS00001B/358-405